Violated

Violated

Sexual Consent and Assault in the Twenty-First Century

Julie L. Fennell
with J. Remy Green

ROWMAN & LITTLEFIELD
Lanham • Boulder • New York • London

Published by Rowman & Littlefield
An imprint of The Rowman & Littlefield Publishing Group, Inc.
4501 Forbes Boulevard, Suite 200, Lanham, Maryland 20706
www.rowman.com

86-90 Paul Street, London EC2A 4NE

British Library Cataloguing in Publication Information Available

Library of Congress Cataloging-in-Publication Data

Names: Fennell, Julie, 1981– author. | Green, J. Remy, 1987– author.
Title: Violated: sexual consent and assault in the twenty-first century / Julie L. Fennell,
J. Remy Green.
Description: Lanham: Rowman & Littlefield, [2023] | Includes bibliographical refer-
ences and index.
Identifiers: LCCN 2023059128 (print) | LCCN 2023059129 (ebook) | ISBN
9781538180877 (cloth) | ISBN 9781538180884 (ebook)
Subjects: LCSH: Sexual assault. | Sexual assault—Prevention. | Sexual assault—Law
and legislation. | Sexual consent. | Sexual consent—Law and legislation.
Classification: LCC HV6556 .F45 2023 (print) | LCC HV6556 (ebook) | DDC
364.15/3—dc23/eng/20240119
LC record available at https://lccn.loc.gov/2023059128
LC ebook record available at https://lccn.loc.gov/2023059129

Contents

Preface

Since you've picked up this book, chances are, you're personally invested in sexual assault prevention for one reason or another. Maybe you or someone you care about has been sexually assaulted. Statistically speaking, you'd have to have a pretty limited social circle *not* to know someone who has experienced sexual assault. Maybe you're coming at this from the other side: you think you've callously or unintentionally hurt someone else (or are worried that you might in the future) and are hoping to become more reflexive. Or maybe you're just a little weary of the consent conversation you're used to hearing and are hoping this book does what it advertises and gives you something fresh to think about and talk about with the people who matter to you.

Maybe you're none of those things, and I'm just projecting different aspects of myself onto my readers—because to tell you the truth at the outset, I am all of those things at once. (And perhaps you are as well.) I've had my consent violated, I've been terrified of violating others' consent, and I also desperately want the conversation my friends have been having about consent to change.

I may as well come out at here at the beginning and say that I'm pansexual, meaning I've had sex with people with a wide range of genders and bodies. As a woman propositioning both men and women, I'd have to be really oblivious not to notice the staggeringly different ways men and women learn to talk about, ask for, and get sex. And once you start noticing those differences, it's kind of hard to stop. My coauthor, Remy Green (who uses the gender-neutral pronoun "they"), meanwhile, is queer, trans, and assigned male at birth, meaning in this case that they were raised to be a man and came to early adulthood presenting that way but have since transitioned to become increasingly feminine over time. Remy and I have a broad range of experiences in negotiating sex, sexuality, and consent, and those experiences have taught us that our cultural discourse about those things is deeply and problematically heteronormative (which is just a fancy way of saying people tend to look at this issue only from the perspective of straight people). With this book, Remy and I are hoping to violate some of your core expectations about consent and sexual assault, encouraging you to think way outside the box and look at those things in ways that you may have never looked at them before.

A quick note about language conventions here. Like many writers on this topic, I choose to ruthlessly alternate between the words "survivor" and "victim" because so many agencies that deal with sexual assault use different words. Usually, I'll use "victim" when I'm talking about statistical experiences and "survivor" when I'm talking about psychosocial elements. I don't think there's a right word here—our language and culture are both still in flux and in contention. Similarly, there's no easy language convention to talk about sex and gender. Here, I have made the same awkward choice as many writers for predominantly straight audiences: using "women" and "men" as a shorthand for "cis women" and "cis men," meaning people who identify with the gender of their sex assigned at birth. Neither I nor my coauthor loves this linguistic choice, but I'm assuming most of my readers are from a heterosexual cultural context that expects this convention.

The topics I'm covering in this book are messy. They're legally messy, they're socially messy, and they're psychologically messy. If you're coming to this book as a survivor, I hope you will only use this book in a way that is healthy for you. As the author and a fellow survivor, I give you permission—indeed, I encourage you—from the start to skim over things that aren't good for you to get to the parts that are. This book isn't a self-help book for individuals, and it's not intended as cathartic reading (although I would be very happy to learn that it was for some). I'm particularly worried that some people reading this book may feel like I'm occasionally blasé about the seriousness of many consent violations and sexual assaults. But I'm trusting at the outset that you're smart enough to know that *plenty* of consent violations are black-and-white stories (I've experienced a couple myself) where one person is wrong and the other was wronged—*the end*. So instead of walking you through a set of incredibly simplistic moral, legal, and philosophical facts I'm assuming you're already on board with by virtue of being a decent human being, I'm going to delve right into the murky gray stuff that ends up muddying those black-and-white stories by association. I'm going to respect you enough as a reader to believe that you don't need me to tell you that having sex with someone who's saying "no" is wrong, and that it happens far too often; I hope you'll respect me enough as a writer and thinker to believe I know that, too.

Instead of being a self-help book for individuals, this book is a self-help book for society and the law. And if you imagine all the work it might take to help you change yourself in whatever ways you want, then multiply that by everyone in the country, you might get *some* sense of how much harder it is to fix society than it is to fix just yourself. On the other hand, you have a lot more people to help you do it.

So let's do it together.

PART I

How Did We Get Here?

Chapter 1

Quantum Consent

Once upon a time, a gay friend of mine I'll call Al found himself in an awkward situation. He was staying in a packed RV out of town, but all his (also gay) roommates for the weekend were out. Al was completely sober and trying to sleep in the top bunk when his roommate Bob—who Al barely knew—came in, drunkenly stumbling into the bottom bunk. Al really just wanted to go to sleep, but Bob was in no mood to sleep. Bob was as insistent as only the very drunk can be that Al should fuck him, despite the fact that they had never done anything sexual before. Desperate to go to sleep, Al finally gave in to Bob's demands for sex. When Al tells the story, he gets a vengeful gleam in his eye when he notes that the only condom he could find was a Rough Rider (the viciously textured kind) and no lube. Al briefly fucked Bob before Bob finally passed out. (It's unclear to me, as I think it was to the teetotaling Al, whether Bob *actually* passed out or if he simply fell asleep.)

When Al initially told me this story, he was clearly full of resentment and frustration about what had occurred. As he continued the story, my mouth dropped further and further open until I finally said, with more than a hint of uncertainty in my voice, "I'm so sorry you were . . . *raped?* . . . I'm not sure what to call that, but whatever it was, I'm sorry it happened to you."

"I just wanted to go to sleep!" he complained.

Al's story is bad for a variety of reasons, but it's painfully illustrative of the ways our culture inconsistently assigns blame and victimhood in experiences of sexual assault. And it's also painfully illustrative of how people in our culture experience such events. Our culture tells us that Al, being sober, is supposed to be the person who rationally rejects a drunk person's relentless sexual advances, which means he was the violator, not the violated. Especially since Al fucked Bob into apparent unconsciousness, Bob doesn't come off as someone who was really aware of what he was doing. Moreover, because he was the person doing the penetrating, our culture tends to assume Al had more "power" in the scenario, especially when it came to the power to "make it stop"—again framing Al as the violator. On the other hand, we

3

also frame relentless sexual advances from drunk or sober men as harassment, which would make Bob the violator. But perhaps the messiest complication of all is that we don't talk much as a culture about what sexual assault looks like between two men, who we tend to assume always want sex no matter what they say. If they didn't want it, their dicks wouldn't be hard, right? (*Wrong.*)

This story becomes even more revealing of our cultural inadequacies if we alter certain details of it. If, for example, both men had been about equally drunk, I'm not sure we would know what to make of the scenario. If one drunk man pressured another drunk man into fucking him, I don't think our response would be particularly indignant or strong. On the other hand, if sober Al had been the tremendously reluctant recipient of drunken Bob's lubeless Rough Rider condom, I believe that as a culture, we would be much more likely to perceive Al as the victim of a sexual assault.

The situation becomes even more dizzying if we leave absolutely every-thing else about the story the same, with slight changes in sexual orienta-tion: imagine sober Al was *straight* and drunk gay Bob had pressured him into fucking him. I think we immediately consider the situation much more "rapey" (while simultaneously quietly doubting the "truth" of Al's heterosex-uality) when we think a man's sexuality was violated on top of his consent. And perhaps even more complex, imagine straight drunk Bob had pressured gay sober Al into fucking him. I believe we instinctively add a false narrative to this version where we assume that gay Al must have been making token protestations but was actually pleased at the opportunity to have sex with a straight man, while "straight" Bob "just needed to get drunk" in order to be willing to have sex with a man. Notice that none of these stories have altered the fundamental fact that one person pressured another one into having sex, but intoxication, gender, sexuality, and sexual roles interact in complex ways to affect our assessment of the situation and "who was violated."

The previous versions are pretty complicated, but let's try playing the same basic story out with different genders and see if we respond differently. I doubt our responses change much if drunk lesbian Bianca pressures sober lesbian Amy into fucking her. I suspect that culturally, we tend to view the situation as "less serious" because we tend to think that lesbian sex is "less real," but the rest of the assumptions hold.

However, if we change the story so that drunk straight Bridget pressures sober straight Andy into fucking her, I think our reactions tend to shift dra-matically. Our culture typically claims that (drunk or sober) men should resist the sexual advances of drunk women because the women "can't consent" or "don't know what they're doing." In particular, the idea or image of a man having sex with a woman who is passed out drunk is constantly held up as a model for a classic fraternity rapist. Change the intoxication here, and we still tend to think of this as Andy's fault: if drunk Andy pressures sober Bridget into letting him fuck her (and possibly even if he pressures her into fucking him with a strap-on), I think we're pretty likely to see Bridget as the victim.

As with the two men, things get weirder here if we throw sexual orientation into the mix. As long as the drunk person is gay, I think we're kind of okay with what happens (drunk lesbian Bridget pressures straight sober Andy into sex, or drunk gay Andy pressures straight sober Bridget into sex) because again, for some reason, we start drifting into the delusion that sexual orientation is related to sexual consent here. If we switch it so that the drunk person is straight, however, I think we respond to the situation more negatively (drunk straight Bridget pressures sober gay Andy into sex, and much worse if drunk straight Andy pressures sober lesbian Bridget into sex).

Before going further, it's important for me to pause here and say that when I talk about these "cultural tendencies," I'm not necessarily talking at all about *what people actually think*. For example, statistically speaking, if you're a college-educated straight woman, you're more likely to (at least claim that you) view those scenarios as similar to each other than if you're a college-educated straight man, who's much less likely to be sympathetic toward a gay male victim than a straight female victim (Davies, Rogers, and Whitelegg 2009). I'm talking more about what the media, broader cultural discourse, and maybe even our peers and respected others tell us *we're supposed to think*. I'm sure plenty of people reading this had only one reaction to the story of Al and Bob: that gay sex is gross and immoral and that consent is irrelevant to the ick factor (although I don't know how many of them will have kept reading as far as this paragraph). Meanwhile, I'm pretty sure a lot of people reading about Bridget and Andy assume that in all the situations, Bridget was clearly asking for it because she was slutty enough to be rooming with a guy in the first place. But because these people know the answers that are culturally expected of them, there's a decent chance that in polite society or on a survey, they'll still give the "right" (aka "socially desirable") answers: "Al was in a tricky situation" or "Andy took advantage of Bridget."

And that, dear readers, is where things get really messy. Because it turns out that especially when it comes to sex, what people say they believe and what they actually do are sometimes wildly at odds. Historically, our culture has maintained a sexual double standard that favors men with regard to numbers: men are allowed to have sex with as many women as they want without suffering social judgment, but women are penalized for having sex with "too many" men (England and Bearak 2014; Allison and Risman 2013). (Note that there's a parallel orientation double standard that favors women: women are allowed to have drunk sex with a lot of women and still label themselves straight, but men who have any sex with men, drunk or sober, get labeled gay [Rupp et al. 2014].) But in the last couple of decades, as I'll explain in much more detail later, at least in educated liberal circles, the superficial evidence overwhelmingly suggests that both men and women have shifted toward a *reverse* sexual double standard. That reversal means if you ask for people's opinions on a survey or in response to an abstract situation, they tend to be more negative about men having a lot of sex partners than they are about women (Papp et al. 2015; Marks and Fraley 2005).

However, when you head out into the real world and actually talk with people about how they interact and what they really do, it's viciously clear that both men and women still judge women much more negatively than men for the same kinds of sexual exploits and experiences (Farvid, Braun, and Rowney 2017; Allison and Risman 2013). Thus, it's entirely possible that we *say* Andy should be held accountable for "taking advantage of" Bridget while simultaneously thinking, "Gee, I hope my son doesn't marry a girl like that," and imagining accountability to be a brief scolding. When we're faced with real-world people instead of abstract vignettes, all of Andy's friends might decide that Bridget is a conniving bitch, for example, while all of Bridget's friends might think Andy is a rapey asshole—or maybe both Bridget and Andy were too embarrassed to tell any of their friends what happened at all.

These scenarios introduce many of the themes we'll discuss throughout the rest of this book: a lack of vocabulary to articulate and describe experiences of sexual assault, gender roles, biological sex roles, sexual power, intoxication, shame and stigma, communication failures and complex ambiguities in "consent" and "assault," and finally, the utter failure of the current legal system to manage these complexities. Most of all, I hope you see a theme of what I'll call "quantum consent," meaning consent often isn't a simple yes-or-no proposition. In physics, a "quantum effect" (very, very simplistically) refers to the idea that we can change matter simply by observing it. Famously, depending on your perspective, light can be either a particle or a wave. Attempt to interact with it, and suddenly it will flip from wave to particle or particle to wave. Much like quantum matter, consent seems straightforward and easy until we actually try to look at it head-on, and then it starts getting messy quickly. In most of the scenarios I've just described, the Al character *technically* agreed to what happened, but do we think they really gave meaningful consent? And from whose perspective should we evaluate that question? Al's? Bob/Bridget's? A "neutral" observer's? Moreover, we've seen that it's easy to (mis)interpret "consent" differently in these scenarios depending on the gender, orientation, and sexual role of the person giving it. But theoretically, consent is supposed to be universally applicable and objectively knowable . . . So what happens if it really isn't?

Rather than trying to brush off the complexities of consent, this book is going to embrace them. Instead of saying, "Well, this is too complicated, so I guess we'll just never know if this is a particle or a wave," I'm going to accept the quantum nature of consent as one of its fundamental properties and then use that to explore how we can improve social and cultural standards, as well as both civil and criminal law. If you're hoping for a few quick takeaway messages with simple solutions, you're probably going to be disappointed. Anyone who tells you solving our social problems with consent and sexual assault is easy—"Just tell men not to rape!" or "Just tell women not to drink so much!"—probably doesn't really understand the nature of the problem. There are lots of pretty simple solutions that would make a huge difference in dealing with sexual assaults that get as far as the police (like, say, actually bothering to test rape kits, which forensic investigators only occasionally do [Harding 2015]). But in order to actually implement those solutions, there are a lot of questions we need to be asking ourselves first, like whether and when we want the police and courts involved in sexual assault at all. And *especially* when a solution is blindingly obvious and simple, we need to ask: well, why isn't it happening?

The sources of our problems go deep into broader issues of sexual shame, gender inequality, alcohol/drug use, education and communication, and outdated laws. Moreover, the problems are disconcertingly similar across many different social and cultural contexts, including in places where gender equality and sexual education are actually pretty darn good (Iceland) as well as ones where gender equality is "fine" and sexual education is terrible by the standards of the industrialized world (the United States). When a problem is that vast in scope, we have to look for multiple complex, structural solutions to it, not just pithy slogans to go on billboards.

WHAT EXACTLY IS "THE PROBLEM"?

If you've read this far, I assume that at least on some level, you're on board with the idea that your social circle/society/culture has a collection of related social problems around sexual consent and assault. Even though the count-less academics, lawyers, journalists, and social commentators who've written about these issues pretty much all seem to agree that there is *a* (collection of) problem(s), they seem at best to have arrived at a mediocre consensus about what those problems are. Most writers start from the premise that the fundamental problem is that too many women experience sexual violence from men and that our culture doesn't take the devastation and criminality of those experiences seriously. That premise feels intuitively appealing and often initially looks like it's backed up by statistics—until we start digging beyond the surface and asking harder questions like: what do we really mean by "sexual violence"? Is sexual violence being kissed when you didn't want to be, or does it have to be more overtly "sexual" than that? Does sexual violence include experiences like that of Al, where someone gets pressured into saying yes to sexual activities they didn't want, or does it only include activities someone always said no to? What about sexual activities someone said neither yes nor no to? And most of all (although generally ignored in this debate), what about sexual activities that occurred while *both* people were intoxicated—which, as far as scholars can tell, seems to be the *vast* majority of nonconsensual sex (Grigoriadis 2017)? If both people are really, really drunk, who's responsible for getting and giving consent?

You might reasonably be thinking, "Sure, but even if we narrow down the concept of sexual violence to include only the most unequivocal examples of sexual assault, we're still going to find that most of the victims are women and most of the perpetrators are men." Perhaps. Especially if we look at crimes of nonsexual violence, around the world, nearly all are committed by men between the ages of sixteen and twenty-four. So it stands to reason that crimes which include both nonsexual violence (e.g., beating and weapons) and sexual violence would probably also be committed by this same group, and the statistical majority of these offenders are almost certainly heterosexually attracted, because most people are. I'll use existing legal terminology to refer to this type of crime that includes both sexual and nonsexual violence as "aggravated sexual assault." I don't think there's an easy answer to the question of whether these aggravated sexual assaults are simply another type of violence (along with robbery, assault and battery, and homicide) or whether they're at the far end of a continuum that includes the drunk guy who just keeps ruthlessly having sex with a drunk girl who says "stop." Regardless of how we instinctively want to categorize such crimes, I think the *very* limited research suggests that aggravated sexual assaults are much more likely to conform to the old feminist aphorism that "rape isn't aggressive sexuality; it's sexualized aggression" than the drunk guy who doesn't stop when he's supposed to (Scully and Marolla 1985). Equally tentatively, I think the evidence we have suggests that those drunken nonconsensual sexual encounters mentioned earlier are actually mostly aggressive sexuality and *not* sexualized aggression (Grigoriadis 2017). So if they have such different underlying motivations, do they even count as the same social problem? Do they have the same solutions? We'll explore these questions throughout this book, with the general answer of sort-of yes but mostly no.

Once we exclude aggravated sexual assaults, we might find that most of the remaining sexual violence starts looking a lot less like how we usually imagine "violent crimes." But if men are the ones mostly responsible for violent crimes and most sexual violence isn't actually so "violent" (Jones et al. 2004), there's a very real possibility that women might be committing acts of sexual violence a lot more often than we expect. And indeed, much-ignored data on sexual assault collected in the United States by respected nationally representative agencies such as the Centers for Disease Control grimly support this perspective (Stemple and Meyer 2014; Stemple, Flores, and Meyer 2017). These data find eerily similar numbers of adult women and men reporting experiences of forced/unwanted sex in the last year, and contrary to expectations, most of men's unwanted sex happens at the hands of women. Indeed, even the stereotype of prison sexual assault—pitting a male inmate against another male inmate—appears to be misinformed, with research finding that female staff are actually quite likely to perpetrate sexual assaults against both male and female prisoners, and female prisoners are more likely to sexually assault one another than male prisoners are (Stemple and Meyer 2014). I realize this information utterly contradicts most of what you've always heard, and I promise I'll spend a lot more time going over it in chapter 3. Other numbers I'll go over in chapter 7 will show that at present, there is no statistical evidence that race significantly affects any quantifiably measured aspect of sexual assault, but being a bisexual woman vastly increases someone's odds of being assaulted and not being taken seriously by the police. I know some of these numbers can be hard to swallow (I spent months uncomfortably digesting many of them myself), so I want you to start getting a sense here at the outset for the way that you may have misunderstood and been misled about the nature of sexual violation.

I warned you earlier that this book was going to embrace all the ambiguities and complexities around consent and sexual assault, so if you're feeling a little overwhelmed right now, don't worry—I am too. The scope of "the problem" is much more complicated and rather different than we've generally been led to believe. Despite all those complications, the goal of this book is relatively straightforward: to propose social, cultural, and legal changes that should help reduce nonconsensual sex and create better strategies for addressing it when it happens.

GOING ROGUE: THE #METOO MOVEMENT

By 2017, it felt like the world was paying attention to all of these issues in a way it never had before. That year, the #MeToo movement exploded around the world, as women on the internet and in real life began sharing depressingly similar stories of sexual harassment and assault at the hands of men—especially men in positions of power over them. Media and culture both seemed shocked that so many women had endured sexual violations from men who apparently never suffered any real consequences for them. Although it went largely unnoticed, this cultural earthquake had actually been preceded over the previous several years by a number of foreshocks in intriguingly disparate places: college campuses, the porn industry, and the BDSM (Bondage & Discipline/Dominance & submission/Sadism & Masochism) subculture. In all those original pockets, as in the eventual larger mainstream movement, women usually began by "calling out" a male "violator" on social media (especially Twitter), publicly shaming him, and demanding that others join her in doing so. As the movement progressed, some men were arrested and charged with actual crimes; others lost high-profile jobs (seemingly for good); others briefly retired into obscurity, only to return once the initial outrage died down; and many others suffered no material consequences at all.

Underlying this strategy of public shaming ("calling out") was the belief that conventional social institutions—particularly the criminal justice system—would dismiss or disregard these complaints as lies or say that they did not meet the sometimes demanding criteria for criminal sexual assault. None of the women making the initial complaints in 2014–2015 fit an easy conventional social profile as victims of sexual violence. Emma Sulkowicz, a college student at Columbia University, alleged that a fellow student had anally raped her after the pair had engaged in consensual oral and vaginal sex; Columbia refused to punish the accused man despite her repeated demands (Grigoriadis 2017). At almost exactly the same time, Stoya, a popular feminist porn star, posted accusations of abuse online against her long-term porn star (now ex-)boyfriend James Deen. Other female porn stars also made accusations of sexual abuse against Deen—at least one about their private relationship, and another about an interaction that should have been professional on set. And then, in the land of BDSM, a socially prominent rope bottom (someone who gets tied up) named Gorgone posted accusations on the internet against a prominent male rope top (someone who ties people up): during a performance, while tying her, he had fingered her without her consent. Once her accusation became public, it became apparent he had been making a habit of doing the same thing to a number of women for many years.

Those stories felt uncomfortably ambiguous to many of the people reading them (although clearly not to the people who had lived them) as, by their own accounts, the victims/survivors had all started off in consensual sexual or erotic interactions, with a boundary or ten eventually being crossed. The bulk of the evidence indicates it's depressingly difficult to get legal authorities to pay attention to instances of sexual violation where there was *ever* any hint of consensual interaction; basically, once someone has consented to *some* sexual or erotic interaction, authorities seem to have little patience for the idea that *any* "violation" has occurred (Lundrigan, Dhami, and Agudelo 2019). These women were all staking a claim for much firmer boundaries than society had historically granted them—arguing in the strongest possible way that "no means no" and that consenting to a particular sexual or erotic interaction with someone doesn't translate to consenting to *every* sexual or erotic interaction with them. The truth of that statement seems self-evident, but these women were demanding something else as well: social censure and serious consequences for men they said hadn't understood and respected their boundaries. Emma wanted her alleged violator expelled from school, Stoya wanted James Deen fired from the porn industry, and Gorgone wanted her alleged violator expelled from the BDSM community. (Columbia refused to expel Emma's alleged violator; many prominent porn companies very publicly broke with Deen, although many didn't; and the BDSM community kicked out Gorgone's alleged violator.) These women framed their concerns as public matters deserving public sanctions, not just private quarrels and hurts. And semiexplicit in their accusations was the threat that if these men weren't properly sanctioned (it eventually transpired that all of them had at least one other accusation leveled against them), they'd just keep hurting other people.

You might be reasonably wondering why I've started my history of the #MeToo movement so differently than the Wikipedia entry. That article (as I expect most encyclopedia articles will continue to do) traces the beginning of the movement to the revelation that Harvey Weinstein, one of the most prominent producers in Hollywood and a staunch liberal, had been sexually abusing women for decades. Many of those women not so coincidentally happened to be movie stars. I've gone back further because I think focusing on Weinstein gives the wrong impression of the shape of the #MeToo movement, which was fundamentally a grassroots effort and always more closely resembled an internet mob than a well-organized social movement. (Before you get too angry at my choice of the word "mob," let me hasten to quote Martin Luther King Jr., who wisely said that "a riot is the language of the unheard.") Weinstein, unlike nearly all of the men who eventually got "MeToo'd" (the verb that emerged for men, especially more powerful ones, who were publicly accused of sexual harassment and abuse), ultimately faced criminal charges, was found guilty, and was penalized. Moreover, the evidence against him was unequivocally damning and overwhelming, coming from multiple sources who all had considerable social prominence themselves. Although the high-profile cases of powerful men sexually harassing and abusing their female employees sometimes echoed what had happened with Weinstein, most of the rest of the #MeToo movement didn't really fit that profile.

Instead, the stories that emerged again and again more closely resembled those of the women who "called out" their abusers in those initial pre-2017 public shaming rituals. These stories and activists were challenging society to reshape its vision of what a "victim/survivor" of sexual violence looked like to encompass anyone who had had a serious boundary crossed, not just the traditional understanding of rape that included only sober women who were violently raped by a stranger in an alley. And they were also arguing that if traditional social institutions like the law continued to fail them, they were going to seek alternative forms of sanction and redress (typically in the form of public shame). But the court of public opinion is notoriously fickle and possibly even more unreliable than dubiously reliable juries; moreover, this unofficial court was in no position to mete out consistent, continuous, or equitable punishments. The court of public opinion was in a terrible position to decide how long someone deserved to be expelled from the good graces of society for any particular offense, and it lacked a coherent system for enforcing that expulsion or for reliably determining whether the accusations leveled against someone were fair and reasonable. In effect, the thrust of the #MeToo movement became: "Our institutions of justice have failed us and will continue to fail us, but we still hurt. So we ask you, our society, to grant us a different kind of justice." And to greater and lesser degrees, parts of society did—at least for a little while.

But I think that's a deeply problematic goal for a social movement aimed at trying to reform problems associated with sexual violation (Koh 2022). Breaking faith with basic social institutions like the law encourages an atmosphere of intense social distrust, which is bad for society at the interpersonal level as well as the broader institutional level. In particular, breaking faith with core social institutions makes it harder for people to trust each other in everyday interactions, and it makes it harder for people to trust their governments and institutions of authority. And while blind faith in the government is a terrible way for any democracy to function, a reasonable degree of trust is necessary to have a functional society. As citizens, and as people who just want to live amicably with one another, we can't afford to simply disregard the importance of the law and other institutional authorities. I admit there's good cause to be concerned that trying to reform rape laws might be futile—hotly debated but discouraging international evidence suggests that after rape law reforms in the 1990s, rape reporting and convictions actually went *down* considerably (Larcombe 2011). But I believe that the previous reforms (which I'll explain more throughout this book), while very well intentioned, were insufficient and misguided. And even those reforms were still decades behind the times, meaning our "modern" rape laws are even further behind.

All of which is to say, a constellation of social problems have led to the outrages that inspired the #MeToo movement. To go back to King's quote that a riot is the language of the unheard, we need to ask ourselves, "What have we as a society been failing to hear?" The answer is: our basic social institutions at every level from families to schools to the media to the law have failed to respectfully and satisfactorily address the realities of sexual violence. The only place people who were hurt and hurting found a sympathetic audience was the internet, so that was where they went to vent their understandable anger. But we have to make other more conventional and regulated social institutions become more receptive to these complaints, because at the end of the day, the internet is a very unstable place for managing society and justice. And if we're serious about changing social institutions' attitudes toward sexual violence, we have to take the time to understand how they got the way they did, which I think mostly comes down to two things: a poor delineation of and differentiation between legal and ethical standards, and gender inequality (but probably not in the way you expect).

LEGAL VERSUS ETHICAL STANDARDS

After acknowledging so much complexity and ambiguity in consent, I think it's important to pause and note that there are *plenty* of stories of sexual violence that aren't ambiguous at all. Whether because Person B literally held a gun to Person A's head, because Person B was in a position of power to threaten and coerce Person A, or because Person B ignored or deliberately avoided hearing a "no," there are legions of appalling stories where Person B unquestionably did an immoral and often illegal thing. And by the time we narrow down our scope of consent violations to those that are actually reported to the police, we're pretty sure that the majority of them aren't very ambiguous at all, even if they usually fail to conform to a cultural stereotypical vision of stranger rape at gunpoint in a dark alley. But almost no sexual assaults are ever reported to the police in the first place, and that's true around the world (and still true even if we narrow our focus to rich countries like the United States, Western European nations, and Australia). On the rare occasions when sexual assaults are reported, the police rarely take them seriously. Even more rarely do they make an arrest or bother to examine the "rape kits" that collect biological evidence to support the reported crime. When the police do make an arrest, the perpetrators are rarely charged in court, and much more rarely found guilty. In fact, in most of the US states I looked at for numbers, in a given year, the number of people found guilty of rape or first-degree sexual assault was often so low that you couldn't really calculate reliable statistics around it. But don't be fooled into thinking that means rape and sexual assault are uncommon—it just means that our criminal justice systems are failing to create justice when it comes to rape and sexual assault. And that failure is both practically and symbolically significant, since it means rapists might (correctly) assume they can do whatever they want with impunity—and it means that it looks like society and the government just don't care.

As infuriating and frustrating as these statistics can be, as a society, we need to have some thoughtful debates about what we think constitutes actionable criminal behavior in general and with regard to sexual violations in particular. Part of why so many sexual assaults are never reported in the first place is that they're committed by someone the victim knows (and sometimes even really likes or loves). If your girlfriend steals $100 from you, are you going to call the police? What about $1,000? $10,000? Your car? Are you going to report her for assault if she slaps you across the face but doesn't seriously injure you? What if she was drunk or on drugs at the time, was clearly in violation of probation or parole, and will immediately be sent to prison if you make that call? While people do get the criminal justice system involved in some of these problems, they often don't—and I personally don't think that's necessarily a problem. A lot of sexual violence comes down to domestic disputes, and the criminal justice system isn't equipped to handle those well. We can imagine a well-developed system of noncriminal support hotlines and social workers which are probably much better candidates than the police and criminal justice system for managing many sexual violence and other domestic issues.

One of the major arguments I'll be making in this book is that the current cultural and legal conceptualization of "rape and sexual assault" is much too blunt to encompass the reality of these types of problematic experiences. As we'll discuss more throughout this book, activists originally introduced the term "sexual assault" to try to counter the specific cultural "stranger rape in an alley at gunpoint" image associated with the word "rape"; depending on whose analysis you believe, this change was possibly successful. But to keep up with the times, I'm proposing a different term and concept, "sexual viola-tion," which includes a wide range of nonconsensual experiences many of us might reasonably hesitate to label "sexual assaults" (much more on this idea in chapter 9). As a culture, we have developed higher expectations about what sexual consent should look like over time, and our language and laws should reflect those changes. Many Americans still live in states where overt vio-lence is required in order for a nonconsensual encounter to meet the standards of "rape" or "sexual assault," and I hope I don't have to work very hard to convince you that nonconsensual sex should be illegal— the end. Throughout this book, when I'm discussing existing statistics and laws, I'll use the term "sexual assault," but when I'm discussing broad experiences and shifting cul-tural ideas, as well as proposing new terminology, I'll use "sexual violation."

Presumably, society believes there are different levels of offenses war-ranting different types of punishment, whether that punishment is losing your romantic/sexual partner, general social disapprobation, losing your job or being expelled from school, losing custody of your children, fines, or imprisonment. We approach most other criminal-ish offenses with this sense of scale, and it seems reasonable to approach sexual violence the same way. Logically, there must be sexual violations of general moral and ethical stan-dards that warrant some degree of social disapprobation; sexual violations severe enough that organizations would want to distance themselves from the violator for pragmatic (e.g., safety), symbolic (e.g., "this reflects badly on our organization"), and/or financial (e.g., "if we don't fire you, we're going to get sued") reasons; and sexual violations serious enough that they warrant intervention from the criminal justice system, again for pragmatic, symbolic, and financial reasons. Although I think the way the criminal justice system currently treats many victims of sexual violence is appallingly bad, I also think that in a well-organized and orderly society, relatively few sexual violations *would* be reported to the police because it's in the best interest of survivors, perpetrators, and society as a whole for those violations to be addressed with counseling and remediation rather than prison (which, statistically speaking, only occasionally helps survivors feel better and almost never rehabilitates perpetrators).

As we consider reforming organized social institutions to address problems of sexual violence, we need to think about the roles that are appropriate for victims/survivors. Should their interests be the central organizing principle for justice, or should we also consider the best interests of perpetrators and society as a whole? For example, do we think that prosecutors should be able to prosecute a crime without the official complaint or support of the victim (in general, and for sexual violations in particular)? I don't have easy answers to those questions, because there aren't any. But we'll consider these questions and their social, legal, and philosophical implications from all sides in part II of this book.

In general, throughout this book, I want to challenge you to think about the types of sexual violations you think the criminal justice system should get involved with, and the types you think could be better addressed in other ways. I'll also challenge you to think about whether the *standards* for "violations" should be the same in a legal versus a social/ethical context. For example, returning to our opening anecdote, we might reluctantly concede that Bob's behavior was legal, since he eventually annoyed Al into agreeing to have sex with him—but we still might deem it socially undesirable and rather unethical. Presumably, in an ideal world, illegal behavior should always be unethical and undesirable, but many undesirable and unethical behaviors don't necessarily have to be illegal. As we consider these standards and laws, we can even imagine them in the context of a utopian system without racism, sexism, or class prejudice before we start dealing with the nitty-gritty realities of what the criminal justice system actually looks like later, in part II of this book. But before we do any of that, let's turn to preview the second reason I argued that so many social institutions are unsympathetic toward victims of sexual violence: gender inequality, but probably not in the way you think.

THE GENDER CHASM AND CONSENT

To return yet again to the story of Al and Bob and their many-gendered varia-tions, I hope we start to recognize that society and culture often think consent doesn't really mean the same thing for men and women. And if consent means something different when women give it (or don't) versus when men give it (or don't), that logically means we're probably going to have a *lot* of misunderstandings about what consent looks like in heterosexual interactions. We're even likely to see plenty of misunderstandings in same-sex interactions because so many of the "sexual scripts" (the sociological term for social rules and expectations of sexual interactions) were written by and for straight people, with all their messy ideas about sex and gender. And unsurprisingly, we definitely see those kinds of misunderstandings all over the place.

You might be understandably resistant to the word "misunderstanding" there, since plenty of (and perhaps even most) sexual assaults are obviously *not* good-faith misunderstandings—they're willfully committed crimes. Lots of men who sexually violate women haven't misunderstood anything and are just bad people, and many of them are complete assholes to women and to other men as well. If we focus on the kinds of men responsible for aggravated sexual assaults, we find many of them are just violent people in general. But if we look at, for example, the men reported for sexual assault on college campuses, like those profiled in Vanessa Grigoriadis's *Blurred Lines* (2017), we find many of them just seem like really average human beings who may or may not have done a bad thing. Grigoriadis admitted she was somewhat staggered by how profoundly traumatized many of the accused college men she interviewed were by the idea that they might have violated a woman and/or the perceived unfairness of the accusation. We're used to imagining "violators" as irredeemably terrible people, and I've certainly personally met a couple in my life who were. But many of them (even the ones who I know for a fact did something wrong) weren't.

As shocking as this seems to be for many women—who have often spent an inordinate amount of time in their lives thinking about sexual assault and protecting themselves from it—in my experience, a lot of guys have barely put any thought into it at all. I don't just mean they've spent little time think-ing about the possibility of being assaulted; I mean they just haven't really thought much about the idea of sexual assault—period. And if you haven't thought much about the complexities of something, it's dangerously easy to assume it's simple. The *vast* majority of men seem to understand that "good guys aren't rapists," but most of them have just learned to think of rape as "you put a gun to her head, and your dick in her pussy." Telling them to redefine rape as "failing to ask nicely before ripping her clothes off the way they do on the cover of her romance novel" and then making the connection to the thing they themselves did when drunk may require some serious cultural work.

Women, meanwhile, for all that they've often spent a lot of time thinking about how *not* to get raped themselves, have often put very little thought into how not to sexually violate men (or other women). Women learn to think of themselves as unthreatening because society tells them they're "physically weaker than men"—a phrase people repeat to me so often when I talk about consent that I've wished it could be banned from the language. Yes, women *on average* are physically weaker than men on many measures, but that doesn't mean they can't use weapons or have deep social power over men to coerce or "merely" humiliate them. A male friend of mine was literally raped at gunpoint by a woman, and when he complained to the (male, Canadian) police about it, their response was, "Why didn't you take the gun away from her?" Women learn to think of themselves and their physical beings as unthreatening, and men learn to think much the same—with the end result being that people often seem to doubt that a woman even *could* rape a man.

Again, I don't mean to imply that *all* men view consent and sexual violation in a specific way, or that *all* women do. Rather, I mean that society gives us gendered lenses with which to view these things, and if we want to change the lenses, we generally have to make an effort. Studies show substantial gaps in the way college men and women perceive these issues (Davies, Rogers, and Whitelegg 2009; Davies and Rogers 2006), but if we had studies with broader samples, I suspect we'd find similar gaps off college campuses too. Until we adjust our lenses to be more similar to one another, we will continue to have messy, spiraling, meandering, angry, and often pointless conversations about the meaning of rape and sexual violation. For so many women, their actual and potential sexual violation by men is a constant threat and reality that permeates their lives and consciousness. But for many men, the things women concern themselves with just don't seem like a big deal at all, because if someone did those things to them, they either wouldn't care or would be happy (with the notable exception that straight men feel theoretically vulnerable to sexual violation by other men).

I think many activists advocate for everyone trying to see the world of consent and sexual violation in the terms women do in this context, but I personally think that we'd all probably be better off taking a more informed third path. For their part, women are taught to think of their bodies and emotions as excessively vulnerable and fragile, and to overvalue their bodies and sexual "purity," while men are taught to think of themselves as strong and tough, and to undervalue their bodies but overvalue sexual "experience." *Many* people in each binary gender category don't absorb these norms and values, but they absorb a cultural awareness of them, feel their pressure or gravitational pull, and on some level usually recognize when they don't conform to them. If we want to imagine a gender-free vision for consent and sexual violation—and I think we should—we should imagine one for people who are neither weak nor strong, who are neither fragile nor tough, and who value consensual sexual experiences even when they're bad. The standard should consistently apply, regardless of the gender, bodies, or roles of the people involved. But to have sophisticated conversations about those standards, we have to be honest about our gendered and personal standards without simply condemning each other, silently or loudly.

As you read this book, I ask you to consider your own experiences, biases, and points of reference. What assumptions do you make about words like "rape," "rapist," "consent violation," "sexual assault," "sexual assault victim," "sexual assault survivor," and "sexual violence"? I don't know what your personal answers are, but I've got some psychological studies that let me guess. And with those guesses at hand, I'm going to ask for your consent, dear reader, to let me violate some of your assumptions and expectations about the context, meaning, and application of those words for the next nine chapters. On the off chance that you already agree with most of what I'm about to say, I hope I can at least add nuance to your thinking and help you better articulate your ideas. Regardless, I hope this book can change the tone of some of our cultural and legal conversations about sexual consent and assault.

But before we can dive into the nitty-gritty complexities of gender, the law, and major social change, we need to start with a short history lesson to establish some background and social context. So let's begin with a brief history of rape.

Chapter 2

A Brief History of Rape

Take a moment to think back to your middle or high school English class. There were probably a lot of books you were supposed to read, and at least a few that you actually did. One of the books you were almost certainly supposed to have read is Harper Lee's *To Kill a Mockingbird* (2014 [1960]), which remains one of the best-selling books of all time in the United States, won the Pulitzer Prize, and is widely read abroad as well. The story centers around Scout, a young white girl growing up in Alabama in the early 1930s, as she learns about disability, social class, and racism. The plot pivots around a scandalous trial in which Scout's lawyer father heroically (and unsuccessfully) defends a Black man accused of raping a poor white woman. As a book that is sort-of written for children (it at least maintains a quality of childlike naivete in its narrative perspective), it circumvents most of the more graphic elements of the rape accusation. The rape trial in the story is mostly just a means to illustrate Southern racism and classism, as the Black defendant is inevitably found guilty for the apparent crime of being nice to a white woman who is in fact probably being abused and molested by her own father.

Although it is fictional, Lee's story was grounded in grim fact. In 1931, nine Black teenage boys who became known as "the Scottsboro boys" were found guilty of raping two white women (who were probably prostitutes) in Alabama in sensational trials that have been the subject of much legal and cultural shame ever since. Lengthy social histories of rape in America usually note the influence of both the actual cases and Lee's fictionalized rendering of them as central to the overarching story of rape in America, which has always emphasized the defense of white women's virtue (Bourke 2007; Sanyal 2019). As in many other countries, race and social class have remained key points in American cultural conversations about rape, and we will revisit them many times throughout this chapter and the rest of this book (especially in chapter 7 when we examine their contemporary statistical validity). But I want to highlight one point that may be easy to overlook amid the glaring dimensions of race and class: I suspect for many young people in the United

States, *To Kill a Mockingbird* is their first in-depth exposure to the legal concept of "rape," and in that story, a *woman* levels a *false rape accusation against a man* to physically and socially protect herself. Put another way, the American cultural story of rape that is widely agreed to be the most enduring, poignant, and powerful is one of a woman lying about a rape that didn't actually happen.

IN THE OLD DAYS . . .

Once upon a time (and unfortunately, continuing today in some very gender-unequal countries), rape was culturally framed as a crime against society, a family, and/or the common good rather than against an individual person. This framing is entirely logical in societies with arranged marriages, since sexual consent isn't really a property of an individual in a cultural system where elders (usually fathers) can tell their children who to marry and thus have sex with. In societies where nonmarital sex was uncommon and always looked down on (which was, to lesser and greater degrees, most large societies prior to the advent of birth control in the mid-twentieth century), "rape" was socially and legally treated more like a property crime. In societies that heavily stigmatized unmarried pregnancies (i.e., most of them), women usually faced much harsher social stigma than men for having nonmarital sex, so men were freer to try to seek sex than women. Facing extremely negative consequences for nonmarital sex, women were not very motivated to say yes to men seeking sex from them. Indeed, women's motivations were so strong to say no that society and the law basically took for granted that of course an unmarried woman would say no. Hence virtually all older rape laws assumed women must put up a violent struggle in order to be able to accuse a man of rape, because how else could they prove exceptionally sincere resistance (Bourke 2007; Sanyal 2019)? Thus could men could become thieves of virtue (the term "rapist" did not even appear in English until the late 1880s), compromising the honor of families, fathers, or husbands, especially if the women involved were of higher social status.

This system provided few protections for unmarried women of lower social status, whose families were presumed to have little honor to protect and respect, and who often lived and worked in the homes of rich men. Moreover, their families usually could not afford to chaperone them, so they were much more vulnerable to the (wanted or unwanted) sexual advances of rich men. As appalling as it is to read that the law did not recognize rape of Black slaves in pre-1865 America (Bourke 2007; Sommerville 2005), class discrimination meant that servant girls in Britain were only slightly better off (Barber

1993) in an era where a substantial percentage of the population worked as live-in servants.

Historically, rape laws tended to require women to demonstrate they forcefully rejected a man's sexual overtures, that they repeatedly said no, *and* that they were able to provide one or more witnesses to the crime (Bourke 2007). A woman needed a darn good reason to accuse a man of rape, since by doing so, she risked the public perception that she was "damaged goods" and thus might become unmarriageable. Moreover, the punishment meted out to men for raping women was often that the pair had to marry, which sounds like a punishment for the woman as much as the man. As perverse as such penalties sound to modern readers, we must keep in mind that they originally served to ensure that the woman and any children sired as a result of the rape would be taken care of—and it might be very difficult for her to find a husband once it was clear that she was the mother of an illegitimate child. Moreover, it's not entirely clear that every "rape" in this era always meant what we imagine; some might have simply meant a woman had (consensual) sex with a man without the grace of marriage or her father's permission, thus dishonoring her family.

There is little evidence that any legal system has ever been particularly helpful to women who experienced rape in any sense of the word, but it was still kinder to women who were raped than men who were. Since "sodomy" was illegal in many countries until very recently, a man who was raped by another man and dared to complain about it was probably as likely to find himself charged with the crime of sodomy as he was to see any justice done against the man who raped him.[1] Fascinatingly, older European cultures seem to have recognized the idea of women taking sexual advantage of men in a way that modern society almost seems to have forgotten. From Lancelot's sexual entrapment by Elaine in Sir Thomas Malory's *Le Morte D'Arthur* (a French medieval telling of the King Arthur story) to women sneaking in darkness into the beds of men they love to force them into consummated marriages in William Shakespeare's *Measure for Measure* and *All's Well That Ends Well*, numerous stories from this era show women sexually manipulating or forcing men. Indeed, there are indications that the colloquial use of the word "rape" at the time even encompassed these actions, even though that idea had vanished by the time rape was coded into English-language law. But since men couldn't get pregnant and thus potentially dishonor their families with unwed pregnancies, neither the law nor society as a whole seems to have ultimately been very concerned with their sexual protection.

---

1. Even reporting nonsexual crimes could be risky for gay and bisexual men. In 1952, Alan Turing famously complained to the British police that his house had been burgled by a friend of Turing's male lover. Instead of investigating the theft, the police charged Turing with "gross indecency."

A COLLECTIVE OFFENSE BECOMES
AN INDIVIDUAL ONE

Over time, the cultural and legal meaning of "rape" changed along with larger cultural shifts in most rich countries around the meaning of marriage (and accompanying shifts in sex and love; Frank, Hardinge, and Wosick-Correa 2009). Marriage became increasingly focused on individual love and romance, and less on collective family economic bargaining (Santore 2008; Giddens 1992). (You can witness this transition occurring, and the resulting social conflicts that emerged, in Jane Austen's 1813 novel *Pride and Prejudice*, where everyone is constantly debating the virtues of marrying for love versus economic security.) As marriage became more of an individual choice and experience, a social concept of individual sexual autonomy also emerged. Gone were the days when fathers could tell their children who to marry (and have sex with): now, socially and economically independent children expected to make those decisions for themselves. You can also see this shift in patriarchal societies by looking at marriage proposal traditions. Long ago, young men asked a woman's father for permission to marry her—the end. By Austen's era, young men asked a woman to marry them, and if the woman said yes, *then* the man asked her father's permission. At some point, the idea of parental permission seemed to drift out of this social script altogether (or at most became a token afterthought). By the time Helen Fielding was writing a modern adaptation of *Pride and Prejudice* (*Bridget Jones's Diary: Edge of Reason*) in 1999, the young man didn't bother to ask the woman's father for permission to marry at all.

These marriage traditions are all connected to larger social trends where women and men in most rich countries came to expect to date ("court") independently of their families, and a few decades after that, to have sex with whoever they wanted. It's difficult to exaggerate what a massive social shift this idea presented. We tend to talk about the "sexual revolution" of the 1960s in terms of sexual exploration and orgasms, with a vague understanding that by the time it was wrapping up in the 1980s, it was no longer a big deal if women were married when they gave birth or if unmarried opposite-sex couples lived together. Those changes are all tremendously important, to be sure, but accompanying them is a basic ideological shift where most modern young people in rich countries have come to believe that their sexual and reproductive bodies are their own, to play with however they choose. In the first set of these shifts toward sexual autonomy, young people started to stake fairly basic claims: neither their parents, the government, nor larger social institutions like the church got to claim ownership of their semen/uterus or of their right to have sex (or not!) with the people they chose. Not long after, women began to insist they should even be able to claim sexual and reproductive autonomy from their husbands as the concept of "marriage" became more and more distant from that of "childbearing." In the most recent step toward sexual and reproductive autonomy, young people even began arguing that they should have the right to change their social gender presentation and perhaps ultimately their genitals, reproductive hormones, and secondary sex characteristics—and thus has emerged a fight for (and backlash against) trans rights.

These shifts were all inextricably tied to social, economic, and technological changes that were directly and indirectly relevant to the cultural and legal understanding of rape. Among others, these included: urbanization and its accompanying privacy/anonymity and economic independence from family farms and businesses; the shift toward independent living arrangements and away from living with parents or servants/masters; the invention of automobiles and the accompanying dating freedoms; the increasing availability of effective birth control and safe abortion; and steadily increasing college enrollment. Each of these factors contributed to shifts in our social understanding of rape. Collectively, these trends meant that young people enjoyed greater social and economic freedom from their families while also being much less protected, sheltered, and chaperoned by them. In short, there were many more opportunities than ever before for people to be raped by someone they didn't live with (i.e., other than their family members or employers—who they were probably unlikely to report or complain about because of emotional ties and/or economic security). At the same time, the previous potentially disastrous consequences of rape—unmarriageability and illegitimate children—faded as women obtained easier access to birth control and abortions and as society largely ceased to care about "illegitimacy."

Once society had more or less agreed people had the right to decide for themselves who they were having sex and children with (instead of being ordered around by their family members), the crime of rape started to move from an offense against the family to an offense against the individual (Frank, Hardinge, and Wosick-Correa 2009). If we imagine a woman birthing and raising a child who was the product of a rape nowadays, I assume most of us imagine she made a "choice" to "keep the child," rather than instinctively focusing on the taint to her family name from an illegitimate child with an unknown man. Socially, culturally, and legally, we tend to conceptualize rape as a violation of an individual and their body, not a violation of their family and honor.

NO MEANS NO

Along with the shift in social norms that meant people (especially women) now had more sexual autonomy came a shift in sexual scripts that meant women could now meaningfully consent to or refuse sex. Reading over a lot of historical accounts (Bourke 2007), it's hard to imagine most women were terribly enthusiastic about most of the available sex. The sex advice—written by men for other men—tended to take the tone of "don't take too long and try not to make it hurt too much," and no one seemed to be writing much sex advice for women until the 1960s. Indeed, even today, in a much more sexually enlightened era where sex advice books for all genders abound, women's sexual enjoyment in casual heterosexual encounters seems to be extremely underwhelming, especially compared to men's (Armstrong, England, and Fogarty 2012). So even if they weren't facing the possibility of dealing with an unwanted pregnancy (a possibility that was *much* higher before reliable birth control was invented and safe abortion was available), women's motivations to say yes to sex with men without some incentive other than sexual pleasure probably wasn't too high. Moreover, as I mentioned in the last chapter, most societies have stigmatized and penalized women's promiscuity far more than men's. Thus, women have faced at least three major disincentives for saying yes to sex with men that they might theoretically want to have: dubious physical pleasure, fear of pregnancy, and fear of social stigma.

The result of these cumulative disincentives is that women have historically had very few motivations to say yes to sex, and have probably often presented extremely mixed signals to men they were with—perhaps appearing very aroused, but still saying no to sex that men in a similar position would almost certainly have said yes to. I don't think most men have ever really had the insight to understand women's disadvantages in these regards, and so what men collectively saw was women who were clearly very turned on, excited, and possibly even in love who were still saying no to sex—and thus was born the idea that women saying no to sex really meant "convince me." For much of history, women saying no to men's offers of sex probably really did mean no, but there were also probably *many* occasions in which no meant "I would love to have sex with you if I thought it would be worth the risk, but it's probably not." And here's the complication many modern folks would like to not think about too hard: many of those women probably really *did* want to be convinced. Society taught women to be at war with their own sexual desires, and women brought those battlefields with them in all their interactions with men. Imagine an internal dialogue that goes something like, "Wanting to have sex with you would make me a slut and being a slut is bad, but I do kind of want to have sex with you, but I don't want to admit that I'm a slut, and if you think I'm a slut, you won't love me anymore, so please convince me to have sex with you in such a way that we can both tell ourselves that you persuaded me to it." Indeed, one interpretation of the lyrical situation in Frank Loesser's 1944 (published in 1949) song "Baby, It's Cold Outside" seemingly describes a very similar sentiment. I will return many times in this book to the theme that open sexual communication is impossible without true gender equality. But the consequence of an extreme lack of gender equality may have been that a woman's no was much more nebulous and flexible in the past than it is today in modern societies.

With so few healthy sexual outlets available to women, it seems grimly plausible that many women may have become enamored with the idea of nonconsensual sex. To modern readers, it seems appalling and illogical that many of the male commentators of the 1800s wrote about how women often actually "wanted" to be "raped" (Bourke 2007; Sanyal 2019). But given that women were generally socially denied any real sexual outlets at all (even masturbation), the idea of sexual contact they didn't have to take any responsibility for may have started to take on a forbidden allure. Even in a modern era, the majority of women and a substantial minority of men admit to fantasizing about being raped (Lehmiller 2018). I can only imagine that these fantasies were all the more intriguing to some people in an era where the only prospect of having sex at all (or with someone other than one's spouse) was from a nonconsensual encounter. Repression and inequality sow confusion, dishonesty, and desperation, and women were probably very uncertain about what they wanted sexually—breeding further confusion in the men they interacted with.

WHICH CAME FIRST: CULTURE OR LAWS?

Figuring out if laws or culture came first is a chicken-or-the-egg problem that is basically unsolvable. Culture informs and creates laws, but laws also shape and inform culture in a constant iterative process. Not all laws get enforced; in the United States, many of them explicitly do not. If you do a Google search for "crazy laws in the United States," you'll get a wide array of examples, from not being allowed to play bingo while under the influence to women needing to ask their husband's permission to obtain false teeth. Even long after cultural norms have changed enough to make old laws wildly obsolete, people sometimes don't bother to change those laws (which may have never been enforced in the first place). Meanwhile, people often don't have strongly formed opinions about many issues (sometimes even including highly controversial ones like abortion), so their opinions can be easily swayed by friends, a single passionate conversation, or the mere thought that "well, that's the law, so it must be right."

Historically, most rape laws in rich countries developed from cultural conceptualizations of rape as a physically violent crime perpetrated by an unknown man against an innocent young woman, resulting in nonconsensual vaginal intercourse. This version of rape originated from a time when young women often led sheltered, very chaperoned lives with limited contact with people outside their own close social networks. I think we can probably safely assume women of the past were very unlikely to publicly accuse men close to them of sexually assaulting them, just as women of the present are. Thus, society and the law mostly only had to address sexual assaults where the man was unknown to the woman and her social circle. Moreover, many young women had so few opportunities to socialize privately with young men (and were often so strongly stigmatized for doing so) that complaining about having been sexually assaulted by a young man they knew would have raised a lot of awkward questions about why they were alone with him in the first place.

Two of the underestimated consequences of modernization are a general increase in privacy, along with a semi-related increase in coeducational socialization. I assume most of the people reading this book have learned to take for granted that women and men can use the same entrances for buildings and sit together interspersed in public places, but many cultures still expect them to be separated for these things, as for most other aspects of their lives. (The modern legacy of these anxieties of protection persists with public bathrooms and locker rooms, which still remain separated by gender/sex in most societies, often with the specific rationale that public coed bathrooms would make women vulnerable to rape [Schilt and Westbrook 2015].) However, it is specifically the *combination* of increased coed socialization and privacy that has created a whole new world of opportunities for people to be sexually violated, but less and less in the form society and the law were accustomed to envisioning in their notion of "rape." Alone together in cars, on dates in their own dorm rooms and apartments, in the dark corners and back rooms of coed parties full of strangers and near-strangers, inside coed bathrooms and showers, and even in overtly sexual spaces like sex parties, people in modern societies now enjoy much greater sexual freedoms than in the past—but also have fewer formal social and institutional protections for their sexual bodies.

The more a sexual assault deviated from the original specific cultural script of violent stranger rape, the more society and the law struggled to place it in proximity to its vision of "rape." Encounters started to look less like this version of rape if:

- There was no evidence of physical violence (such as bruises, scratch marks, etc.).
- The woman's "innocence" had been "compromised" in some way before the encounter took place (particularly if she was intoxicated or not a virgin).
- The woman and the man knew each other, and especially if they had engaged in other sexual activities (even kissing).
- The woman and the man were in an established relationship, especially if they were married.
- The genders of the people involved were anything other than a cis man attacking a cis woman.
- The nonconsensual sex was anything other than vaginal intercourse.

As men and women came to socialize more privately in ways that exposed them to sexual violation, the cultural (and eventually legal) concept of "rape" slowly expanded to encompass more and more situations outside this traditional vision of stranger rape.

Throughout the 1970s, anti-rape feminist groups in the United States pushed hard to change US rape laws that mostly only acknowledged or were heavily geared toward this older vision of what rape meant (Klein 2008). By the end of the 1970s, changes in most states had removed requirements for evidence of physical violence, introduced "rape shield laws" that reduced the likelihood that women's (victims') sexual histories could be brought up during rape trials, and expanded the list of sexual acts that counted as "rape" (Bevacqua 2000). Slightly later changes made spousal rape illegal and made it possible for men to be the victims of rape (although usually only if they were penetrated—more on that later). Beginning in the 1960s, the National Organization for Women (NOW) began pushing for lower penalties to be associated with rape, in the hope that more rape cases would be brought to trial and conviction. (In the 1950s, as in the 1930s world of *To Kill a Mockingbird*, several states kept the death penalty for rape convictions, which activists feared created hesitancy among prosecutors and juries.) Other rich countries changed rape laws throughout the 1980s, with poorer countries following suit. By the end of the twentieth century, nearly every country in the world had changed their rape laws (Frank, Hardinge, and Wosick-Correa 2009). Although I want to keep our focus centered on the United States, I also want to look at other wealthy countries—especially Britain and Germany—for purposes of comparison and contrast.

RAPE LAWS IN OTHER COUNTRIES

Statistically speaking, Western European countries tend to rank much higher in terms of gender equality than most other countries in the world (including the United States). You might therefore reasonably imagine their rape laws are more sophisticated, more nuanced, and better enforced than those in the United States and other countries. However, on average, that is not the case, and many twenty-first-century Western European rape laws look a bit like US ones did in the 1950s (minus the threat of the death penalty). As of late 2020, Amnesty International reported that only half of European countries defined rape as sex without consent, instead mostly framing rape as a sexual crime that requires violence or coercion (Amnesty International 2020). I should caution that many of these laws are being hotly debated as of this writing, so by the time you read this book, there's a decent chance the laws in some of these countries might have changed a lot.

Let's start our short world tour with Germany, which generally ranks extremely high in the world for both gender and income equality. Moreover, sexual culture in Germany is quite different even from many of its surrounding countries—prostitution is legal there, and Berlin is famous for its sex clubs. We might imagine the combination of relative equality and an extremely liberal sexual culture would create a nation with sophisticated rape laws, but somehow until quite recently, German rape laws managed to get left behind in the previous century. Germany reformed its rape laws in 1997 to become more gender neutral, broaden the scope of culpable sexual offenses, include psychological coercion, and allow for the possibility of marital rape. Despite these reforms, until 2016, when a series of famous cases prompted outrage at home and abroad, German law maintained that rape victims had to show evidence of physical resistance, not merely say no. Contemporary German rape laws now encompass any nonconsensual sexual contact and broadly penalize many forms of sexual exploitation and coercion (Sanyal 2019).

Let's continue our European tour and head next to France, where equality and sexual tolerance are also high. In 2021, France saw a wave of rape law reforms sweep the country, including expanding the definition of what counted as "sex" for purposes of rape to include oral sex. Unlike most rich countries, until that time, France didn't have a legal age of consent. With some apparent controversy, they reluctantly settled on fifteen as an age of consent, with provisions for age differences between the people involved (Doezema 2018). Around the same time, they also voted to extend the statute of limitations on rape charges (meaning they extended the amount of time victims have to report a crime and the government has to file charges). However, even after these reforms, rape law in France still requires evidence of violence, coercion, threat, or surprise. Interestingly, French rape law includes a provision that the accused perpetrator must have been aware of the victim's lack of consent, which is a concept we'll discuss in more depth when our tour arrives in the United Kingdom.

As we continue our tour of Europe, let's go next to the Nordic countries, which have extremely high levels of gender equality but vary in how they legally address rape (Amnesty International 2019). For example, Denmark only legally determined that "no means no" in 2020, while Sweden made the same conclusion in 2018. Even compared to its neighboring countries, reported rapes in Sweden in particular are extremely high and have been since the 1990s. International comparisons are complicated here, because Swedish authorities have been pretty generous about what they classified as "rape" for a long time (despite only recently changing the law to "no means no"). Moreover, living in a very gender-equal country, Swedish women probably feel much safer reporting instances of sexual violation to authorities than women in other countries. On the other hand, as discussed earlier in this chapter, greater gender equality may create more opportunities for women to be raped as they experience greater sexual freedom in general. Furthermore, there may be some odd cultural discrepancies at work, since the majority of convicted Swedish rapists are foreigners (Khoshnood et al., 2021)—a likely by-product of a law historically emphasizing "stranger rapes" in a small country where so many native-born citizens already know each other.

Let's make our final European stop in the UK, which has extant and continuous laws regarding rape dating back to the 1700s. British rape laws are much more encompassing than those in many other European countries, instituting expansive charges by 2003 to ensure women could be accused as rape perpetrators and men as victims (McKeever 2019), and to legally enshrine the idea that "no means no." The UK also maintains a controversial provision for "rape by deception," meaning that someone can be charged with rape if they "misrepresent" themselves in some fashion, and many critics have argued the provision is dangerously broad (even infamously being applied to a transgender person who supposedly "lied" about their gender [Sanyal 2019]). The other major controversial aspect of British rape law pertains to *mens rea* (Bourke 2007; Alexander 1995), a topic we'll discuss in great depth in the second half of this book. Basically, *mens rea* refers to the mentality, understanding, and consciousness of a criminal. If Person A believes that Person B has consented to have sex with them, is Person A still a rapist? British law rather strictly says no. This legal provision was intensely argued in the British court system in *DPP v. Morgan* (1975). There are conflicting accounts from all the parties involved in this case, but the outline is something along these lines: William Anthony Morgan invited three friends back to his house to have sex with his wife. The three friends claimed he said that she was "kinky" and would enjoy being pretend-raped by them. (Morgan denied this claim.) A violent gang rape ensued, and Daphne Morgan immediately went to the police to say she was raped. All four of the men involved were convicted of rape, and the convictions held upon appeal. However, the appellate judges determined that if the defendant sincerely believed the victim had consented, the defendant would not be guilty of rape. In this specific case, they determined based on the circumstances of the case, no sincere belief was held, and thus the defendants were guilty. The argument from the case that has remained highly controversial is the judges' declaration that there was no objective or "reasonably held" standard for these assertions: the defendant merely had to believe the other person had consented (Bourke 2007).

The same general trends of British law apply to rape laws in British Commonwealth countries like Canada and Australia. The key difference is that in contrast to the UK, where *mens rea* was applied very broadly, some Australian states have determined the defendant's belief in the victim's consent must be "reasonable" (and this distinction was made in British law officially in 2003). Meanwhile, in 2022, the Canadian government passed federal legislation to ensure that intoxication could not be used as an excuse for committing a crime, specifically targeting sexual assault in the legislation (Department of Justice Canada 2022).

RAPE LAWS IN THE UNITED STATES: A SAMPLING

Like Canada and Australia, the primary way the United States creates and enforces law against rape and sexual assault is through its many individual jurisdictions (for these purposes, mostly states). In the United States, the majority of criminal cases (including sexual assault) are handled at the state level. There is some federal law on the subject—mostly limited to governing conduct within maritime jurisdictions or in prisons—and because it is at least uniform, I'll start with those federal laws to see how sexual assault is legally organized in the United States. So we'll look at those federal statutes first, and then briefly compare and contrast those to a handful of states.

US federal law doesn't have a provision for "rape" per se. Instead, the federal government (again, applicable within "the special maritime and territorial jurisdiction of the United States or in a Federal prison") has several levels of charges that start with "aggravated sexual abuse." For this charge, USC, Title 18, Part 1, Chapter 109A declares that a person must have engaged in a "sexual act" with someone using force or threatening serious bodily harm, or rendering someone unconscious or intoxicated. In these statutes, a "sexual act" is defined as

(A) contact between the penis and the vulva or the penis and the anus however slight; (B) contact between the mouth and the penis, the mouth and the vulva, or the mouth and the anus; (C) the penetration, however slight, of the anal or genital opening of another by a hand or finger or by any object, with an intent to abuse, humiliate, harass, degrade, or arouse or gratify the sexual desire of any person; or (D) the intentional touching, not through the clothing, of the genitalia of another person who has not attained the age of 16 years with an intent to abuse, humiliate, harass, degrade, or arouse or gratify the sexual desire of any person.

While these designations for "sexual acts" are clearly intended to be relatively gender neutral, as with most legal designations around the world, they make it very difficult to charge someone with the crime of forcing a person to penetrate them.

The next level in the federal government's scaled offenses is "sexual abuse," which includes a sexual act accompanied by threats that do not pertain to grievous bodily harm, in which the other person is "physically incapable" of "communicating unwillingness" or that simply occurs without the other person's consent. The law also contains provisions for "abusive sexual contact," which is basically the same general set of conditions as aggravated sexual abuse but involves genital touching "with an intent to abuse, humiliate, harass, degrade, or arouse or gratify the sexual desire of any person" instead of being included in the aforementioned list of "sexual acts." Thus on our international scale of countries where "no means no," the United States seems to pass, for all that the federal government intentionally doesn't have a specific statute for rape.

Let's compare these federal statutes to the wildly varying ones between the states. Michigan, which is now considered a moderate state, was often used as a model for sexual assault laws in the 1970s (Spohn and Horney 1996). In Michigan, sexual assault in the first degree occurs among adults when there is a sexual act (involving broadly defined "penetration") and: the defendant was in a position of authority (such as teacher) over the victim; the defendant was armed or was in any way able to threaten the victim; the victim suffered grievous bodily harm; the victim suffered physical harm and there was mental incapacitation; *or* the defendant was in the process of committing another felony (such as theft). Sexual assault in the second degree occurs when any of these circumstances apply and there is no penetration. Third-degree sexual assault involves penetration and force/coercion (without injury) or an incapacitated victim (again without injury). Fourth-degree sexual assault involves the same circumstances without penetration and also applies when the defendant works for the department of corrections and the victim is an inmate (i.e., prison guards raping prisoners). In the 1970s, Michigan instituted a series of amendments specifying that victims didn't need to show signs of resistance, their testimony didn't require corroboration, victims' previous sexual conduct was usually inadmissible as evidence in court, and victims' names should be publicly protected.

Let's go next to California, whose rape laws look so different from Michigan's that it's a little hard to believe they're from the same country dealing with the same crime. California is an extremely liberal state that is home to more Americans than any other. The state's rape laws go on for many pages, so I'll have to do some very reductive summarizing. Offenses are separated by acts rather than degrees, divided out by "rape" (vaginal intercourse), "sodomy" (anal intercourse with a penis), "oral copulation" ("copulating the mouth of one person with the sexual organ or anus of another person"), and "fondling" (touching "intimate parts" of another person for sexual arousal, gratification, or abuse). The law starts with the basic premise that these acts are criminal if the victim was unable to consent because of disability that "reasonably should be known" to the defendant or if the victim was unconscious, if force or threats or coercion were used, if the victim was intoxicated (notably, it doesn't require the defendant to have drugged the victim), or if the defendant pretended to be someone else. California's statutes have been amended so many times that they've become increasingly difficult to parse, but in 1979, the state declared, "The essential guilt of rape consists in the outrage to the person and feelings of the victim of the rape. Any sexual penetration, however slight, is sufficient to complete the crime." In 2017, they added, "all forms of nonconsensual sexual assault may be considered rape for purposes of the gravity of the offense and the support of survivors." They defined consent in 2022 to mean "positive cooperation in act or attitude pursuant to an exercise of free will," and specifically added that if consent is contested, "a previous dating or marital relationship is not sufficient to constitute consent."

The next stop on our US tour will be Texas, which is also home to a significant percentage of Americans but is much more conservative. Texas's sexual assault statute was written after 1983, was repeatedly amended as recently as 2021, and is unusual in its inclusion of a provision for "forced to penetrate." Somewhat like Michigan, Texas's system is scaled according to the nature of the offense. Thus, "aggravated sexual assault" occurs there when a person uses force, threats of force, or a deadly weapon; intentionally intoxicates another person; or takes advantage of a disabled person and in so doing

> intentionally or knowingly: causes the penetration of the anus or sexual organ of another person by any means, without that person's consent; causes the penetration of the mouth of another person by the sexual organ of the actor, without that person's consent; or causes the sexual organ of another person, without that

person's consent, to contact or penetrate the mouth, anus, or sexual organ of another person, including the actor.

Note that Texas statutes are also the first in our US tour to specify a requirement to take the *mens rea* of the defendant into account within the statute (as opposed to through a default state-of-mind provision that applies across the criminal code), detailing that the defendant must "intentionally or knowingly" violate the victim. The next level offense in Texas is "sexual assault," which is most of the things associated with aggravated sexual assault, but at a lower level (e.g., taking advantage of an intoxicated person rather than intoxicating them yourself). It also includes a lot of provisions for various professionals who might take advantage of their charges, like teachers, healthcare providers, and clergy. In 2019, Texas added a misdemeanor charge of "indecent assault," which encompasses nonconsensual sexual touching and contact.

For the final stop on our US legal tour, let's go to New York, which is a large and very liberal state, and probably has the most finely gradated rape laws in the country, with separate charges for rape in the first, second, and third degree; criminal sexual act in three degrees; sexual abuse in three degrees; and aggravated sexual abuse in four degrees, as well as distinct charges for sexual misconduct, forcible touching, facilitating a sex offense with a controlled substance, and sexually motivated felony. You might imagine that contained among this litany of offenses we would find subtlety, nuance, and a sophisticated recognition of the complexities of sexual consent, but alas, such is not the case. New York simply felt compelled to create entirely different charges for various sexual acts (rape = vaginal intercourse, criminal sexual act = oral and anal sex, sexual abuse = sexual contact, aggravated sexual abuse = insertion of digits and foreign objects) and then graded most of them in some very particular ways. Thus, first degree addresses victims who are "forcibly compelled" or are "incapable of consent by reason of being physically helpless"; second degree, victims who are "incapable of consent by reason of being mentally disabled or mentally incapacitated"; and third degree, "lack of consent by reason of some factor other than incapacity to consent." The law further specifies many conditions under which people are deemed to have reduced capacity to consent due to situations of authority and care over their charges (such as prison guards, healthcare workers, and police officers). In contrast to California's intentionally broad notion of sexual consent, New York's looks awkwardly obsolete, specifying that "lack of consent" comes from "forcible compulsion, incapacity to consent," and the wide range of aforementioned unequal power dynamics. However, conspicuously absent from these many sexual offenses is the simple concept that "no means no." New York is hardly alone in this problem. By some counts, the majority of American states don't have solid consent laws, although many state legislatures have been working in recent years to reform these statutes. For example, Indiana changed its laws in 2022 so that a person who "physically, verbally, or by other visible conduct refuse[s] the person's acts" has legally been the victim of rape (Lange 2022). *Thus, only some Americans live in areas where no means no.*

REFORMS AND THEIR CHALLENGES

With so many rape law reforms sweeping nations and states throughout the 1970s and '80s, many activists were optimistic there would be meaningful and positive changes in rape reporting and conviction rates, hopefully resulting in a reduction in the number of rapes and better treatment of survivors (Frank, Hardinge, and Wosick-Correa 2009; Bevacqua 2000). Unfortunately, it's really hard to know if that's happened (in the United States or elsewhere). Reports of rape to the police have certainly gone up—and in many places skyrocketed—over the last fifty years. But since so many places expanded what "counts" as rape, it's very hard to know if those changes occurred because sexual violence increased or because acknowledgment of it increased. Frank and colleagues (2009) conducted the largest multinational comparative study, demonstrating incontestably that rape law reforms improved reports to police and that this change was about twice as strong in rich countries like those in Europe and North America as it was in poor countries in other parts of the world. Inevitably, as police reporting rates have gone up, overall conviction rates in many countries have plummeted, for reasons that are difficult to assess. Are many of the reports from cases that are unlikely to secure convictions? Are criminal justice personnel unprepared to deal with the massive backlog of "rape kits" (the physical specimen kits that are collected when a person reports themselves a victim of rape)? Does the criminal justice system just not care much about rape victims, as many activists have complained? Or are rape convictions about on par with other forms of violent simple assault, as other analysts have claimed? In the United States, for example, the *vast* majority of reported rapes do not involve a weapon (Statista n.d.), and these "simple rape cases" (as opposed to aggravated rape cases) are much less likely to result in conviction (Spohn and Spears 2006).

I'll attack more of these statistical complexities in chapter 5. For now, I'll summarize by noting that all anyone can say with confidence is that reported rapes have gone up a lot over the last thirty years and that reported rapes appear to lead to convictions less often than other violent crimes, but given that about 90 percent don't involve any sort of weapon, from a legal perspective, the level of "violence" for reported rapes does tend to scale pretty low (Statista n.d.). Presumably, other violent crimes also usually carry much less psychological and social damage for the victims than rape does, so reporting them and dealing with police and the public is quite a different matter. A homicide trial never has to deal with the victim making an appearance, but a rape trial subjects victims to what has become known as "second trauma" as they are repeatedly examined physically and verbally, then interrogated in front of the community (Corrigan 2013). The legal system is slow and usually doesn't care much about how victims feel. One can imagine someone who experienced a rape lasting perhaps fifteen minutes being reluctant to spend the next two years repeatedly telling their story to police, social workers, prosecutors, and juries. Rape law reforms have done a lot to protect victims from what used to be the most obviously terrible parts of this process (especially dragging their sexual histories out in front of an entire community) but have done little to erase the gross indignity of having your genitals inspected by a stranger to collect a rape kit mere hours after being violated.

Rape activism in the United States declined precipitously by the end of the 1970s, reemerging in the 1990s as feminists began to introduce phrases like "date rape" and "acquaintance rape" into the popular vocabulary (Bevacqua 2000). Activists wanted these terms and concepts to highlight rapes that occurred at the hands of someone the victim knew and perhaps even liked, in contrast to the persistent vision of rape as mostly occurring with violent strangers. Although activists were successful at raising public awareness in the United States and a few other countries about the high frequency of nonconsensual sexual encounters that happened in these more intimate contexts, their work appears to have had relatively few direct effects on the law. Instead, the US government expanded its vision of Title IX, which provides support for colleges and universities and demands gender equality at those supported schools. The government directed universities to establish a collection of increasingly byzantine collegiate Title IX panels, which exist in a bizarre grey zone that is only sort-of part of the court system. These panels have been the subject of intense criticism, as their rulings can ruin the lives of students or professors but are not subject to clear standards of evidence or accountability (Sanyal 2019; Grigoriadis 2017). Moreover, none of these panels address date or acquaintance rapes that occur outside of universities, which has produced an incorrect feeling in both popular media and culture that date/acquaintance rape is mostly a problem only on college campuses.

As the #MeToo movement swept through the United States and other countries in 2017, it helped encourage major shifts in European rape laws but few legal changes in the United States. Most of the changes in the United States were relatively subtle, such as California removing its separate charge for spousal rape in 2021 and instead integrating marital rape charges with existing rape statutes. Other states, such as Hawaii, changed the statute of limitations for many sex crimes. In many places, legislators wanted to look like they were doing *something*. A few high-profile cases went to trial as well, most notably the infamous movie mogul who had helped push the social movement in the first place—Harvey Weinstein, who was found guilty of multiple counts of rape and sexual assault.

THINKING BACK TO THINK AHEAD

As we wrap up our whirlwind review of the history of rape laws in the United States and Europe, their variations, and their changes, let's take a moment to consider some of the successes and failures of previous reforms. One of these was that many states removed the word "rape" from their statutes altogether to try to escape the cultural baggage of the term, replacing it with "sexual assault." This decision was a conscious one that many activists encouraged (Bevacqua 2000), but the difference seems to have largely failed to sink into popular consciousness. These changes are decades old now, and it's a little hard to understand why activists were so unsuccessful at changing the cultural conversation to match the changes in the laws. While many people changed their vocabulary to include the new legal term "sexual assault," it mostly just expanded the sexual acts that the culture now counted as violations rather than shifting the imagined social context (i.e. strange violent men hurting women) of the crime.

We have seen in this chapter that most of the previous attempts at reform of the legal system with regard to sexual assault have focused on levels of violence/brutality, the nature of the sexual acts, attempts at gender neutrality (discussed more in the next chapter), dismissing evidence of the accuser's sexual activity and the need for supporting witnesses, and illegalizing marital rape. These reforms were essential and revolutionary for their time, but the motivations for most of them date to half a century ago. Our entire sexual world has changed since then, with many more young people actively identifying as gay, lesbian, bisexual, trans, or queer; many more people going to college and marrying much later or not at all; massive changes in sexual expectations in dating and courtship; increased access to better birth control and reduced access to abortion; and the internet's creation of an entirely new way for people to date and "hook up" (a term that didn't even exist in 1980). We need to be having a serious cultural conversation about the way these changes might demand updates to existing laws and social expectations around sexual assault. We'll explore some of those possibilities in the second half of this book, but I want to leave you with those ideas as we turn our attention now to focus more specifically on gender.

Chapter 3

Double Standards and a Culture of Mistrust

IT'S NOT "RAPE" IF IT HAPPENS TO A MAN

You can learn a lot about American ideas about consent by watching movies and TV. I don't mean that you can learn *good* models for consent, but you can learn a lot about the way we view consent. Scenes where women's consent gets violated are played for horror, sadness, and disgust—but also for sex appeal and arousal. You can find examples of every one of these in the extremely popular series *Game of Thrones*: from Daenerys's relatively peaceful rape at the hands of her royal new husband (whom she eventually falls in love with) to Sansa's repeated violent rapes by her insane husband (whom she eventually kills) to Cersei's apparent rape by her brother-lover Jaime (in whose arms she ultimately dies). Cersei's rape scene in season 4 (2014) especially stands out on that list because the director claimed it wasn't a rape scene—even though Cersei repeatedly says no to sex, appears to struggle, and never says yes—a fact that caused considerable cultural commentary at the time. That scene follows the general pattern of rape scenes played for sexiness in films and TV, which usually start with a woman saying no, then showing her (supposedly) becoming physically into what's happening to her. Just like the rest of our culture, Hollywood seems to believe that women's consent is either serious and a Really Big Deal . . . or kind of meaningless, depending on how turned on she is.

It's a lot harder to find scenes where men's consent gets violated. Those scenes are sometimes serious—especially when men get violated by other men, such as in *Outlander*—but are often played for comedy when men are violated by women. These scenes have become conspicuously less common in TV and movies over time, and most of the examples are now quite old.

The last example I can find from a major wide-release film is *Get Him to the Greek* (2010), where a male character is orally and anally fucked with a dildo against his will. He immediately tells his friends, "I think I was just raped," and they laugh. Part of the humor here is apparently supposed to be the extravagant size difference between the small woman and the big man. Even one of the 2010 blog entries I found online harshly criticizing this scene still included the observation that "in reality, he could have easily tossed her off him" (Sowisdral 2010). The scene became so notorious that it even has a section on the film's Wikipedia page; a movie critic for the *Los Angeles Times* wrote disgustedly, "Can't we just agree going forward that no matter who the victim is, rape jokes never work?" (Sharkey 2010). This attitude shift was a stark change from merely five years earlier, when *Wedding Crashers* was the highest-grossing comedy of 2005, and no one seemed particularly concerned about the well-being of Vince Vaughan's character, who is literally tied up to a bed and raped by a woman. He even tells his friend the next day that he was "raped" the night before, but the scene is played entirely for comedy, and he ends up cheerfully marrying his rapist at the end of the movie. The scene seems to have made remarkably little impression on many viewers, and even a 2018 *GQ* article discussing whether the movie "held up" to the sociopolitical scrutiny of time argues that it decidedly does not because of its sexually exploitative humor (Meslow 2018). And yet. The author of that piece only mentions Vaughan's rape in passing and *doesn't mention it as one of the problematic aspects of the film.* In fact, when I Googled "Wedding Crashers rape," one of the only places on the internet where people were complaining about the scene was a men's rights activist (a viciously conservative men's group) forum on Reddit. Ouch.

In season 10, *South Park* (2006) viciously mocked this gender disparity in attitudes toward sexual violation of men in an episode where Ike—a kindergartner—has sexual relations with his female teacher. In the episode, Ike's brother Kyle goes to the police to report the situation, and the police are ready to take notes when they initially assume that a male teacher is molesting a female student. But when they learn that a female teacher is molesting a male student, their response is just to say, "Niiiice," adding, "We need to track this student down and give him his Luckiest Boy of America medal right away." Later one of the policemen complains, "Where were all these sexed-up teachers when I was a kid?" The police only reluctantly agree to arrest the teacher because "the lady principal insisted," with the strong implication that only a woman would think a woman molesting a young boy was actually a crime.

Hollywood mostly seems to have gotten the memo that male rapes aren't funny anymore, and the most recent famous portrayal of a heterosexual male rape, in *Bridgerton* season 1 (2020), isn't played for laughs. Indeed, the show writers went out of their way to turn a very disturbing scene of fairly blatant sexual manipulation in the original 2000 source book into a *slightly* more ambiguous encounter in which it's not clear the female character fully understands what she's doing. She intentionally gets on top of her husband in what begins as a consensual sexual encounter, then, after he tells her to stop (so he can pull out), she refuses so she can force him to orgasm inside her. The show is a historical romantic comedy set in the early 1800s, and it would be extremely ahistorical for him to accuse her of "raping" him. However, in the book, he does accuse her of taking advantage of him, which he notably does not do in the show. The TV show's scene caused quite a stir online, with the general consensus finding it problematic that the show didn't treat her behavior as more obviously objectionable.

Although it seems we've made progress toward more gender equity, we should ask ourselves why we as a culture tend to understand rape scenes so differently when we change the genders of the violators and the violated? I don't think there's a simple answer to that question, so we're left with a bunch of complicated, multilayered answers. Those answers start with the assumption that men always want sex (with anyone of the gender[s] they're attracted to), and a corollary assumption that women only sometimes do, making women the sexual gatekeepers in heterosexual interactions. And then (like the blogger commenting on *Get Him to the Greek*) we assume women are physically weaker than men, which means women can't pose a real threat to men in terms of sex or violence. Lastly, we're constantly bombarded with cultural and supposedly scientific narratives claiming that men are rarely the victims of sexual assault, so we don't learn to worry about them as potential victims. These ideas all combine so that women learn to think they can't really pose a sexual threat to men, and men learn to think their sexual consent doesn't matter very much. Interestingly, these same weird ideas about gendered consent still apply in convoluted ways in gay and lesbian interactions, not just straight ones, but I'll get to that later. For now, let's break down each of these assumptions in more detail.

ASSUMPTION 1: MEN ARE ALWAYS ASKING FOR IT; NO ONE KNOWS WHEN WOMEN ARE

A male friend of mine, who was sexually assaulted by a woman in college, grimly summarized his confusion about the experience by explaining, "Men are expected to be in a perpetual state of consent." He said he felt the admission to himself (let alone others) that at some moment, when presented with the opportunity, he hadn't wanted to have sex with a woman, undermined his own masculinity and heterosexuality. (As it turned out, he was gender nonconforming and pansexual, so he was already struggling there a bit anyway.) In short, our culture expects that heterosexual men always want to have sex all the time with basically any woman they can, and that the only reason they don't is because . . . rules and laws say they can't, women restrict their sexual access, their dicks will give out eventually—or some combination of these reasons. This cultural attitude basically asks skeptically, *why would any man ever say no to sex with someone of a gender he's attracted to?* It was probably best summarized in the 1989 film *When Harry Met Sally*, when Harry tells Sally, "No man can be friends with a woman he finds attractive. He always wants to have sex with her." Sally responds, "So you're saying that a man can be friends with a woman he finds unattractive?" and Harry says, "No, you pretty much want to nail them too." While the phrase "she was asking for it" floats around the culture (often just sarcastically at this point), the equivalent phrase for men just doesn't even exist *because we assume men are always asking for it*. It doesn't warrant comment.

Yet while we assume men always want to have sex with anyone of a gender they're attracted to, we expect women to be a lot pickier and to say no to sex a lot more often. In general, society tends to assume men just want and think about sex a lot more than women do, but it's actually pretty hard to test or measure this assumption empirically. One of the few studies that actually tried with a remotely meaningful methodology asked college students to keep track of their daily thoughts about sex, finding that men thought about sex about twice as often as women did (Fisher, Moore, and Pittenger 2012). But it also found that men thought about food and sleep about twice as much as women, so maybe men just think about their bodies more than women do. Moreover, it found that "erotophilia"—the person's general comfort with sex—was a much better predictor of how often they thought about sex than their gender was. This finding in turn suggests that most of the difference in sexual thoughts between men and women just stems from how comfortable they are with sex, not their gender per se.

We also tend to assume women will be much more likely to say no to sex with random men than men will be to say no to sex with random women, and science has supported this assumption pretty well with many different kinds of data. However, it turns out you can greatly reduce that gender gap in unenthusiasm in some very interesting ways. Various experiments combined (Conley et al. 2011) show that straight women turn down sex more than men for three main reasons: (1) they think the guy asking won't be a good lay, (2) they're worried about being stigmatized as a slut, and (3) they learn to be choosier because they're usually the ones being pursued rather than doing the pursuing. If you even out these three conditions, women and men seem to be equally likely to accept a proposition for casual sex. Creating situations where women think men are as good in bed as men think women are, where women aren't worried about being stigmatized as sluts, and where both are equally likely to proposition one another is staggeringly unlikely in the real world. So outside of psychologists' laboratories, we shouldn't be surprised that women seem to be turning men down for sex a lot more often than men are turning down women. Consequently, just purely by the numbers, women probably have a lot more opportunities to have their sexual consent violated (since they're the ones saying no) than men do. Probably.

While plenty of activists have argued for empowering women as sexual pursuers, the idea that men want sex all the time is so deeply ingrained and unquestioned in the culture that no one seems especially worried about addressing it. For example, a few recent films and TV shows, such as 2018's *Blockers*, have gone out of their way to positively portray women as enthusiastic sexual pursuers. But even that film (which is a relative paragon of gender nuance in the unsophisticated world of teen sex comedies) still mostly takes men's consent and interest in sex for granted. Thus we get the following exchange between two teenage characters (virgin Kayla and more experienced Connor) who don't know each other very well:

Kayla: Before I drink this [cocktail], I just want to let you know that I'm fully planning on having sex tonight . . . with, with you.

Connor: Yeah, I-I mean, wherever the wind blows us.

Kayla: Well, the wind's gonna blow us there.

Connor: Wherever the night takes us, it's . . .

Kayla: It's gonna take your penis into my vagina.

Connor: Okay, uh, you know, if the universe wills it.

Kayla: And the universe *will* will it.

Connor [laughing]: Thanks for letting me know, I guess.

The exchange is certainly amusing in the context of the film, partly because it so thoroughly violates our expectations about women as sexual pursuers/ pursued. But Kayla (and presumably the audience) just takes Connor's consent for granted, even though he doesn't seem especially enthusiastic about the idea of having sex with her. And I suspect we'd view this exchange as pretty sleazy or creepy if we continued our earlier exercise of reversing the genders here. If a teen guy simply informed a teen girl he's on a date with that he was going to have sex with her tonight, adding, "It's gonna take my penis into your vagina," I think most people would be more annoyed than amused.

Similarly, in season 8 of *Game of Thrones* (2019), virgin Arya begins blatantly hitting on her longtime crush Gendry by asking how many women he's "been with." After he eventually admits, "Three," she says, "We're probably going to die soon. I want to know what it's like before that happens." They stare at each other for a moment before he stutters, "Arya, I—" and she cuts him off by kissing him and undressing him. Gendry never says yes, and Arya (and presumably the audience as well) seems to take for granted that of course he wants to have sex with her. While it's great to see women shown in positions of active sexual desire and relative empowerment, these scenes seem to empower women *at the expense of* the men they're with instead of empowering the women *with* the men. Only tweaking half of the original grouped assumption (men always want sex/women only sometimes do) sets a problematic precedent where men's sexual consent is *still* disregarded, but now there are more opportunities for it to be violated.

ASSUMPTION 2: WOMEN JUST AREN'T A THREAT

Whenever I get into debates with people about sexual violation and consent, someone inevitably brings up the idea that women are physically weaker than men. In case you've never bothered to look for numbers to back up that claim, it's mostly true. Statistically speaking, by many measures, even unusually strong women are usually only stronger than most men; for example, the women's world record holder for running speed wouldn't quite qualify to participate in a men's Olympic running event. So in an even fight, it seems reasonably fair to say that a majority of men could physically overpower a majority of women (and this is probably as true for trans women as it is for cis women). Yet there are countless ways to make such a fight uneven. A woman with a gun, for example, is almost certainly a greater threat than a man without one. Another way to make the fight uneven is cultural conditioning, which teaches men they're not supposed to hit women; I've talked to a depressing number of men who were in physically abusive relationships with women, but said they just tolerated the abuse because they "couldn't hit a girl." Women can also take advantage of men while men are sleeping or intoxicated; one of my male friends was raped by two different women who had sex with him in his sleep. And yet, remember that as we saw in the previous chapter, for most of American history (and still to this day in many other states as well as countries), women legally could not rape someone.

Women can also be in official positions of power over men, as teachers or prison guards or medical professionals, which allow them to coerce men into sex. At least one study from the US Bureau of Justice found that contrary to what one might imagine, female prison guards were surprisingly likely to rape their young male charges—claiming that 89 percent of male juveniles reporting rape victimizations on a survey said a female prison guard was responsible (Beck et al. 2013). In more informal contexts, women can simply have a lot more power in their romantic relationships with men (probably most often by being their primary or sole source of emotional support), which means they can emotionally manipulate men into having sex with them. Thus, in contrast to the stereotype of adolescent relationships that imagines heartless, horny boys constantly pressuring girls into having sex with them, high-quality in-depth research has actually found that boys often have much less sexual power in relationships with girls than generally imagined. This research shows that girls frequently have a gaggle of friends in addition to their boyfriends, while boys often only have their girlfriends, making boys emotionally dependent on their girlfriends (Giordano, Longmore, and Manning 2006). Boys' emotional dependence on their girlfriends may make them very vulnerable to doing whatever their girlfriends want.

Our culture also tends to literally and figuratively frame vaginas as weak, with the implicit accompanying idea that they pose little sexual threat to men's (stronger) penises. In American culture, "being a pussy" means being weak, while "having balls" means being tough (and "being a dick" means being an asshole). There's not a lot of inherent logic to this system—to quote a popular question widely attributed to Nitya Prakash, "Why do 'balls' equate to toughness and 'pussy' equates to weakness when even the slightest flick to the 'nuts' sends a guy to his knees and vaginas can push out an entire human being?" Society views penises as so sexually threatening that sociologists actually created the term "penis panics" to refer to persistent societal fears associated with having penises in vulnerable locations (particularly women's bathrooms; Schilt and Westbrook 2015), and judges have occasionally deemed the act of penetration by a penis to itself be an act of "force" in rape cases (Fried 1995). Regardless of its logic (or lack thereof), women and men both learn that vaginas are unthreatening as well as being extremely desirable. If a man flashes his dick at a woman on the subway, society teaches her to view that as a gross and threatening power move on his part, but if a woman flashes her pussy at a man on the subway, society teaches him that he should be at best delighted that this horny slut was willing to show off her pussy, and at worst merely annoyed. Superficially, these gestures are basically identical, but society teaches us to interpret them entirely differently.

But most importantly, society teaches both women and men that there's just no real risk of harm from a pussy. Rape, in our legal and cultural logic, is still about being penetrated against one's will, and vaginas aren't going to penetrate someone against their will unless their owner is very sexually creative. So neither women nor men learn to view women as potential rapists.

ASSUMPTION 3: ERECTIONS EQUAL CONSENT

There are some very good reasons why we mostly assume men aren't the victims of sexual assault: we're constantly bombarded by statistics claiming most victims of sexual assault are women, men are almost never the accusers in legal rape cases, and there's not exactly a big social activism circuit on behalf of male sexual assault survivors (Stemple and Meyer 2014). I always personally found myself scratching my head a lot over those statistics, since the men I know seem about as likely as the women I know to have been sexually assaulted—but I used to just shrug and assume I knew an odd bunch of people. (I do.) Yet it turns out that better data show that my friends aren't so unusual after all, and the apparent disconnect was a case of selective presentation of statistics.

Let's start with the law itself. As we saw in the previous chapter, in the United States, the Federal Bureau of Investigation (FBI) revised its definition of "rape" in 2012 to be "the penetration, no matter how slight, of the vagina or anus with any body part or object, or oral penetration by a sex organ of another person, without the consent of the victim" (US Department of Justice 2012). Before that, as in many European countries and many individual American states today, only women could be raped (Stemple, Flores, and Meyer 2017; Weare 2018). But the FBI's definition, while a big improvement over what it used to be and over many alternatives, still focuses exclusively on the experience of being nonconsensually *penetrated*, not being nonconsensually *forced to penetrate*. That means the friend I mentioned in the first chapter, who *was literally forced to have sex with a woman at gunpoint* by penetrating her vagina with his penis, still wasn't legally a victim of rape according to the FBI—even by modern standards. So most statistics that depend on the legal definition of rape exclude men like him from their count of victims. While his experience does seem to have been unusually bad (one study claims that only about 7 percent of male or female rapes involve the use of a weapon [Weiss 2010], although these numbers vary), he certainly doesn't seem to be alone. The National Intimate Partner and Sexual Victimization Survey, which has collected nationally representative data for several years on a wide array of nonconsensual sexual experiences in America, has consistently found that in the previous year, nearly identical numbers of adult women were penetrated against their will as adult men who were made to penetrate against their will. Indeed, the numbers look far more similar than we're generally led to believe for a variety of types of sexual violence, from unwanted groping to forced sex involving intoxicants. Cumulatively, looking at different years of the survey, about 5–6 percent of adult women and 4–5 percent of adult men report experiencing some kind of sexual violence in the last year. According to these findings, women are certainly more likely to experience sexual violence, but not so dramatically that men's sexual victimization is simply irrelevant.

Interestingly (tellingly?), most of the basic summary reports from this survey don't mention these numbers. Instead of talking about what happened in the last year, most reports from this survey emphasize how likely men and women were to have experienced rape in their lifetimes (Stemple and Meyer 2014). In those statistics, we find that at least 18% of women experience rape or attempted rape (and 13% sexual coercion), and about 6% of men experience rape or are forced to penetrate someone (and 6% sexual coercion), during their respective lifetimes. Why such a vast disparity between what happens across someone's lifetime versus what happened in the past year? Well, there are probably a number of reasons for that gap, but the most significant is that women on this survey were much more likely than men to have experienced rape when they were minors, so they've had a much longer time to accumulate a lifetime's worth of rape victimizations. Another might be that people don't always remember everything that happened to them twenty to sixty years ago very well, and men (especially much older men) may be less likely than women to remember rape experiences as they age. Related to that memory gap is a cultural/personal framing gap: men who grew up in an era where what happened to them wasn't "rape" probably didn't/don't frame it that way for themselves. (For example, in one of the more surreal moments of my professional life, in 2012, I interviewed a seventy-ish-year-old man who recounted—seemingly cheerfully—being tied up and forced to perform oral sex on his aunts when he was four, with nary a mention of words like "rape" or "molestation.") But the results from this survey that adult men and women are startlingly likely to have experienced nonconsensual sex in the last year are less vulnerable to these complex cultural trends, and have been damningly consistently across time.

If you're wondering why these numbers look so different from those found in several surveys of college students (such as those in Hirsch and Khan's *Sexual Citizens* [2020]), which find women are much more likely to be the victims of sexual assault than men, the answers are a bit complicated (Thomas and Kopel 2023). First and foremost, there are methodological issues: the revised Sexual Experiences Survey (SES), which is the gold standard used in many of these studies, does not include any specific wording about "forced to penetrate" and includes only language about nonconsensual fondling, oral sex, and penetration. All the nationally representative studies mentioned earlier agree that without language about "forced to penetrate," we end up vastly underestimating men's sexual assault victimization. Notably, the original SES only ever sought to measure women's victimization at all, and the revised SES awkwardly changed some of its language to try to be more "gender neutral." To give you a sense of how *not* gender neutral this language is, one question specifically asks the respondent to note if "a man put his penis in my butt, or someone inserted fingers or objects without my consent." This phrasing not only represents a bewilderingly broad range of experiences, but also awkwardly initially introduces a gender for the perpetrator ("a man") then subsequently tries to elide it ("someone"). Second, as Hirsch and Khan explain, there may be some basic facts about college sexual and gendered life that make women more vulnerable than men, including distorted sex ratios in college (60 percent women/40 percent men), which end up privileging men, as well as institutional regulations that mean male fraternities get to throw wilder and potentially more sexually exploitative parties than sororities.

We learn not to question numbers like these for many reasons, including a lot of vicious cultural mythology around the physics of male rape. That is, many people insist men can't get hard if they didn't want sex. (I presume that these are often the same people who say if a woman orgasmed, she wasn't raped.) It's hard to dispute this unscientific speculation with actual science, since it turns out to be spectacularly unethical to stick men into a laboratory against their will and then see if they get hard when you stimulate their dicks. But I think anyone who's ever spent much time in the company of people with penises should have observed that dicks often don't do what their own-ers would like for them to—whether that's awkwardly getting hard in times of high emotion, or failing to get hard in moments of high sexual arousal. I think we can safely skip the unethical lab experiments and simply turn to the nearest person with a penis and ask if they've ever gotten hard at some point when they didn't want to be; my bet is that as long as they're being honest, they'll answer with an emphatic *yes*.

In short, men definitely can be sexually assaulted in the conventional sense of the word—although, thanks to the legal definition, they are rarely techni-cally "raped" in most countries—and the available data suggest it happens much more often than you've been led to believe.

THIS IS ACTUALLY A PROBLEM FOR EVERYBODY

Society is so in the habit of not giving a shit about men's sexual consent that I'm afraid a lot of people reading this might be yawning right about now and saying, "Who cares? Those men were probably mostly fine, and that's why they don't remember those consent violations years later." Perversely, there's limited data from college students suggesting the people least sympathetic to the sexual violation of straight men are other straight men (Davies, Rogers, and Whitelegg 2009). So let me explain why this is a problem for a group that society seems ostensibly much more sympathetic toward: women. When we set up such a vicious cultural double standard, we teach men to become unconsciously callous toward women's complaints about sexual violations. When women talk about how bad they felt when a sexual violation happened to them, straight men often seem to respond in word or thought with, "What's the big deal? If that happened to me, I wouldn't care and neither would any-body else." Men learn to think their own consent doesn't matter, and it's often hard for them to understand why someone else's matters in a context where their own wouldn't.

I'm not sure it's a coincidence that both of the scenes I mentioned earlier (in *Blockers* and *Game of Thrones*) of women's purported sexual empower-ment were both written by men. The only vision of women's sexual "empow-erment" many men seem able to make sense of is one where women get to take advantage of men the way men are used to taking advantage of women. But real sexual empowerment should mean that everybody's bodies and con-sent are respected equally, regardless of their gender or sexual roles. So much consent-focused education is based around the idea of telling men, "Don't rape!" And while that's solid advice, statistically it doesn't appear to work very well (Grigoriadis 2017). Multiple studies have found that one of the most effective ways to teach straight college men to start thinking seriously about consent is to put them in situations where they imagined being harassed and assaulted by another man (Foubert and Newberry 2006). The reason this strategy is so effective is because it teaches *empathy*. When men aren't being asked to judge abstract scenarios but rather—for probably the first time in their lives—to imagine themselves as victims of unwanted sexual advances, they get more compassion for what unwanted sexual advances actually look like. I can confirm based on my own experiences teaching college students that you can make a much bigger impression on men by talking about consent in a context where their own becomes more valued and meaningful than you can by simply repeating over and over again, "Don't rape."

That's right: I follow Stemple (2008) in proposing the wildly counterin-tuitive idea that one of the most effective ways to minimize men's sexual consent violations of women is by empowering men to say no to sex. I'll come back to this proposition in part II of this book, but for now, let's turn to another highly problematic set of sexual double standards that disempowers both men and women and causes all kinds of communication confusion.

THE "FAG" AND "SLUT" PENALTIES

To some degree, two very different parallel social pressures affect men's and women's sexuality and sexual consent, regardless of their sexual orienta-tion: the fag penalty (men) and the slut penalty (women). The fag penalty stigmatizes men for saying no to sex, while the slut penalty stigmatizes women for saying yes. I'll explain each of these separately, then talk about how disastrous the combination is together.

Remember my male friend quoted earlier in the chapter who said that "men were expected to be in a perpetual state of consent" because of course they always wanted to have sex? The fag penalty is the leftover baggage from that idea, implying that any man who *doesn't* always want to have consensual sex with anyone from a gender he's attracted to must not be really masculine—in other words, a "fag." The threat of this penalty might sound trivial to you, especially if you're a woman or a man from a position of class privilege. But sociologists and anthropologists have documented widely different contexts around the world where men viciously police their own and other men's conformity to strict standards of masculinity, and the consequences for failing to meet these standards can be literally life threatening (Moussawi et al. 2011). In America, sociologists have shown how casually teenage boys insultingly label one another "fags"—a highly offensive term to adults—for any behavior they perceive as insufficiently masculine (Pascoe 2011). Importantly, it's not just bisexual or gay boys who are subject to this verbal abuse: in fact, the statistical majority seems to be straight boys harassing other straight boys. Mind you, it's generally worse for gay and bi boys, but not always in the way you might think. Recent surveys of American high school students found that teens who weren't heterosexual reported much worse bullying for failing to conform to conventional gender expectations than for their sexuality, and this problem was worse for boys than girls (Kosciw et al. 2018). But men often do far worse than hurl insults at other men they perceive as unmanly: they also physically assault them and sometimes even murder them. Many gender-nonconforming teens are literally afraid to go to school because of the abuse they'll suffer from their peers, and while adulthood is generally saf*er*, it certainly isn't always safe for them.

As dire as these consequences sound, the penalty for violating gendered expectations goes even deeper than bullying, teasing, and the implicit or explicit threat of physical violence that often accompanies it. Men who don't live up to these expectations also face the fear of being isolated from male peers, as well as having difficulty finding romantic and sexual partners. You might reasonably hope that this kind of social pressure doesn't affect gay men, but alas, you'd be wrong. While the pressure is undoubtedly lessened somewhat, research in the United States and abroad still shows gay men furiously policing one another's masculinity, stigmatizing more feminine men, and rewarding more masculine ones (Miller and Behm-Morawitz 2016). The cumulative effect of all these social pressures is that even if they can convince themselves they don't care what other people think, men often still have to deal with the voices in their own heads telling them they've failed in some fundamental way if they don't uphold social expectations about what it means to be manly.

All of which means that men have something to prove—and potentially gain—by not saying no to sex.

The slut penalty, on the other hand, induces exactly the opposite effect in women. Most of the analyses I've read about the relationship between "slut-shaming" (social pressures that directly or indirectly try to make women feel bad for having sex with lots of people) and sexual violation emphasize that women learn to feel guilty for having put themselves in a position where they could be violated in the first place. Consequently, women often end up blaming themselves for having been sexually violated (and society often seems to blame them too). This problem is serious and real, and I don't want to trivialize it in any way. But there's a simple and important fact that gets lost in a lot in these discussions: women's consent couldn't get violated so much if they didn't feel like they had to say no to sex so often. Now, let's pause. I know someone is going to take that sentence wildly out of context and try to act like I'm saying that if women were just sluttier, they wouldn't get raped so much, but that's not what I'm saying at all: *I'm saying that social circumstances and pressures create costs and broader consequences for women saying yes to sex.* As we saw earlier, the three main reasons why women end up saying no to casual sex are that they're generally the ones being pursued and asked, they (correctly, according to statistics on pleasure from casual sex [Armstrong, England, and Fogarty 2012]) assume that they won't get much pleasure from the person asking, and they fear the social stigma of being labeled a slut (Conley et al. 2011).

As with the fag penalty, much of the social consequence of the slut penalty is what sociologists call "homosocial," which is just a fancy way of saying that it comes from people of the same gender. Women are mostly the ones who judge and police each other's sexuality and "sluttiness," mocking, shaming, and alienating one another (Farvid, Braun, and Rowney 2017). However, men also seem to be less receptive to being in serious relationships with women they perceive as having slept with "a lot" of people—and they think "a lot" for women is less than "a lot" for themselves (England and Bearak 2014). Thus, I once interviewed a cohabiting heterosexual couple where the woman told me in a hushed voice that she had slept with more than thirty men in her life, but she would never tell her partner that. He obviously couldn't condemn her for what he didn't know, but she clearly expected rejection if he ever found out (and from having spoken with him myself, I think her fear was reasonable). The evidence that the culture perceives sexually experienced women as questionable romantic partners pervades popular culture too, from the famous scene in *Clerks* (1994), when a male character reacts with apparent pride to the idea that his girlfriend "only had sex with three different guys" followed by exaggerated comical horror in response to the revelation that she "sucked thirty-seven dicks," to the entire premise of *Easy A* (2010), in which Emma Stone's character deals with the consequences of a fake reputation as a slut in high school.

In addition to social condemnation, women are constantly threatened with the idea that once they're branded as sluts, they're ironically more vulnerable to sexual assault; society declares that once they've consented to sex with too many men, that must mean they've consented to sex with all men. Thus, there have been actual legal cases declaring that prostitutes couldn't be "raped"—at worst, they could have "services stolen" (Harding 2015). And of course, as with the fag penalty, the cumulative effect of all these social pressures is that women can still face feelings of anxiety and problems with self-worth in the face of so much social stigma if they feel like other people feel like they've slept with too many people.

All of which means that women have a lot to prove to themselves and others by saying no to sex.

TRYING TO NEGOTIATE AROUND
DOUBLE STANDARDS

Most people I talk to seem to be at least abstractly aware of the slut penalty against women, although they seem less aware of its effects on women's willingness to consent to sex on a broad scale. On the other hand, they generally seem consciously unaware of the fag penalty, or at least the assumption grounding it (that men want sex all the time). The combination of these competing pressures means that in a heterosexual situation, if both people are only kind-of sort-of interested in having sex with each other, women are likely to prefer not to have sex, while men are likely to prefer to do it. Imagine an abstract scale of wanting to have sex with someone, where 0 is *no way* and 10 is *OMG YES.* Because of their different social pressures, Joe will probably be happy to have sex with Joanna at a 3, but she might not be happy to have sex with Joe unless she's at a minimum of 7. Indeed, plenty of women would probably say no even at a 10 because they've been told that if they say yes, the guy won't get into a serious relationship with them.

Moreover, as I will discuss much more in the conclusion, I think our society tends to apply two very different standards to our understanding of sexual consent. In one version, all sex is rape unless consent is provided to make it otherwise. In the other version, all sex is consensual unless non-consent is provided to make it otherwise. This is a conceptual, philosophical, and legal chasm that creates havoc with our personal and cultural understanding of the fundamental nature of consent and sexual assault. But the part that really fucks us up is that (culturally, at least) we apply two completely different standards based on gender: women get an all-sex-is-rape-unless-they-consent model, and men get an all-sex-is-consensual-unless-they-say-no (and maybe not even then) model. Trying to communicate across this chasm is extremely challenging, and trying to establish consistent laws and norms across it is practically impossible.

These different social pressures and conceptualizations create chaotic misunderstandings as men and women try to negotiate sex with each other. When women constantly say no to sex they seem to want, some men feel led on and think, "Well, I guess women are inscrutable and capricious" or "I guess she just doesn't want me" rather than, "She wants me exactly as much as I want her, but she doesn't want me badly enough to risk her reputation and relationship prospects." These types of misunderstandings can lead men to cynicism, thinking women are just using them for free drinks because they are saying no to sex men would cheerfully have. Conversely, when men constantly pressure women for sex, women think they are "creepy" and "sleazy." What women often don't seem to know is those guys have probably only *ever* gotten laid by hitting on every woman they meet. And so women get cynical about men in general, thinking they're horny and sex obsessed, and the cycle of messy gender dynamics continues.

When we watch how these social pressures play out among gays and lesbians, we find predictable, extremely gendered consequences. Gay male culture depends heavily on extremely casual sex ("cruising"), and the back rooms of gay men's clubs often just assume that sexual "consent" is automatic (Orne 2017). In the same vein, the cautious unwillingness of lesbian women to initiate sex or even engage in explicit flirting is a common meme on the internet that is also backed up by studies looking at their willingness to engage in casual sex and to proposition one another online (Gordon 2006). Being outside of heterosexual pressures doesn't let people off the hook from gendered pressures, and many gay men and lesbians complain a lot about these expectations in their respective cultures and communities.

The irritation and cynicism that both straight and gay (as well as bi) people experience in these contexts is problematic in and of itself, but for darker reasons as well. As we become so cynical about the genders we want to have sex with, I think we become more willing to believe these differences are innate, inevitable, and inescapable, instead of understanding them as the products of socialization and culture. Moreover, when we buy into these cynical "truths," it makes it so much more difficult to see the lies they cover—that many men experience sexual consent violations, that many women would be happy to have more casual sex if social circumstances were more favorable to it, and that society is generally disinclined to punish men pushing consent boundaries, among other things. We have to start looking at consent and sexual violation in a more multifaceted way if we want to be able to have a conversation across the gender chasm our society has created around the issue.

Unfortunately, as we'll discuss next, it's not just gender socialization differences that make that conversation so difficult—it's also the messy combination of alcohol and shame.

Chapter 4

Toxic Cocktails of Anomie and Alcohol

Does anyone really know how to date anymore? When I ask my (very liberal) undergraduate students how they expect to go about finding people to date and be in a relationship with—and even more elusive life partners, husbands, and wives—they usually respond with blank looks and shrugs. They mumble something vague about meeting people online or going to parties, but it's clearly not getting most of them partnered off in a serious way; like so many college students these days, they don't seem particularly concerned about their singlehood either (Wade 2017). This hazy dating land of confusion is a pretty recent cultural reality, and it's closely tied to some really fuzzy social rules about when two people are "allowed" or "expected" to have sex. As discussed in chapter 2, in the not-so-distant-past, our culture had a well-established system for deciding when two people were allowed to have sex: either the man married the woman, or the man paid the woman. Although the latter was illicit (and often illegal), it at least established a clear boundary and expectation. The idea of marital rape simply didn't exist, so a marriage license was basically a certificate of social and legal sexual consent (and queer sex was illegal or grey-legal under pretty much all circumstances).

Somewhere along the way, those expectations very gradually started breaking down. As birth control became readily accessible to prevent pregnancy, condoms prevented HIV, and new antibiotics treated most STIs, the idea of waiting until marriage to have sex started to seem quaint to the vast majority of people in rich countries with easy access to healthcare. But the sexual and dating norms they were accustomed to were not replaced overnight with well-devised and well-managed social systems to thoughtfully acknowledge and handle these social changes in sex and relationships. On the contrary, traditional institutions like religion and schools were dragged kicking and screaming into the late twentieth century, with the Catholic Church *still* refusing to support birth control—which the United Nations has long since agreed is a basic human right—as of this writing. One is hard-pressed to find a mainstream religion in the United States or Europe that has wholeheartedly embraced the idea of sexual exploration, fulfillment, passion, desire, and—simply put, nonmarital sex. US schools barely teach sex education, and while the situation is much better in many European nations and Canada, the complaints of young people in those countries are still quite similar to those of Americans (Laverty et al. 2021). Sex education feels disconnected from reality, with adults who grew up in a completely different sexual and relationship universe seemingly unable and unwilling to help young people navigate a sexual landscape no one even gave them a map for.

At the same time as official institutions continually bombard us with a stubbornly unrealistic moral perspective on how young people ought to do relationships and have sex, we're bombarded in the other direction by a bizarrely unrealistic portrayal in popular media about the way young people actually do relationships and have sex. Most older adults are shocked to learn that young people nowadays in all rich countries have less sex later with fewer people than young people did when they were their age (Paquette and Cai 2021). On the one hand, I think most adolescents and adults realize that teen sex comedies spanning the decades—from *Fast Times at Ridgemont High* (1982) to *American Pie* (1999) to *Blockers* (2018) to *Sex Education* (2019–2023)—are comedic and fantastical representations of young people's sex lives, but on some level, most people I've talked to truly believe that even though those fantasies weren't true for them, they were somehow magically true for "everyone else." How is anyone to reconcile such crazily conflicting information: traditional social institutions like religion and schools eschewing responsibility for changing social norms and teaching a century-out-of-date version of sexual reality, while movies and TV shows portray, idealize, and model an equally unrealistic version of sexual reality that becomes aspirational and absurdly unattainable for most.

ANOMIE AND THE CONTEMPORARY LAND OF DATING CONFUSION

When social norms get this far out of whack, sociologists describe the situation as "anomic." Broadly speaking, "anomie" refers to social worlds where the rules are vague and illogical, the consequences for breaking these fuzzy rules are also unclear and/or feel arbitrary, and the rule enforcers are hazy, unreliable, and/or untrustworthy. In some of the worst situations, the rules may be unclear but the consequences for breaking them may be dire. Sometimes entire societies can become anomic (for example, much of the world in the early stages of the COVID-19 pandemic, or any society in the midst of civil war), or sometimes smaller social systems can (for example, the many American Protestant Christian religious denominations that have argued and splintered around allowing LGBTQ marriage and pastors, while debating legitimate authority). Sociologists have been a bit slow to observe the anomic conditions of dating and partnership formation in modern life (Yoshida 2023), but it seems increasingly clear that (for better and for worse) our society has lost its traditional road map to sex, love, relationships, and marriage.

One of the surest situations that gives rise to anomic conditions is when official social norms (which sociologists call "formal norms") conflict with casual social norms ("informal norms"). Most of the time, when social expectations change, people have the good sense to change their laws and official rules, but sometimes, for a variety of reasons, it doesn't happen. Thus you can end up with bizarre social situations like that of the United States, where for many years it has been normal and expected for teenagers to drink booze and smoke pot (the informal norm), yet it remains completely illegal for them to do so (the formal norm). Many of their parents still get mad at them for doing these things—which they often did themselves—and schools often still punish teens for doing them as well. Kids who are poor and/or Black even get arrested and put in juvenile centers or prisons for these things. Never mind that all their friends were doing them, all the movie and TV teenagers they ever watched were doing them, and even their parents and school authorities expected them to do them. No wonder that American teens often seem a bit confused!

It's hard to overstate the negative social and individual consequences of anomic social environments. They're strongly associated with feelings of social isolation, uncertainty, stress, depression, anxiety, increased heavy drug use, and suicide (Bjarnason 2009). As a species, humans like a balanced degree of structure, order, and rules—we don't thrive with too little, and we don't thrive with too much (Bjarnason 2009). Obviously, when the rules get fuzzy for something that's relatively minor and specific (say, the process for renewing our driver's licenses), we merely get stressed and annoyed. But when the rules get fuzzy for things that start to affect the fundamental way we function as human beings (say, family formation processes, access to love and friendship, or secure access to food and shelter), it's really bad for us. We become uncertain about how to act, and we start avoiding the situations (and people) where we'd have to engage in this uncertain behavior, which can take a serious and dangerous toll on our overall mental health.

To get a sense for what this kind of anomie can look like without the life-threatening stakes of global pandemics and civil wars, we can look at the experiences of an extremely conservative religious group that lives largely outside of mainstream American society: the Amish (Stevick 2014; Reiling 2002). The Amish live much the way people in the United States did in the mid-1800s: forbidding nearly all of their members high school or college education, maintaining strict traditional gender roles for men and women, having large families, farming, and forbidding adults from driving cars. But they also maintain a quirky social practice generally known as "rumspringa," in which Amish sixteen-year-olds are encouraged to break the strict rules of their sect and experiment with mainstream American life. They drink, have loud music parties, sometimes have sex, get cell phones, drive, and occasionally even live apart from their families. It's a really sociologically weird thing to do: tell people they're expected and *supposed to* engage in "immoral" behavior. Amish culture doesn't tell them any of these things are okay for them, it just tells them it's a phase they have to pass through, and hopefully they won't go to hell for it. Amish society tells people this "simmie" (foolish) period is a necessary part of growing up; without it, more adults might be tempted to do things their culture normally forbids and thus weaken the strength of the community. "Get it out of your system when you're young," they say, "and then come back to us wiser and more committed to our ways." This simmie period usually ends two to five years later when young people "join church" and become full-fledged Amish adults (and contrary to what you might imagine, about 90 percent of them do). When we study these Amish teenagers (we aren't allowed to study the adults, who won't usually interact with outsiders much), we find they're often very depressed and anxious. They're doing things they feel and understand to be *wrong*, but their society expects them to do those things anyway. They don't really have the social or psychological resources to "enjoy" the rebellious experiences they're having, and most of them seem to head back to a quieter adulthood with rueful acceptance.

Mainstream Americans have a somewhat voyeuristic fascination with Amish culture in general and rumspringa in particular. Rumspringa is a pretty extreme example of contradictory social norms, but I think mainstream Americans do much the same thing to their own young adults (just at a lower point on the same scale) without noticing their own hypocrisy. For (mostly middle-class and higher) American teenagers who go away to live at college, the experience can have a certain rumspringa-esque quality to it. Like rumspringa, college begins with a clear moment (enrollment and arrival) and has a clear moment of conclusion (graduation). During that time, young adults are expected to do things that their society tells them is "wrong"—drink a lot, experiment sexually, party, and keep relatively unstructured weird hours. To a large degree, we tell college students, "We understand you'll experiment sexually and hope you like what you find, but please don't tell your elders because they don't want to hear about it or advise you. As a society, we'll probably mostly look the other way as you break a lot of rules we never followed either—unless you just happen to randomly get caught or do something particularly egregious that forces us to pay attention. We expect you'll drink a lot even though it's against the law and can get you expelled from school. Just try not to get caught, okay?" Given our very human love for clear rules, it's little wonder that young adults in college, like those young Amish adults, are often depressed, anxious, and confused (Lipson et al. 2022). In short, we create a drinking and party culture among young adults in college that's a rich breeding ground for anomic opportunism.

THEN VERSUS NOW

In her *Pink Carnation* novels, historian and romance novelist Lauren Willig (2005) cleverly observes that "the Season" in early nineteenth-century Britain (think *Bridgerton*), with its structured mating ritual of parties and social events for rich elites, had a lot in common with modern college dating. Her observation is especially true for overstudied elite universities, which have historically predominantly attracted upper-class students. In both cases, elders carefully selected pools of socially acceptable young adults, threw them together in a rampant party atmosphere, and let them sort themselves out into mated pairs, confident the couples would be "suitably" matched.

There are obviously a great many differences between those two systems, and the differences matter a lot for thinking about sexual consent. In those olden days, adults usually diligently chaperoned young women (but not men) at parties, and any preengagement sex was seriously frowned on. If anyone broke those rules, they were expected to marry or face social disgrace. (Think about "poor Lydia's situation" in *Pride and Prejudice* [Austen 1813], when a young woman dares to run off and live with a man without marrying him. Her entire family bands together to force him to marry her and is mortified by the incident.) A marriage license was a license for sex, and nonmarital sex among the upper classes was so uncommon that the only normative system for arranging it was prostitution.

Nowadays, the mating norms for richer young adults are much fuzzier but still have general patterns. College students often expect to go to parties where they'll get tipsy or drunk (and possibly high on pot too), meet potential partners, and have casual sexual encounters that may or may not involve penis-in-vagina sex (Wade 2017). These collegiate flirtations and sexual experiments might or might not lead to more serious relationships later. Although many colleges try to regulate parties in accordance with laws forbidding people under twenty-one from buying booze and pot, they're not very successful. Many elite colleges also make rules requiring freshmen to live on campus with roommates in dorms under the supervision of "resident assistants" (who are other college students). These pretty weak rule systems are the closest modern young adults get to being chaperoned the way rich young women were in the past.

As it has become increasingly unfashionable for young, privileged adults to marry soon after college graduation—the average age of marriage for all American adults these days is pushing thirty—most of them continue dating after college. The party life fades and transforms into a dating life increasingly centered around meeting people through friends and work as well as on dating apps. People go out together to relatively public venues for drinks or dinner (which usually also includes drinks), and then, if they like each other, head to one or the other person's place for more privacy and possibly some kind of sex (Lamont 2020). People tend to progress from "dating around" to dating one person exclusively to living together to marriage and childbearing (Lamont 2020). But dating adults usually expect a fair degree of independence in this process, without chaperonage or tentative arrangements from elders.

If you feel like I've been holding out on you by not telling you much about how poor and working-class people used to date and how they date now, it's because the research about them is much more scant. As best I can tell from older accounts like Rubin's *Erotic Wars* (1990), which includes interviews from the 1950s, working-class American young adults usually got married because the woman got pregnant. For a long time, the defining difference between a "lady" and a poor woman mostly seemed to be how much society prized her "virtue" (i.e., virginity and sexual innocence). These class differences persist into the present day, with poorer teenagers having sex younger than richer teens (Karney 2021). Working-class young adults tend to have less time and money to date than richer adults, and most of them never went to the kinds of colleges where people live away from their parents. For poor women particularly, without likely access to college graduation ceremonies or career advancement trajectories, the threshold to cross into adulthood is having a baby (Edin and Kefalas 2005), and for most of them, that necessitates having sex. Poor and working-class folks lack a highly selective mechanism like a college admissions process to help them choose their partners, and they're more likely to meet partners in very public venues like stores and bars; these meetings tend to more quickly lead to sex (and much more quickly to childbearing) than middle-class dating does (Karney 2021). Marriage has become increasingly uncommon or extremely delayed among poor and working-class Americans, who often feel it's simply beyond their means (Miller and Sassler 2019).

There are a few important things to notice in this class comparison of dating norms as they relate to sex and consent. First, for all that the chaperonage systems in place to protect young women in college are intentionally pretty half-assed, they do exist (for example, American sororities still strictly limit parties, but fraternities get to go wild); by contrast, no one is really even making that much effort on behalf of poor and working-class women. Second (and relatedly), there are officials other than the police that young women in college can complain to if they experience sexual assault at school. Again, those officials might be unsupportive and ineffective, but they do exist. Meanwhile poor and working-class women mostly only have the police to complain to, and that makes them more dependent than richer young women on the formal justice system (Zaykowski, Allain, and Campagna 2019). Third, and most importantly, middle- and upper-middle-class women grow up with the idea that they have a future in education and employment to safeguard, and they usually feel that having an untimely baby (and thus, potentially, having sex) will get in their way (Edin and Kefalas 2005). But poor women especially grow up with basically the exact opposite attitude: having a baby is the future they're expecting, so sex carries fewer risks (Edin and Kefalas 2005). Returning to the previous chapter's theme that women in general have more motivations than men to say no to sex, for a variety of reasons, we can layer class onto this idea and suggest that middle- and upper-middle-class women have more motivations than working-class and poor women to say no to sex.

"WOULD YOU LIKE TO HAVE SEX WITH ME NOW?"

With some very specific exceptions, regardless of social class or where people originally met, few people expect to have explicit conversations about whether sex is happening. Shumlich and Fisher (2020) studied Canadian college students and found that most of them perceived direct conversations about sex as signs of inexperience. Only extremely liberal students who had been exposed to educational programming emphasizing the importance of verbally saying yes to sex (i.e., "affirmative consent") had explicit conversations. Hirsch and Khan's (2020) exhaustive study of students at Columbia University in the United States resulted in similar findings, with quotes from respondents like one from a young man who said, "I don't think I've ever asked, 'Can I have sex with you?' 'cause that would be pretty awkward, but it's pretty obvious that it was consensual" (126). Other studies have found that many young adults believe a woman accepting an alcoholic drink is a sign she's horny, and almost everyone agrees that people consent to sex at the point where they agree to go home with someone (Livingston, Rerick, and Davis 2022; Shumlich and Fisher 2020). People mostly expect context to shape sexual consent rather than explicit verbal communication.

Even if people aren't trying to get explicit consent from their partners, men in heterosexual encounters usually try to get implicit consent from women. In study after study (Hirsch and Khan 2020; Hunt et al. 2022), women mostly seem to give interviewers blank looks when asked how they ask their male partners for their consent. Women point out that they expect the men to be doing the propositioning, so they don't really expect to have figure out how to get men's consent when men were the ones asking them for sex. Interestingly, the men in these studies *also* seem to find the idea that women would try to get their consent weird—even though many of these men have stories about women violating their sexual consent (Griswold, Neal Kimball, and Alayan 2020; Herbenick et al. 2019). In interviews, men whose consent had been violated didn't usually tell stories framed as "women don't care about men's consent"; rather, they tended to frame individual women as problematically aggressive or uncaring. Not only do many young men have stories about women blatantly violating their consent, plenty also report recent sexual encounters that were technically consensual but unwanted (Willis, Jozkowski, and Read 2019). Although young women were more likely than young men to report this type of ambivalent consent, it was still common for men to do so.

There are multiple gender dimensions that overlap to make young men more vulnerable to unwanted sex than most of us would expect. First of all, as Lamont (2020) explains, many men superficially say they would love it if women hit on them—but if you keep talking to them long enough, it turns out most of them admit that if they think a woman's hot, they'll probably hit on her themselves. Even worse, they report that the kinds of women who *do* hit on them are usually women they find unattractive. Consciously or unconsciously, the available data suggest that men start to assume the only women who're available to hit on them are women who aren't desirable enough to be picked up by other men. In psychological experiments where women hit on men, they find that men suddenly get a lot pickier about the women who are hitting on them (Finkel and Eastwick 2009). But this nuanced information is the kind that only social scientists who are good at their jobs really have access to—a lot of everyday women only ever hear casually that guys would be thrilled if women hit on them. We can additionally layer onto this misimpression the assumption we previously discussed about men always wanting sex and needing to prove their masculinity by always being up for sex, along with the normative reality of women not knowing how to ask for consent and men not knowing how to give it. Altogether, you end up with a disastrous combination that results in men being less likely to want to have sex with the kinds of women who are more likely to hit on them, men still feeling very pressured to do it anyway, and neither women nor men being clear how to manage consent in those situations. Thus it becomes easier than one might imagine for men to end up in situations where their consent gets violated.

And of course, a sizable proportion of those encounters are occurring under the influence of alcohol and/or pot . . .

. . . BUT LIQUOR IS QUICKER

As messy as gender norms make consent, the significance of those messy gender norms almost certainly pales in comparison to the intoxicated reality of young people's sexual worlds. The available data strongly suggest the majority of initial sexual encounters (and possibly even most sex among young adults with established partners [Willis et al. 2021]) occurs under the influence of alcohol, pot, or both. In 2015, there was an infamous public service campaign which tried to frame sexual consent as being like offering someone tea, basically with the point that if someone turns down your tea, you shouldn't keep trying to convince them to drink it. (Of course, in many ways, it's actually a good metaphor for sexual consent in that people often feel obliged to drink tea just because someone has offered it because of existing social norms and power structures, but that didn't really seem to be where the ad was trying to go.) Obviously, it is indeed problematic to keep pressuring someone to try to drink tea they don't want, or to have sex they don't want. But the real thing that campaign was missing—which *most* sexual consent campaigns seem to be missing—was any hint of the extremely common reality of a drunk person propositioning another drunk person. Not directly, mind you, because as we just established, most sexual consent conversations are indirect. In my mind, I like to imagine converting that video to a more real-world portrayal, with a drunk guy sloppily sliding a cup of tea across a table to a drunk woman and trying to gauge her interest in it while she tries to figure out if that tea will taste good and if she'll be negatively judged for drinking it. That's much closer to the reality of so much heterosexual sexual consent.

It is *impossible* to overstate the importance of alcohol in contemporary sexual lives. Regardless of social class, most people (possibly regardless of sexual orientation) expect their newish partners to be at least "tipsy" when having sex (Hunt et al. 2022; Lamont 2020). General consensus says there's a line where someone is "too drunk" to consent to sex, but good studies of college students drinking heavily found that line is *far* past where we might expect it. One study (Jozkowski et al. 2023) looked at how drunk people thought they were, how drunk they thought their friend was, and if they thought they or their friend were too drunk to agree to have sex with someone if propositioned. It turns out that people were terrible at assessing their own and their friend's level of drunkenness, and that their tolerance for agreeing to sex for themselves or in support of their friend was usually well beyond the legal limit to drive (which is, by most standards, quite drunk indeed). When people said "too drunk to consent," they mostly seemed to mean "barely conscious," because even things like "obviously walking poorly" weren't always sufficient to discourage them. People understood "tipsy" to be fine to consent to sex, and hazily agreed that "extremely drunk" people couldn't consent to sex, so there was further consensus that the most troublesome zone for consent is "moderately drunk," where it's not necessarily obvious just how drunk someone is (Hunt et al. 2022). In general, both men and women openly admit to being confused about whether moderately drunk people can ethically consent to sex.

There are three complicating gender norms hiding under the cover of "too drunk to consent" (Cowley 2014). The first, as I've mentioned several times before, is that "men always want sex," so regardless of their level of intoxication, "of course" they would consent. The second, also previously mentioned, is that if women drink a fair bit, they're assumed to be horny and looking for sex. The third (utterly perverse) one is that if women want to have sex with someone they're not in a serious relationship with when they're *not* drinking, they must be sluts and thus undesirable. (Keep in mind that if women drink too much, they're also perceived as sluts and thus undesirable, so this is a fine line to walk.) Altogether, these norms mean that people feel like they shouldn't have to work very hard to ensure consent from a person who's intoxicated. They assume the woman wouldn't have been drunk and in a private place with a man she didn't want to have sex with—because that's supposed to be what women do when they want to have sex with a man—and they assume men want to have sex all the time anyway.

Surprisingly, given the wildly different drinking norms and sexual social-ization projects (explained below) in many countries, these norms are *remarkably* similar across rich countries. Most European countries have much more laid-back attitudes about alcohol in general than Americans do, and children in Europe are allowed to start legally drinking at a far younger age. The awkward anomic situation of young adults being expected to drink but not being legally allowed to isn't really a problem in Europe; and yet, the expectations for tipsy/drunk sex remain much the same. Indeed, some of the best research on the topic of drunk sex (Pedersen, Tutenges, and Sandberg 2017) has been done in Denmark, which is a very liberal country with much more equal gender norms, but where alcohol and sex still go hand in hand in ways that are completely familiar to Americans.

It's easy to miss the fact that this is, sociologically speaking, very weird. Age of first sex, rates of unintended and adolescent pregnancy, and age at first marriage and childbirth—to name but a few related statistics—all vary considerably among these many countries. But somehow, the basic idea that sex and alcohol should mix stays the same. Of course, it's possible that drunk sex is just better than sober sex, so everyone who can afford to have drunk sex (i.e., people in richer countries) does. However, the numbers don't really bear that conclusion out. With a large sample of young adults, Herbenick and colleagues (2019) found that only half as many drunk sexual encounters were wanted "very much" as compared with sober ones. Given these differences, it's probably unsurprising that alcohol also massively reduced people's experiences of sexual pleasure. About 15 percent of people in encounters where one or more partners were drunk reported "very pleasurable" experiences, compared with 20 percent of men and 27 percent of women in encounters where one or both partners were "drinking but not drunk" and 40 percent of people in sober encounters. Men often report that alcohol reduces their sexual performance (giving birth to the colloquial term "whiskey dick," meaning a guy can't keep a hard-on because he's too drunk), and both genders report that alcohol increases their "sexual regrets," meaning they wish they hadn't had sex with that person (Palamar et al. 2018). These data don't exactly present a ringing endorsement for the physical or emotional joys of drunk sex.

On the other hand, being drunk seems to mean people in many different cultures feel "allowed" to experiment with low levels of sexual "deviance"— most especially threesomes and low-key BDSM (Pedersen, Tutenges, and Sandberg 2017). For example, Herbenick and colleagues (2022) interviewed young women about their experiences with choking during sex, which often occurred while intoxicated. The concept of sober threesomes barely seems to exist in mainstream culture at all. Even though threesomes and BDSM are the two most popular sexual fantasies in America (Fox et al. 2022; Lehmiller 2018), people in both the United States and European countries seem to feel these fantasies challenge respectable sexual norms too much to manifest while sober. With all that said, although people tell stories of drunken sexual escapades as fun and adventurous, it's clear that sexual pleasure is often almost incidental to these experiences, which frequently seem to be focused more on having a good story to tell later (Pedersen, Tutenges, and Sandberg 2017).

Another reason for this cross-cultural norm of drunk sex is that in modern life, young people have fewer and fewer places to casually socialize. Because they are much less likely to participate in organized religion or even secular organizations than earlier generations, bars and clubs serving alcohol have become some of the only places for young adults to meet new partners in person. Thus, young people would have been incidentally drinking before having sex because they met in places where drinking was expected. While social environments undoubtedly shape these drunken sex norms, they don't seem to be a complete explanation, since *even people in existing sexual relationships* still usually drank before their most recent sex (Willis et al. 2022). A perhaps more convincing reason for these widespread drunken sex norms is that popular media from rich countries around the world show drunken sex as normal (Marcantonio et al. 2022), and thus the idea of poorly negotiated drunken sex gets exported to and spread around many different countries.

I'm sure all these factors individually accumulate and encourage people to have sex under the influence, but I'm hard-pressed to believe they sufficiently account for just how widespread these norms are. I suggest that two other things are actually happening simultaneously. First, there are many norms that actively promote drunk sex (most importantly, that's what friends and potential partners do, so drunkenness becomes almost inevitable in the quest for sexual partners). Second, I think there's also a negative push that creates drunk sex by filling a normative void. The overall social breakdown of dating and relationship norms has created so much anxiety and awkwardness around sex and relationships that people drink to minimize their anxieties. Even in rich countries that have much more relaxed attitudes about sex than the United States does (i.e., much of Europe), relationship norms have still broken down in much the same way (Perelli-Harris et al. 2017). This normative breakdown (anomie) creates widespread social anxiety—even among individuals who perhaps personally feel no particular guilt or anxiety about sex and relationships. Many people in the United States drink (and use other drugs) in sexual situations to deal with their guilt about having sex at all (Grigoriadis 2017; Hirsch and Khan 2020). But I think people in many different countries now use alcohol to try to deal with the feeling that *they don't know what they're supposed to do* in sex and dating situations. Remember that two of the most common responses to anomic social conditions are drug use and avoidance; well, in many rich countries, we're seeing a retreat from sex and dating (Julian 2018), and we've certainly witnessed plenty of drinking and drug use with sex.

So what do all these drunken sexual escapades mean for consent? First, for all that most sex seems to occur under the influence, sexual violations seem to occur much more often when people are *drunk* and especially when they're very drunk (Tutenges, Sandberg, and Pedersen 2020). Even if we look at instances of "sexual compliance" (where the person agreed to sex but didn't want it) with new partners, the most common reason people give for doing so is they were drunk (Willis et al. 2022). Few studies have tried to figure out just how important intoxication is in determining the likelihood of being sexually assaulted, but one of the only studies that has tried (Herbenick et al. 2019) threw every factor the researchers could think of into their analysis and consistently came up with intoxication, gender, and sexual orientation as being the most important factors by far in predicting who experienced sexual assault. (As we'll discuss in chapter 7, bisexual women are more than twice as likely to be sexually assaulted as straight women, and that heightened risk is entirely from men [Marcantonio and Willis 2023].) The risk of intoxication isn't as simple as merely being drunk: the really risky thing is being drunk *and* high on pot at the same time (Willis et al. 2021). These studies are all extremely recent, so researchers have only barely begun to untangle the mechanisms leading to their results. But I don't think you need a great imagination to see how *social norms assuming that women drink because they want to have sex combined with norms discouraging explicit conversation about sex would lead to drunk women having sex they didn't ask for or want.*

In general, it's really hard to tell if people have drunk sex because they enjoy it, because they're just following the lead of those around them, because they don't know any other way to do it, or because they're trying to calm their anxieties around sex and sexual situations. Even if people have no shame about sex per se, they might still feel anxious about another person seeing and judging their naked body, about the risk of rejection from someone else when seeking and experiencing physical intimacy, about how someone else might judge their sexual performance, etc. etc. When it comes to sex, there's a lot to feel anxious about, which is probably why people often say they like drinking *some* before sex because it "helps them relax." But tipsy sex and drunk sex don't appear to be much the same in terms of either social context or personal experience; the data make it hard to believe most people enjoy drunk sex in terms of physical or romantic pleasure—mostly they seem to enjoy the fact that it makes them feel allowed to have sex at all, and to manifest sexual fantasies they would never dream of manifesting sober.

The question, "Do people really want to be having drunk sex?" should be a haunting one for anyone interested in promoting better consent practices and education. If the answer is an unqualified yes, then our goals as consent advocates and educators are simply to help them figure out how to negotiate and manage sexual consent as safely as possible while intoxicated, and to help them develop realistic expectations about imperfect consent in those situations. But if people are having drunk sex for much more neutral or negative reasons, then one of the long-term goals of consent advocacy and sex education is to try to help them better navigate social worlds so they can more plausibly and comfortably have sober sex. We'll return to these themes in the second part of the book; for now, let's consider what contemporary sex education looks like.

SO DOES FORMAL SEX EDUCATION, LIKE, *DO* ANYTHING?

I can't find much evidence that school- and community-based sex education programs in most countries are terribly forthright about the fact that so much sex happens while intoxicated. I even found one author (Grigoriadis 2017) who claims that US colleges are forbidden from providing sex education that addresses alcohol (although I haven't been able to independently confirm this). Given this essential omission in sex education, I was pretty skeptical about how useful most sex education programs really are. Moreover, formal sex education programs tend to be fairly brief (and often awkward) hours in young people's lives compared to their constant exposure to friends, family, media (especially porn), and the internet. How much does sex education in school really matter when there's a much more sophisticated universe of sex education online that teens can consume in the comfort and privacy of their own homes?

The answer is a resounding *some*. For all that sex education in US schools has become one of the hot political battlegrounds for liberals and conservatives to fight over (along with racial issues and abortion), the research demonstrating the success of "comprehensive sex education" as compared with "abstinence-only sex education" was sketchy for many years (Slominski 2021; Luker 2007). On the one side, conservatives wanted schools to teach kids as little about sex as possible—just tell them to wait until marriage and leave it at that (abstinence-only sex ed). On the other side, liberals wanted schools to teach kids how to have safe and responsible sex, pointing out that the vast majority of them were not going to wait until marriage (comprehensive sex ed). Ironically, many abstinence-only programs even fail to teach kids how to say no to sex, and the number of students who get education in saying no has fallen across time (Lindberg and Kantor 2022). To be clear, support for these opinions is hardly even—the majority of Americans support comprehensive sex ed, but its objectors tend to be very, very loud (Luker 2007).

Over time, it has become clear that comprehensive sex education is better at achieving the two chief goals of American sex education—namely, reducing adolescent pregnancies (Fox et al. 2019) and STIs (Slominski 2021; Goldfarb and Lieberman 2021). However, these effects aren't as large as we might expect, nor are they even incredibly consistent. Regardless, the majority of American teens still get abstinence-based education, and this situation hasn't improved much over the last decade (Lindberg and Kantor 2022). There are still some lingering questions about whether comprehensive sex education encourages kids to have sex sooner; for example, teens in the UK receive more comprehensive sex education than those in the United States do, but British teens have sex younger, even though they use contraception more (Scott, Wellings, and Lindberg 2020). There are also *a lot* of lingering challenges about just how "comprehensive" most comprehensive sex ed really is. Most of it doesn't seem to include talk about consent (Burton et al. 2023), although when it does, it seems to be very helpful. Hirsch and Khan (2020) found in their small-scale study that "women students who'd received comprehensive sex education before college that included refusal skills training were half as likely to be raped" (266). That is certainly a compelling argument for better sex education, assuming the findings can be replicated with larger samples. Moreover, most "comprehensive sex education" also does not include mention of LGBTQ experiences (MacAulay et al. 2022), or much about pleasure in general (Hirst 2013). Given these omissions, it's not really surprising that whether we look at teens in Canada (Laverty et al. 2021), the UK, or the United States (Pound, Langford, and Campbell 2016), young people are extremely unimpressed with the quality of sex education they receive in school.

I suspect the exact content of sex education programs in schools is much less important than the attitudes and institutional forces they represent and muster. It's true that sex ed in schools can make up for parents and families who don't teach their kids much, and that seems to be the primary goal as far as most schools are concerned. But I suspect the most important role of sex ed in schools is part of a much broader social landscape, telling young people that their community takes their sexual development seriously (or not). It's less about facts and information, and more about giving young people a sense of what their sexual lives are "supposed" to be in the eyes of their society and culture. And from the perspective of the fuzzy social norms that I've repeatedly mentioned throughout this chapter, it seems like a pretty serious gap persists in many rich countries between what gets taught in schools and what young people's lived experiences are.

To some degree, I think we have to accept the idea that school-based sex education will always be extremely limited. There once was a time in human history when the sexual norms of parents closely resembled those of their children, but those days are long gone. Especially as many people become parents later and later, it has become very hard for parents and teens to have mutually agreeable conversations about what sex is and should be. I think we have to reluctantly accept that the best people to educate teens about sex are mostly very young adults, not people their own parents' age. That doesn't mean we have to give up on the idea of formal sex ed entirely. Rather, we need to ask ourselves slightly different questions: How can schools help young people safely explore their sexuality? How do we want to use schools to shape the broader social realities of sexuality and sexual experiences? The United States seems unlikely to take such an open-minded stance in its primary schools any time soon, but colleges could at least give it . . . well, the old college try.

ALL THE OTHER PLACES TO LEARN ABOUT SEX

Perhaps my own doubts about the significance of school-sponsored sex education are biased by personal experience and partly driven by the "sex education" at my private Christian all-girls' high school, which consisted of our (probably lesbian) gym teacher proudly announcing to the class that she was still a virgin and telling all of us that we should stay virgins until marriage. In fact, I have no memory of an adult ever giving me useful sexual information when I was a teenager. But by the late 1990s, my friends and I all had access to the internet, and that was much more useful than the silent adults in our lives whose sexual advice I probably wouldn't have trusted even if they had volunteered it. Besides, they were all apparently straight and monogamous and we weren't, so why would I have taken them seriously? I had much more faith in PlannedParenthood.com to tell me the truth.

My experiences were certainly not unique here in the United States, where sex education has actually gotten considerably worse since the days when I was in school (Lindberg and Kantor 2022), and where parents stubbornly resist the idea of their teenagers having sex even when they abstractly hope they'll someday have happy sex lives (Schalet 2011; Montemurro, Bartasavich, and Wintermute 2015). In stark contrast to parents in countries like the Netherlands, who are happy to permit their children to have opposite-sex sleepovers with romantic partners, most American parents are deeply uncomfortable with the idea (Schalet 2011). They cite fear of pregnancy and STIs, and turn to a flawed American cultural belief that teenage love isn't "real love" to justify thwarting their children's sexual hopes and access. American parents tend to be especially sexually protective of their daughters, with parents of boys more often saying they'd be okay with letting their sons' girlfriends sleep over—except that they're afraid of angering *her* parents. The behavior of American parents in extremely popular TV shows focused on high school girls, like *Gilmore Girls* (2000–2003) and its more recent reference show *Ginny & Georgia* (2021–), must seem especially strange to people from more reasonable cultures. In those shows, liberal mothers who gave birth as teenagers themselves talk to their daughters about sex (which most American parents *don't* [Rothman et al. 2021]), and in the case of *Ginny & Georgia* even get a daughter on birth control—but still refuse to let their daughters openly sleep with their boyfriends. Three parents' absurd quest to stop their daughters—*who are about to graduate from high school*—having sex for the first time is the entire plot of the movie *Blockers* (although part of the point of the movie is that this quest is absurd).

About a third of American adolescents said they got helpful information about sex from their parents (which was more than any other source), but over 40 percent said they hadn't received helpful information from any source in the previous year (Rothman et al. 2021). On the one hand, these numbers show that plenty of parents are talking to their kids about sex, but they also show that most of them aren't doing it very often. When parents don't talk to their adolescent sons about sex, the boys mostly appear to turn to porn (Rothman et al. 2021). Among young adults (ages eighteen to twenty-four), friends, partners, media, and porn become increasingly important ways to learn about sex (Rothman et al. 2021). Race matters a bit here, with white parents talking to their children about sex more than Black parents (Bleakley et al. 2018; Kapungu et al. 2010), but it looks like the gender and sexual orientation of the child probably matter more than any other factor, with parents, health professionals, and peers all communicating quite differently with boys versus girls, and with straight kids versus LGBTQ kids.

Peers and friends seem to be less helpful and communicative than we might imagine. Although college women talk about sex with their women friends fairly often, those conversations focus more on the relationship aspects than the technical details of sex (Pariera and Abraham 2020). Adult American women often don't talk much about sex with *anyone*, even when conflicts about it are destroying their marriages and relationships (Montemurro, Bartasavich, and Wintermute 2015). The majority of adult American men say they feel comfortable talking about sex with other men sometimes, but only about half said that it was "easy" to talk to male friends about sex (Henao, Montemurro, and Gillen 2022). So it's not just American parents and kids who don't talk much about sex—it's everybody.

In addition to family and friends' (not) teachings about sex (and consent) there is, of course, also the behemoth that is the media, which nowadays includes a vast panoply of prime-time TV, streaming TV, movies, podcasts, and blogs as well as news media. Popular films in general tend to reinforce norms of "implicit consent," meaning people don't actually talk about whether they want to have sex, and they're even less likely to have an explicit conversation if they're intoxicated (Marcantonio et al. 2022). An analysis of top-rated prime-time TV shows from 2015 found few storylines dealing with the realities of sex (e.g., risk of sexual assault, contraception, etc. [Kinsler et al. 2019]). It's clear that Netflix, at least, took these criticisms to heart, and its more recent shows targeting teens such as *Sex Education, Heartstopper* (2022–), and *Ginny & Georgia* have confronted these themes of intoxicated sex, consent, contraception, sexual identity and queer experiences, and the accompanying emotional travails head-on (although it's probably no coincidence that the first two are British shows set in England). These shows were produced post-#MeToo, and many of the high school kids in them appear pretty savvy about consent. The social worlds of popular media characters are slowly but surely becoming more aware of their roles in modeling consent norms.

MODEL MINORITY? LGBTQ FOLKS AND
SEXUAL NEGOTIATION NORMS

If the dating, relationship, and sexual norms of heterosexuals seem ambiguous these days, their blurriness is nothing compared to the free-for-all of LGBTQ dating norms. LGBTQ folks often celebrate and revel in how much more flexible their dating norms are than straight people's, for all that bisexuals admit that they tend to slip into more heteronormative patterns when dating the opposite sex (Lamont 2020). For many LGBTQ folks, rejecting those dating norms and expectations is a joy in and of itself—a relief from fulfilling prescribed awkward social expectations. But the free-for-all still has a price in terms of social organization and certainty. Moreover, if *straight* people end up drinking and doing drugs as ways of coping with social anxiety, uncertain norms, and guilt about having sex at all, it seems to be nothing compared to the alcohol and drug norms of LGBTQ people's sexual lives (Hequembourg and Dearing 2013; Orne 2017; Herbenick et al. 2019; McKie et al. 2020). So the intoxicated consent violations that plague straight sexual worlds seem, if anything, to be exacerbated in LGBTQ ones (Herbenick et al. 2019; McKie et al. 2020). The one study that specifically focused on intoxication, consent, and sexual identities found few meaningful differences in rates of intoxicated sex or consent communication between straight people and bisexuals (although bisexuals were slightly more likely to have ever had sex high) but found that bisexuals (both men and women) were much more likely to have ever had nonconsensual sex while intoxicated (Marcantonio and Willis 2023).

The true story that opened this book of ambivalent consent between two men is not unusual; McKie and colleagues (2020) studied gay and bisexual men's experiences of sexual consent and communication with other men and found that they often felt pressured to say yes to sex in order to impress their friends and to conform to norms of "hypermasculinity"—meaning that gay men, just like straight men, are supposed to always want sex. Orne (2017) describes the world of gay men's clubs and bars with a great deal of pleasure and joy, but admits that it's not a world that puts much value at all on explicit consent communication. Instead, Orne argues, consent communication depends heavily on nonverbal eye contact and body signals to indicate sexual interest, willingness, and desire. Given that many gay and bisexual men still experience plenty of unwanted sex from other men (especially while intoxicated; Marcantonio and Willis 2023; McKie et al. 2020), we should probably be careful in assuming the success of this nonverbal model.

The consent communication practices of queer women and trans folks have as yet barely been studied. The one thorough study on the topic is from New Zealand (Beres 2022), and in that context at least, it's clear that queer women tend to be much more attentive than other groups to consent. The common reason for this is perhaps not entirely intuitive: much more than gay male or straight sex, lesbian sex mostly lacks an obviously scripted progression. Depending on the preferences of the people involved, lesbian sex might involve mostly hands, mostly mouths, strap-ons, vibrators, toys, and some or all of these things in combination. One of the respondents in that study said, "You don't know what they're into . . . so you gotta ask" (145). Ironically, of course, that same statement applies to all people, regardless of gender or sexual orientation. But only queers and those in queer-adjacent subcultures seem to have realized that such conversations can free people from the limitations of sexual expectations and patterns.

CONCLUSION: LEARNING ABOUT
SEX IS A PACKAGE DEAL

It's easy to assume that "informal" methods of sex ed, including parents and peers, fill a gap left by institutions (especially schools and religious organizations). Formal sex ed looks like an elegant means and end itself, as if that alone will create better sexual health outcomes for young people. But the evidence overwhelmingly suggests good sex ed doesn't happen in a vacuum: comparing many different European countries with wildly different approaches to sex ed, we find that countries with good sex ed (especially those that legally mandate it) *also* have cultures where parents talk to their kids more about sex—and have better sexual health outcomes (Ketting et al. 2018). I do not in any way want to underplay the importance of having good sex education in schools, but the mere fact of being able to mandate it without excessive controversy usually indicates a country and culture that already has generally sex-positive attitudes. There's clearly an important cycle happening here with sex-positive cultures having better sex ed, and better sex ed cultivating more sex-positive cultures. Meanwhile, here in the United States, most young people's exposure to ideas and beliefs about sex seems to come more from media than from conversations with real people like parents and friends. As we think about how to structure interventions targeting sexual consent practices, we should remember those interventions can happen at any level: schools, media, friends, family, and eventually partners. We can aim broadly to create an overall culture where people talk more freely about sex, and thus hopefully also learn to communicate more openly with their partners about consent and desire.

I also think we should demand better sex education from a major social institution that most people seem to have just given up on for sexual purposes: religious institutions. It's actively bad for societies and cultures if religious institutions promote social norms that are wildly removed from lived experiences. The United Nations has been badgering the Catholic Church for years to finally join the twentieth century and endorse birth control, to no avail (Faiola and Boorstein 2014), and most modern religious institutions have refused to modernize their teachings about sex. Given that so many young people have abandoned organized religion, we should look to the few organized associations they still participate in as other places to try to provide more modern education about sex.

On some level, I think conservatives have understood something about sex education that liberals have been reluctant to admit: real comprehensive sex education isn't just about learning the facts of reproduction or the correct use of contraception—it's about institutions establishing norms of sexual and romantic relationship engagement. As long as we let institutions pretend that young people aren't having sex before marriage, the rules for having sex before marriage remain fuzzy, and no one really understands how they're supposed to do it. And as long as that confusion about sex and dating norms remains, trying to create sound norms for negotiating sexual consent is extremely difficult.

The fact that most people are at least mildly intoxicated while they try to negotiate consent isn't improving anyone's odds of doing it well. And it's only made worse by the way sex ed programs try to bypass that drunken reality in favor of an unrealistically sober one. Nobody wins when society staggers around, drunk on this toxic cocktail of bullshit and anomie.

Chapter 5

Lies, Statistics, and the Failures of Justice

If you're someone who finds numbers boring in general, you might already be wondering why this book has an entire chapter devoted to them. The reason I'm focusing so much on these numbers is that activists have been leveling statistics about rape and sexual assault since the 1970s to justify all sorts of calls to action, but most of the numbers they're depending on run the gamut from being blatantly false to mostly true but misinterpreted. In general, statistics can be a complicated weapon in arguments about any social problem. On the one hand, without them, it can be easy to lose all sense of scale: a problem that may be common among your social circle or community might be virtually unknown elsewhere, and statistics can highlight some of these discrepancies, along with positions of relative privilege or disadvantage. On the other hand, statistics can often be manipulated to make a problem seem much larger or smaller than it objectively is when the numbers are fairly calculated or rationally presented along with other relevant numbers.

Unfortunately, when it comes to sexual assault statistics, "fairly calculated and rationally presented" tend to go out the window. I've spent a couple of decades analyzing complex social statistics, but I've rarely encountered numbers as confusing and often downright sketchy as the available data on sexual assault. The low quality of the numbers is especially discouraging because it makes it almost impossible to genuinely assess the scope of the problem, to judge the relative successes or failures of different legal jurisdictions in addressing it, or to evaluate the success or failure of any sort of intervention trying to reduce the problem. For example, when we find massive differences between college campuses in their rates of sexual assault (which we do), it's extremely difficult to know if the differences result from how survey takers asked their questions, victim/survivor's level of social awareness in answering the questions, or genuine differences between campuses in sexual assault rates.

Hidden in the story of these numbers are some important summary facts. As mentioned before, the sexual violation of men (by women) is almost certainly much greater than typically assumed; depending on statistics about "false reports of rape to the police" to mean much of anything is naive; and rape conviction rates are quite low, but so are conviction rates for all other nonfatal violent crimes. If you have the stomach to learn more about these statistics and how I arrived at these conclusions, read on. But if reading about the sausage factory of these statistics is a bit much for you, by all means, stick to the headlines here and jump ahead.

SEXUAL ASSAULT IS COMMON, BUT NOT THAT COMMON . . . PROBABLY

In the United States, the "best" (I use scare quotes deliberately here) way we have to estimate the real rates of crimes is the National Crime Victimization Survey (NCVS), and most national statistics about crime you see come, in one way or another, from the NCVS. The NCVS mostly focuses on crimes individuals experienced as a victim in the last year, which helps keep the data recent and specific (people's memories tend to get fuzzier with time). It doesn't focus on crimes reported to the police (although it does ask about that too); it just asks people what happened to them. Then it translates those numbers into a "rate" of crime per 1,000 people over the age of twelve. In 2017, the sexual assault rate was 1.4; in 2018, 2.7; in 2019, 1.7; in 2020, 1.2; and in 2021, it stayed at 1.2 (Thompson and Tapp 2022). These numbers are at least logically comparable to one another across time. But, of course, it seems *extremely unlikely* that the sexual assault rate doubled between 2017 and 2018. What seems much more likely is that in the wake of the #MeToo movement, more women reported incidents as sexual violence that they might otherwise have deemed unremarkable or been uncomfortable disclosing. This apparent heightened reporting propensity doesn't seem to have lasted into 2019; after that, of course, we have to approach any numbers in the COVID-19 era with great caution, as isolation and then release from quarantine seem to have had intense and wild effects on crime.

But whatever those numbers might mean, let's not get too comfortable with them. The way the NCVS obtains these numbers is by straight-up asking people if they have been the victim of "any rape, attempted rape, or other types of sexual attack," then following up by asking if they have been "forced or coerced to engage in unwanted sexual activity" (Thompson and Tapp 2022, 22). The NCVS labels people as victims of rape in these data if they report there was a completed, attempted, or threatened "rape, sexual assault other than rape, or unwanted sexual contact (grabbing, fondling, etc.)." And the

NCVS specifically "does not ask respondents if psychological coercion was used, nor make any explicit reference to the victim being unable to provide consent (e.g., in incidents involving drug or alcohol use)" (Thompson and Tapp 2022, 22). The wild variation between 2017 and 2018 almost certainly stems from more people (presumably women) labeling incidents as "sexual assault" in their reports to the screeners that the survey doesn't really ask direct questions about. In fact, the NCVS is mostly targeting incidents of *physical violence* in its survey questions, with a focus on people who were hit, threatened, or had a weapon drawn on them.

Depending on what exactly we want to know, NCVS metrics are probably either great or terrible. If we're interested in sexual violation from a social justice perspective—trying to gauge who has experienced a sexual viola-tion for the purposes of, say, understanding the broad nature of the problem or who might be experiencing psychological issues as a result—the NCVS measure is very bad. It doesn't ask people many questions that would help filter in some of the most common experiences of sexual violation (especially nonconsensual sex while intoxicated), and it emphasizes the types of sexual violations more people tend to think of when they hear the term "rape." It's especially bad for gauging men's experiences as the victims of sexual vio-lence, since they're very unlikely to label their experiences as "rape" or "sex-ual assault." However, if we're interested in who might report a sexual assault to the police, the NCVS measure is just about perfect. Presumably, very few people would report their experiences to the police as a sexual assault unless they *believed* it was a sexual assault (although occasionally nonvictims like friends or witnesses report); thus a subjective measure of sexual assault is great for determining the scope of crimes of direct concern to law enforce-ment. However, the massive spike in reported sexual assaults in the midst of #MeToo emphasizes just how truly subjective this measure probably is.

According to the NCVS, how widespread is sexual assault compared to other violent crimes? From 2017 to 2021, the relevant rates for robberies went down fairly steadily, from 2.3 to 1.7, while the rates for aggravated assaults went down less steadily, from 3.6 to 2.7. Exempting the anomalous (but possibly more accurate) 2018 rates, sexual assault rates average about 1.4; however, I suggest that comparing these rates across crimes is illogical, since the vast majority of reported "rapes and sexual assaults" occur only to women, so keeping a denominator of the entire population is unreasonable. Put another way, everyone is potentially the victim of all other crimes, but "rape and sexual assault" are defined in such a way that usually only women are the (reported and self-identified) victims of them. (As we've discussed, this is often a more or less accurate reflection of both law and culture.) Thus, the rate calculations for crimes should include only the potentially vulner-able population. If we double the published estimate for sexual assaults, that gives us an excessive estimate (since some men are included in the numerator but not the denominator at that point), and we get an overestimate of about 2.8. That puts rapes and sexual assaults slightly lower than aggravated assaults in general and considerably higher than robberies.

By definition (and to some degree by design), the NCVS's definitions of rape and sexual assault are not very inclusive. Many of the numbers you see estimating much broader sexual assault victimization come from other survey measures, mostly using some version of the Sexual Experiences Survey. In contrast to the NCVS numbers, the SES measures are quite expansive in what they count as sexual assault victimization for women. Researchers tend to primarily use the SES on college students; using these measures, across the twenty-year period from 1985 to 2015, there was a slight but significant increase in the number of college women reporting a rape or attempted rape, rising from 28 percent to 33 percent (Koss et al., 2022). Much of that increase appears to have been specifically related to rape by incapacitation via intoxication, which rose from 50 percent of all reported sexual assaults in 1985 to 75 percent in 2015 (Koss et al. 2022).

The SES numbers for women are at least a decent starting point for estimating the actual prevalence rates of sexual violence. But the problem with the SES, as mentioned in chapter 3, is that its standard question formulation makes it a very poor candidate for gauging the extent of men's sexual victimization. Indeed, the original SES didn't even seem to have a notion that men could *be* the victims of sexual violence, which is why older historical comparisons can be done only with women. Anderson and colleagues (2020) found that including questions along some version of "forced to penetrate" on a much-modified version of the SES for a large sample of college students *greatly* increased the number of men who reported being the victims of sexual violation. With those modified questions, 22 percent of college men and 50 percent of college women showed up as victims of sexual violation.

So between just two studies using the SES, we end up with estimated sexual assault rates against college women of 50 percent and 33 percent, which are staggeringly different numbers. I didn't pick these two studies to contrast their findings; I picked them because they are relatively recent studies that both used the SES and had samples of well over one thousand people (which is a pretty large sample, statistically speaking). Who's correct? I have no idea. If I consult another recent book on sexual assault (Hattery and Smith 2019), the authors confidently give victimization numbers of 20 percent for women in college and women in general. But I have absolutely no confidence about whose numbers I should endorse. Furthermore, note that most studies using the SES are surveying only college students, and the rate of sexual assault against college students is—or at least used to be—lower than that against young women of the same age who weren't in college (Sinozich and Langton

2014). The only thing I can say with any confidence about these findings is that *NCVS numbers are probably the only ones that track criminal offenses within the current construction of the law; most other statistics encompass something much more like the idea of "sexual violation" I'm proposing, which by definition tends to fall outside of the scope of present "sexual assault" laws.*

What about the numbers on men? The idea that women are the primary victims of sexual violence is a staple fact of nearly all the writings on gender and sexual assault. Even a recent study (Hine et al. 2021) focusing on male-on-male rape reported to the London police stated that, in general, "90% of rape victims are women." Stemple and Meyer (2014) argue these numbers are wild underestimates resulting from the failure of more surveys to include questions about whether someone was "forced to penetrate" someone else; they add that most noncollege survey samples focus on households and exclude people who are currently in prison, but a large percentage of overall rapes against American men occur in prisons (Stemple, Flores, and Meyer 2017). If we exclude prison rapes (and I think the sociological factors that lead to prison rape are rather different than the ones that lead to rape in general), my educated guess from poring over statistics and talking to a lot of men about their sexual experiences is that adult women experience sexual assault at about twice the rate of adult men, but that hardly makes it solely a crime against women. I don't have much confidence in most numbers about sexual assault prevalence, but the one thing I can say with confidence is that *most of them massively underrepresent men's experiences as victims of sexual assault (at least, assuming we are not using a definition that categorically excludes men).*

Given that the real numbers seem to be so elusive, you might wonder why anyone should care. It's obvious from even casual conversations that sexual assault is depressingly common, and surely that alone should be sufficient to establish it as a social problem worthy of attention. And that's almost certainly true. But if we can't correctly draw an outline of the scope of the problem, we'll have no way of knowing if any measures we take to combat sexual violence have succeeded. Indeed, debates continue to rage among scholars about whether previous attempts at sexual assault legal reform in the late twentieth century were "successful" (defining success in this context is obviously difficult; Frank, Hardinge, and Wosick-Correa 2009). Moreover, as we're about to see, defining the scope of the problem is also important for determining what percentage of legally actionable sexual assaults are actually addressed by the legal system and how much of a problem sexual assault of adults is relative to other serious crimes.

ADULT SEXUAL ASSAULT STATISTICS
COMPARED TO OTHER SERIOUS CRIMES

One of the most discouraging statistical failures of the information on sexual assault in general is the lack of data on child sexual abuse (CSA). In the United States, any authority (teachers, researchers, counselors, etc.) who learns of an instance of CSA is legally required to report it. Unfortunately, the consequence of this legal obligation is that researchers basically never ask about CSA since it compromises their ability to promise respondents confidentiality. As a result, the only knowledge we have of CSA rates in the United States is from the retrospective reports of adults (whose memories might be extremely biased, especially in favor of forgetting the abuse occurred) and from reports to police. I was most interested to learn if children or adults experience higher rates of sexual assault, but there are no reliable statistics to answer this question. Daly and Bouhours (2010) report that internationally, the highest rate of sexual victimization is for children aged ten to fourteen. In the United States, studies show even lower rates of children reporting to the police than adults (Daly and Bouhours 2010). As of this writing, the Centers for Disease Control (2022a) website claims (without a direct citation) that one in four girls and one in thirteen boys will experience child sexual abuse. This is a remarkable claim, since elsewhere the website also says that one in four adult women and one in twenty-six adult men have experienced an "attempted or completed rape" in their lifetime, and then goes on to say that half of the women were raped before age eighteen (CDC 2022b). In case you struggle with fractions, that could mean that 100 percent *or* 50 percent of women victims were raped before age eighteen and that 50 percent of boys' rapes somehow go away by the time they reach manhood. The confusion here probably results from the fact that "child sexual abuse" is a very vague term encompassing a wide array of crimes, whereas the term "rape" is somewhat more specific. But again, so much statistical confusion makes it virtually impossible to know where best to direct our prevention and intervention resources. I think there's little reason to expect that the factors that lead to children being sexually abused by adults are the same as those that lead to young teens being sexually abused by other teens, which are probably still distinct from the factors that lead to adults being sexually assaulted by other adults. As I've mentioned before, some statistics even suggest that adult men and women are sexually violated at similar rates, and all the difference in their lifetime prevalence rates occurs because girls are so much more likely to be raped as children (Stemple and Meyer 2014).

Women's higher victimization from sexual crimes stands in stark contrast to the recent historical reality that men probably used to be much more often the victims of violent crimes in general. This idea was well established among scholars in the early 2000s, although it largely seems to have failed to sink down into popular consciousness. Sanyal (2019) makes the point in her book on rape that focusing on women's experiences as victims of sexual assault simultaneously overexaggerates their experiences as victims in general while also downplaying the grim reality that men are more likely to be the victims of violent crime. It's unclear if that point was ever actually true statistically, but it's almost certain that, aside from homicide, it's no longer true.

Before I really dig into the confusion of these numbers, let's start with the one statistic everyone agrees on: pretty much worldwide (the United States included), *about 75 percent of homicide victims are men, and the people who usually kill them are also men* (Fridel and Fox 2019). However, homicide is quite uncommon compared to all other violent crimes. Assuming all homicides get reported to the police (and we're fairly sure most of them do), the homicide rate per 1,000 people is tiny (.05) compared to the rape/sexual assault rate, which is at least thirty-four times higher (around 1.7). On the other hand, one could reasonably argue that the violent crime that best parallels sexual assault is aggravated assault, and unfortunately (even though the data exist), no one I could find has done a recent analysis for whether men or women are more likely to have been the victims of aggravated assault. In any given year, by far the most common violent crime is "simple assault" (meaning someone injured someone else without using a weapon), but in recent years not only do the rates for that vary greatly from year to year, they *also* vary greatly in terms of whether women or men are more likely to be the victims (Morgan and Truman 2020). And finally, regardless of how often men are the victims of violent crime, women are more likely to be reported to police as the victims of it (Morgan and Truman 2020). Thus women remain the public face of violent crime victimization, regardless of who is actually victimized more. All these facts together make it very hard to say definitively whether women or men are more likely to be the victims of violent crime in recent years. (I suspect men used to be much more definitively victimized in the United States in the 1990s, when violent crime rates were *much* higher)

The other fact that appears to be indisputable in the gendering of the violent crime rate differences is that *men are much more likely to be the victims of violent crimes committed by strangers* (Morgan and Truman 2020). That statistic remains true regardless of how we count rapes—most of which are committed by someone the victim knows. In general, women mostly suffer at the hands of intimate others, and men mostly suffer at the hands of people they know less well.

For most major crimes, there's usually a chasm between how many people experience that crime and how many of them report it to the police (Baughman 2020). (The crime most likely to be reported to the police relative to its occurrence is homicide, which doesn't even get reported by the victim, followed by motor vehicle theft, which usually has to be reported in order to collect insurance money.) In the case of sexual assault, the numbers about how many get reported to the police appear to be the only broad prevalence numbers that are reasonably trustworthy—but even here there are complications. The NCVS gives a statistic of 0.66 per 1,000 people reporting rape or sexual assault to the police in 2018 and 0.56 for 2019. But the FBI, which collects most of the data on police reporting, uses a narrower definition of rape, so its numbers are inevitably different (and indeed, they are different from the NCVS for all major crimes reported to the police); for 2018, the FBI's number was 0.43 (Morgan and Truman 2020, 6). Based on the NCVS's own numbers for 2019, that would mean almost exactly *a third of self-identified rape/sexual assault/unwanted contact victims reported their assaults to the police. But remember that many systems for counting "sexual assault" include lots of people who don't describe what happened to them in those terms, so if we include all those people, that percentage reporting to the police goes way down.*

How do those reporting numbers look compared to other violent crimes? In 2019, the rate reported to the police for robbery was .90, with an actual victimization rate of 1.9 per thousand people (Morgan and Truman 2020), which leaves a reporting percentage of 47. And for aggravated assault, the rate reported to the police was 1.92, with an actual victimization rate of 3.7 (Morgan and Truman 2020), which leaves a reporting percentage of 52. *That means the rate of sexual assault/unwanted contact victims reporting to the police is much lower than for other violent crimes. However, we should remember the NCVS includes a wide array of offenses as "sexual assault" (including "unwanted contact") that many states don't recognize as "rape" or "sexual assault," so there's a lot of ambiguity in these numbers that isn't as much of an issue for other violent crimes.*

REPORTS TO THE POLICE AND "FALSE ALLEGATIONS"

Who actually goes to the police raises the specter of one of the most pernicious and widely abused statistical weapons in the sexual assault numbers arsenal: "false allegations." Especially in the wake of the #MeToo movement, the idea that false rape allegations are extremely rare became a rallying cry for "supporting victim/survivors," with advocates insisting that victim/survivors' accounts of what happened to them should be believed (usually socially rather than legally) without question. Often-quoted numbers on websites and popular media for "false reports" were in the 2 to 5 percent range, or sometimes even lower, and many social and political groups seem to treat this number as reverential scientific truth. But if you ever wondered, *So how do we have a statistic that says what percentage of rape allegations are false?* the answer is, "Um, we don't, really."

Lacking witnesses or recorded evidence, a depressingly high percentage of rape allegations come down to "he-said, she-said" charges that are extremely difficult to confidently sort out. No one is in a position to say with great certainty what percentage of reports are false or not; the best they can ever really sort things into is "reports that appear to be very well-supported" or "not." Saunders (2012), who researched false rape allegations, observes, "The only thing we know with any certainty about the prevalence of false allegations of rape is that we don't know how prevalent they are" (1167). *Unfortunately, determining the truth or falsity of a rape allegation is often more a matter of guesswork than of science.*

So where do these dubious statistics come from? *These numbers are from police data claiming the purported victim either confessed they had lied with supporting evidence that they had done so, or where the police claimed there was egregious evidence of intentional falsehood.* Unfortunately, the basic data quality in these studies is very, very problematic. I don't mean to insult any of the hard work the researchers have done on this topic (which seems to be very good, as far as I can tell), but they've all been working with very small numbers of cases. Although there have been multiple studies on this topic over the years, keep in mind that the *best* study on the topic had 81 "unfounded" cases to work from (Spohn, White, and Tellis 2014), and the second-best study had 136 total cases, with 8 coded as false reports and 19 coded as "insufficient information" (Lisak et al. 2010). To get meaningful statistics on complex subjects, we usually want to see many hundreds of, and preferably more than a thousand, cases in a single analysis, and thousands in a meta-analysis. Moreover, as of this writing, all the available data are very, very old. I could find no published study of an Anglophone country that drew from data collected before 2010, and many were well before that.

In addition to being old and small, these data also depend on the candor and transparency of the police, who don't have a great track record for honest criminal investigative reporting, let alone for turning over documents in full (Shaw et al. 2017). In fact, in one study, the police readily told researchers they used aggressive questioning techniques specifically to "get the victim to recant" or to "break her down and admit to what she was really doing" (Spohn, White, and Tellis 2014). No study I could find had independently tried to reinterview victims reporting to the police to see if the study investigators got different information than the detectives did. Instead, most studies just try to reread and verify that the "false report" labels the police applied to their own information appear to be correct—based on the information from the police. Some of the scholars reinterviewed the police, but that's definitely not the same thing as talking to victims or other witnesses. In short, *the prevalence statistic for "false" reports means almost nothing because the basic data quality (through no fault of the researchers) is very low.*

In addition to the number of reports the police declare "false," a sizable chunk of rapes reported to the police in different countries are also declared "unfounded" (United States) or "no crimed" (England; Venema, Lorenz, and Sweda 2021). What the heck does "unfounded" mean in this context? Well, unfortunately, it's a catch-all category for obviously false reports, victim recantations (which are often just people talked out of continuing with the case), people who knew they were intoxicated and were afraid they were raped but a rape test showed they weren't, cases where the law doesn't cover the conduct (which in many jurisdictions could include blatantly nonconsensual sex that just wasn't violent enough to satisfy the demands of the law, as I'll discuss in chapter 9), and a few reports that for a variety of reasons the police couldn't be bothered to investigate further. But again, no one has data from anyone other than the police themselves to try to untangle these numbers. Keep in mind that reporting here can get pretty messy, especially when victims were intoxicated or suffering from extreme trauma responses. Lonsway (2010) points out many things that make someone look like an unconvincing rape victim to police or others—waiting too long to report, having small inconsistencies in what they say, and vagueness about certain details—are often signs that they were, in fact, raped.

The thing everyone seems to want to use these numbers for is trying to decide, "If my friend comes to me saying they were raped or someone reports a rape publicly, should I believe them?" And the answer is quite unambiguous: these numbers don't tell you anything, one way or the other, about whether to believe your friend or a particular public accusation. Instead, that is a political and personal decision you're getting no statistical help in resolving. I can offer some other things worth considering, though. On one hand, keep in mind that making a false allegation to the police is a crime itself and making a false allegation to a friend is not—so the stakes are very different, and reports to the police presumably filter for incidents the victims themselves assume will be taken more seriously based on legal and cultural biases. But as a mirror to that, there are potential benefits from reporting to the police that one does not get from talking to a friend (namely, legal and social validation). And in addition to not knowing how truthful victims are, we don't know how truthful the police are. In short, all we have are very, very, very messy "statistics" using small sample sizes from questionable sources a very long time ago pertaining to a specific circumstance (reporting to the police) that probably doesn't usefully reflect on the situation we are in when talking to a friend in our living room. *All told, even if we could be confident in these dubious numbers about reports to the police (and we shouldn't be at all), they would still tell us nothing about what to believe in other circumstances.*

CONVICTION/ATTRITION RATES

As staggeringly unscientific as most of the numbers I've reported thus far turn out to be, no popularly quoted statistic on sexual assault turns out to be as mind-bogglingly unscientific as the oft-quoted claim that only about 3 percent of perpetrators of sexual assault in the United States will be convicted of sexual assault or a related crime. It's difficult to find the exact origin of this claim, but most people cite the Rape, Abuse and Incest National Network (RAINN) for it. Let's be clear: RAINN is not a research institution, and it does not claim to have access to statistics that seem to have eluded researchers in the United States since the late 2000s. Instead, after dramatically illustrating that 28 out of 1,000 perpetrators of sexual assault will be convicted of a felony (which is how the statistic often gets quoted), it contains a footnote in an 8-point font at the bottom of its page warning readers: "This statistic combines information from several federal government reports. Because it combines data from studies with different methodologies, it is an approximation, not a scientific estimate" (RAINN n.d.). Even RAINN's own page has added complementary charts showing that based on its own unknown methodology, the supposed conviction rate for sexual assault isn't wildly off from other violent crimes, claiming 20 out of 1,000 for robberies and 33 out of 1,000 for assault and battery cases. Many activists have tried to encourage a sense of indignant rage that the criminal justice system treats sexual assaults exceptionally badly, but those numbers don't really support that conclusion. Even among scholars trying to investigate this issue, there's still a lot of educated guesswork happening. Baughman (2020), who attempted to calculate conviction rates across violent crimes in general, arrived at a rough guess that less than 5 percent of nonfatal violent crimes result in a conviction, but due to data limitations, those guesses are quite old (from 2006 and earlier).

In general, in the United States, conviction rates for almost any crime are extremely difficult to calculate. At every step along the process of this calculation, we often have to move from one data source to another, with each source using a different measurement tool or methodology. Cases trickle out of the legal system at every step, and criminologists talk about the "attrition rate" from crimes reported to a particular institution or agency, all the way down to conviction. The starting number in some ways can be the most complicated part of this statistical process: it can be *either* the number of crimes we believe have occurred *or* the number reported to the police. Determining the number of crimes we believe have occurred is incredibly tricky when it comes to sexual assault, since, as we've seen, different measurements result in wildly different estimates. Even choosing a time frame can be complex, since it often takes more than a year for a serious crime to move through the legal system, so trying to figure out, say, how many people charged with sexual assaults committed in 2018 were eventually found guilty is complicated by time because we can't just look at the numbers from 2018 for complaints and convictions. These statistics are also complicated by the fact that *especially* for sexual assaults, a single person is often charged with for multiple offenses, so we can't just calculate how many people were found guilty versus the number of crimes reported. And then there's yet another complication: people are often found guilty of a related crime but not necessarily this specific one, and deciding what counts as a "related offense" isn't simple either.

We can have a lot more faith in crime statistics grounded in the percentage of crimes reported to the police, rather than vague estimates of how many instances of a crime theoretically occurred (which is what RAINN's numbers are based on). The FBI collects annual data on reports to the police and subsequent arrests made—obviously, arrests can't be made if crimes aren't reported. The percentage of reported crimes resulting in an arrest is called a "clearance rate." In 2019, the percentage of rape cases cleared by arrest was 30.8 percent, which is pretty close to that for robberies (29.7 percent) but much lower than for aggravated assault (50.4 percent). Presumably the gold standard here, such as it is, is for homicide (59.2 percent), and on that scale, 30.8 percent for rape doesn't look amazing, but it also doesn't look terrible (Federal Bureau of Investigation 2019).

If you feel a "but" about to happen to here, that's because there's a *really big* "but" about to happen. Yes, the clearance rates for sexual assault look pretty decent on paper, but the FBI allows for a weird loophole called "cleared by exceptional means," which is supposed to apply to situations where, for instance, the suspect is dead or already being charged with another crime. However, it appears that American police often (mis)apply this designation to sexual assault, especially when the victim "decides" not to continue with the investigation. (There's a great deal of evidence that police often actively or passively discourage victims from continuing to press charges, but we'll get there later.) From 2008 to 2010, 38 percent of sexual assaults were cleared by exceptional means and 62 percent by arrest, versus 12 percent and 88 percent, respectively, for aggravated assault (Pattavina, Morabito, and Williams 2021). Venema and colleagues (2021) used data from 1999 to 2014 and found that in one large midwestern city, 3.5 percent of sexual assault cases were "open" (meaning the police had an ongoing investigation), 42.5 percent were "suspended" (which functionally meant they weren't doing anything about them), 16 percent were "unfounded," 13 percent were "cleared" (meaning there was an actual arrest), and 25 percent were "exceptionally cleared" (NP1 0702). Many of these "clearances by exceptional means" occur from victims choosing not to pursue further investigation (Richards, Tillyer, and Wright 2019). Victims backed out most often when the accused were former or current partners, and least often when the accused were nonromantic family members or when the victim sustained physical injuries (Richards, Tillyer, and Wright 2019). Sexual assault also appears to be a virtually unique situation in which the police consult with prosecutors before deciding whether to make an arrest (and after doing so, very rarely make an actual arrest), sometimes resulting in the dubious designation of "cleared because of failure to prosecute" (Pattavina, Morabito, and Williams 2021; Spohn and Tellis 2019). Prosecutors were most likely to pursue cases perpetrated by strangers, involving any physical injury, and that occurred in a public setting. So the takeaway here is that *sexual assault clearance statistics from the police are uniquely suspicious because the police often don't actually make the implied arrest.*

The next stage in the attrition process is another place where we get a major data mystery. Once the police have arrested someone, prosecutors have to decide what to do with them. Prosecutors can drop charges, try to negotiate a plea deal (which means the person admits to being guilty, often to a lesser charge), or continue to press charges (resulting in a jury trial or, if the defendant requests it in a state that allows it, a "bench trial," meaning a judge hears and decides the case without a jury). Unfortunately, there's not much easily accessible national data for any of these numbers in the United States, and no one has linked those numbers since 2006, which was obviously long before *many* reforms in sexual assault laws. Perhaps most importantly, the statistic we have for the number of sexual assaults reported to the police has gone up considerably since then, partly because what the FBI—the main source of that data—started counting as "sexual assaults" became much broader.

From 1990 to 2005 in the United States, about 65 percent of sexual assaults reported to the police were dropped one way or another, and 35 percent involved some kind of arrest (Daly and Bouhours 2010). For various reasons, another 15 percent got whittled out along the way, and around 20 percent of all reported sexual assaults actually ended up in court, not merely on the prosecutor's desk (Daly and Bouhours 2010). In 2002, the conviction rate for people who were actually charged with rape was 67 percent; 61 percent pled guilty and 74 percent were convicted at trial (Daly and Bouhours 2010). *Overall, from 1990 to 2005 in the United States, of one hundred sexual assaults reported to the police, fourteen reached a conviction* (Daly and Bouhours 2010). Data from 2008 to 2010 in a large-scale US analysis found that 37 percent of those arrested were found guilty, an overall conviction rate from police report to conviction of 6.8 percent (Morabito, Williams, and Pattavina 2019). The only more recent data I have found coming from the

United States is from a single analysis of the state of North Carolina from 2014 to 2018, which found that 24 percent of people charged with sexual assault were convicted (Martin and Taylor 2019). Ten percent of those guilty charges were the result of a jury trial, with the rest presumably mostly resulting from plea bargains, as bench trials had only just become legal in North Carolina at that time (Kate Martin, personal communication). *Across time, each of those conviction percentage numbers is considerably lower than the one before, and it's very hard to know if that's representative of what's actually happening, or if the reduction is because surveys have expanded the conceptualization of what counts as "sexual assault" much faster than the courts.*

Due to the lack of recent data on the United States, we can turn to other Anglophone countries to try to make educated guesses about what might be happening in the United States. Canada apparently experienced an increase in rape conviction rates from 2009 to 2014, when its overall conviction rate rose to 21 percent (Rotenberg 2017). In general, overall conviction rates are presumed to have gone down in most countries in the twenty-first century because police reports of rapes have mostly gone up. We know the most about the UK because the British government and people have been particularly concerned about what was found to be their exceptionally low conviction rate for rapes in the early twenty-first century (Daly and Bouhours 2010; Thomas 2023). The number of people charged with rape in the UK varied wildly from year to year throughout the early twenty-first century, but the one thing that remained constant during that time was the very high percentage who pled not guilty—more than 80 percent. This is an extraordinary percentage of people pleading not guilty compared to other crimes (Thomas 2023), and no criminal justice system is really set up to handle that. Post-#MeToo, jury conviction rates steadily increased in the UK, even as the number of jury trials for rape also increased (Thomas 2023). Alas, I have seen no comparable figures for the United States, even for small jurisdictions.

So if one hundred people report sexual assaults to the police, and somewhere between perhaps seven to fourteen of them end with a conviction for their report, what's different about those seven to fourteen people? In the United States, we tend to assume that "privilege" (in most situations, being white, male, straight, and college educated) is more likely to get you taken seriously by most major institutions, including institutions of criminal justice. We'll talk a lot more about how these assumptions do or don't play out in chapter 7. Suffice it to say for now that being a straight male *definitely* isn't an advantage if you go to the police and complain that you've been sexually assaulted (by a man or a woman). In general, analyses show that privilege doesn't matter in sexual assault cases the way we might expect it to; demographic factors about victims other than age and sexual orientation are never statistically significant in determining whose cases move forward and whose don't in the limited data available. Instead, just as police claim when we interview them, *the most important factor in getting a case continued is having a "cooperative victim"* (Wentz and Keimig 2019; Morabito, Williams, and Pattavina 2019). We'll deconstruct what that means shortly, but cases are much more likely to proceed when police and prosecutors perceive the victim as being prompt, open, honest, and persistent. More specifically, the factors that matter are providing a fast report to the police (meaning under seventy-two hours; Daly and Bouhours 2010); having a rape kit done by a specially trained nurse (Campbell, Patterson, and Bybee 2012); showing signs of physical assault, such as bruises (Venema, Lorenz, and Sweda 2021; Daly and Bouhours 2010); and corroboration from a witness or video (Burgin 2019). On the other hand, police are suspicious of victims who were intoxicated or who failed to provide specific details of what happened to them (Campbell, Menaker, and King 2015).

The takeaways. Conviction rates for rape are very messy statistics. They are extremely low in all Anglophone countries, but they don't seem to be wildly out of line with other nonfatal violent crimes. How low they are depends a lot on whether the attrition estimate starts with the number of sexual assaults reported to survey takers (and how they measure it) versus the number of sexual assaults reported to the police (which is a much smaller starting number). Because reports to the police and survey takers have both gone up a lot in recent years, if we had the numbers on conviction rates during that time for the United States (which we don't), they would almost certainly have decreased a lot. While it's true that very few violent criminals in general are found guilty of a crime, official reports claim about a third of sexual assaults reported to the police result in arrest—however, those numbers are very dubious because such a high percentage of them are "cleared by exceptional means," meaning no actual arrest was made.

WHY GET INVOLVED WITH THE CRIMINAL JUSTICE PROCESS?

The adversarial nature of criminal justice systems in most rich countries means that someone is supposed to be found guilty or not guilty of wrongdoing committed against another, then punished if they're found guilty. But in order to try not to punish the wrong person for something they didn't do, we have a very elaborate legal process to attempt to protect the accused. That process is not in any way designed to make things comfortable or easy for the victim. Indeed, one could reasonably argue that it's set up to make things intentionally very unpleasant for them to discourage them from reporting.

After all, legal processes are expensive and resource-intensive undertakings, so the people involved don't have great incentives to make heavy caseloads even heavier. But as difficult and possibly even scary as it may be to report a robbery and actively participate in the prosecution (especially if, say, you have reason to believe you were robbed by someone who's part of a criminal group that might seek retribution against you for pressing charges), doing the same in a rape case can present all those anxieties *plus* the grim reality of repeatedly having to confront a deeply traumatic experience *in front of other people*.

Consider all the qualities listed above for a "cooperative victim": being open, honest, and willing to subject oneself to a rape kit. Talking about a traumatic experience isn't easy for most people; for some, it's literally impossible. The idea that we seriously expect someone whose body has just been sexually violated by someone else to head down to a local hospital, strip before a group of strangers, and let them stick swabs in their mouths and genitalia (an experience that must surely feel horribly reminiscent of the rape that has just occurred) is appalling. Except for a specialized group of medical professionals who've been specifically trained to help, many hospital workers are annoyed at having to deal with rape victims who aren't obviously injured (Martin 2005). This process is clearly designed for the benefit of prosecutors, not victims (Corrigan 2013).

Along the way, the victim will probably have to tell their story multiple times to various officials, who are required to ask a lot of very personal questions. It's not like victims get to make a single recorded statement and that's the end of it; instead, they're usually asked, again and again, to relive some of the worst moments of their life in conversation with police officers, detectives, and prosecutors. Only 44 percent of women in Canada reporting a sexual assault to the police "felt the first officer [they spoke to] believed them" (Johnson 2017, 49). Even worse, there's reason to believe that lack of support from institutions may itself be a major factor in creating traumatic memories and/or exacerbate existing trauma (Smith and Freyd 2013). Commentators decades ago began referring to this entire judicial process as a "second trauma" or a "second victimization." That means we've created a "justice system" that is very likely to seriously harm the people it's ostensibly trying to help. Numerous social scientists have agreed the entire system around the world needs to be completely overhauled (Cossins 2020, looking at Australia and England; Fohring 2020, focusing on Scotland).

Who would actually sign up for this miserable process? Nowadays, with more women than ever going to the police, women say they do so from a sense of obligation to others and society "to do the right thing" and also to protect others from being hurt by the same person (Brooks-Hay 2020; Johnson 2017). Sometimes they're afraid for themselves and seeking police protection, but more often they say they wanted the person who hurt them "to get help." (Johnson 2017). Perhaps most important is a motivation we will be addressing very seriously in the second part of this book: legitimacy. Despite its myriad problems, society views the criminal legal system as our primary means of showing something "really happened" (Johnson 2017). Reporting a sexual assault to the police is a crucial step for many victims in trying to prove to others (and perhaps even to themselves) that an assault actually took place, and they weren't just lying or exaggerating. But as we have seen in this chapter, few survivors get the social validation of seeing the people who hurt them punished by the legal system.

It's important to keep in mind the legal system is *especially* bad at helping victims of certain classes of sexual assault. Already massively undercounted by the definitions of the law, male victims who meet the definitions are still only estimated to report at less than half the rate of female victims (Hine et al. 2021). People are also far less likely to report or press charges against people they have ever dated and/or previously had sex with, which makes it very difficult for the justice system to address the literal majority of sexual assaults. Despite many legal changes over the years, it's clear that the criminal justice system still zeros in on the types of people our culture imagines as stereotypical "rape victims": sober women who are violently attacked by strange men. Everything outside that bullseye is very hit or miss, and even that bullseye hardly gets a perfect score.

As we begin to shift to the second part of the book, which focuses more on solutions, I don't want to conclude this chapter with the oft-repeated claim that the criminal justice system spectacularly fails the victims of sexual assault. I want to conclude with a less often repeated claim that *the criminal justice system spectacularly fails almost everyone, but particularly the victims of violent crime.* Only murder victims usually get the metaphorical satisfaction of having their day in court . . . and they're dead. It's possible we should be satisfied with the current conviction rates for sexual assault, and we just need to turn our attention to other ways to legally address sexual violation. Let's be very, very careful about framing low conviction rates for sexual assault as a social problem we need to address—especially since mass incarceration is an epic social crisis itself. Instead, for the rest of this book, we're going to talk about all the ways other than conviction for sexual assault that might help mitigate the underlying problem here, which is always, ultimately, that people are hurt.

PART II

Real Change

Chapter 6

The Harm Reduction Approach

Consent Hygiene and Actual Gender Equality

A TIME AND PLACE TO SAY YES TO
AN UNASKED QUESTION

As discussed in chapter 4, long ago, social authorities used to hand you a "license to fuck" the day you got married, and it was awkward to do so beforehand (although many people did), and also awkward to fail to do so afterward. Most people in rich countries nowadays don't expect an institutional authority (or even their parents) to grant them permission to enjoy each other sexually—they just expect to have the right to do what they want. But in the case of sex, doing whatever *you* want obviously still runs up against the potential limitations of doing whatever *the other person* wants. Despite this limitation, we've mostly built some sort of free-for-all where there's no clear moment when someone is supposed to ask for and consent to sex. If anything, the majority of young adults seem to find explicit conversations about sexual consent off-putting. There are really only two ways to get around this problem: reshape sex and dating norms completely to create a mythical sober moment in which two people who've never had sex before can talk about it (which seems extremely unlikely at this point given all the social norms working against that), or change our cultural conversation about consent to reflect reality and downgrade our expectations a bit (which makes it very likely many people will still get hurt).

This normless sexual free-for-all is complicated by social expectations that pretend we still have a clear normative system in place. Even after the days when a marriage license was the only means of bestowing sexual rights, society created some decent substitutions through rules and norms. Most of us grew up with a socially dictated vision that sex was supposed to happen something like this: go on a date with someone and maybe they'll kiss you; after a couple more dates, you might make out, grope each other, and touch each other's genitalia. In public, they'll hold your hand, and you'll declare yourselves boyfriend and girlfriend (at which point you'll definitely be sexually exclusive with one another) and say, "I love you." After a few months of this, you'll probably progress to intercourse, and if you're an adult, sleep in the same bed together; you'll also likely experiment with oral sex. After doing this for some number of years or months, depending on your age and social situation, you'll either break up, or move in together and possibly eventually marry. From a consent-focused perspective, that's probably not an ideal system, but it doesn't seem like a very bad one. Lots of people in it likely end up getting pressured into having sex they don't particularly want to have because they feel like it is socially expected of them (and expected from their partner) "because they're in a relationship." But barring other social or situational pressures, they at least usually have a long time to think about it and see it coming and try to get out if they really want to avoid the expectation.

Ironically, modern American society starts with these relatively straightforward dating/sex expectations—teaching them at a fairly early age—and then proceeds to place endless obstacles in the paths of young people trying to manifest them. There's a lot of understandable concern over the fact that American teens often struggle to get access to reliable birth control or abortion, and many people worry too about how often American adults fail to have real conversations with their children about safe and consensual sex. But there's a lot less conversation about the way we deny teenagers access to physical space to have sex. We just kind of assume that determined teens will find a place to bang, because they usually do. By the time young teens mature into legal adults, we still don't usually provide them with socially accepted places to have sex. College students living on campus find themselves deliberately deprived of easy space for sexual experimentation, with freshmen and often sophomores made to live with roommates in dorm rooms. Poor or working-class young adults, meanwhile, are usually still living with parents (who might or might not support their sexual lives) or sharing crowded living spaces with roommates, a partner, and possibly young children of their own. Where do we (literally) make space for young adults to legitimately have sex?

Answer: nowhere.

While older (twenty-five and up) middle- and upper-class adults seem to have more opportunities to date in ways that conform to the social expectations they were brought up with (Lamont 2020), when young people begin their first forays into sexual life, they end up doing it furtively, without the guidance of social norms or the support of elders. Instead of sexual experiments happening in their bedrooms after dates, they end up fooling around in the back seats of cars, or screwing around at parties that probably aren't approved of by anyone's parents and are unaccompanied by anything that resembles a "date." We create a sense among adolescents that their opportunities for sex are scant so they must seize them when they arise, which doesn't help young people make the best long-term decisions for themselves. They often find themselves in sexual spaces they weren't "supposed" to be at in the first place—say, illicitly drinking at a friend's house with members of the opposite sex. And because they're "breaking the rules," they're now stuck following an alternative social script that no one gave them the guidelines for, leaving them feeling lost and anxious. They don't know what "correct" sexual consent behavior looks like in these situations because no one told them how to behave in these situations at all—in fact, all anyone ever told them was not to be there in the first place.

Hirsch and Khan (2020) document in detail the consequences of these social and sexual landscapes on college students' sex lives. Privacy is conspicuously lacking in the worlds of most college freshmen in particular, but young adults in general often find themselves short on it. There's an unfortunate "sunk cost fallacy" that can emerge at the point where you have to kick a roommate out of your shared living space so you can have sex, only realizing after they're gone that sex with this person wasn't such a good idea after all. (Sunk cost fallacies emerge in a wide variety of situations when you feel like you've invested in something, so you stick it out even though doing so only makes your situation worse—like continuing to watch a movie that's terrible because you paid for the ticket and feel like you have to "get your money's worth.") If you functionally tell, or even heavily imply to, multiple people you're close to that you intend to hook up with someone (and especially if those people have inconvenienced themselves so you can), then it can feel *extra* awkward not to if you come to realize the hookup was a bad idea. If you say no at that point, not only do you not get laid, you also either have to admit that to your friends who got you here, or lie to them.

When young adults finally manage to stumble upon privacy, they often feel like they have to jump on the opportunity to have sex with someone even if they aren't sure they really want to. Many college freshmen feel like they've busted free from restrictive homes where they had few opportunities to have any kind of sexual contact, and then practically overnight they find themselves suddenly elevated to adulthood, with many of its accompanying sexual freedoms. Is it any wonder that such a high percentage of college sexual assaults tend to happen to female freshmen in their first six weeks at college? The literature on college sexual assault refers to this time frame as "the red zone" (Grigoriadis 2017; Hirsch and Khan 2020), but it's only partly the result of college itself. Young people's parents (especially the parents of daughters) frequently follow a counterproductive set of social norms, sheltering and protecting their young ones right up until the moment they shove them out of the nest. I don't know what everyone else did in their first twenty-four hours at college, but I promptly got in a car with a sophomore who drove me to a party at a different college in another state just for the pure, unadulterated thrill of going somewhere and not having to tell anyone where the fuck I was going.

And of course, the novelty of freedom helps breed the college party culture, and so layered on top of the weird limitations of "few places and times to have sex" are the illegal alcohol and drugs that tend to accompany parties. Whether in college or not, Americans under age twenty-one aren't allowed to buy alcohol or pot, so any time they consume these drugs, they do so illegally and surreptitiously, without the support or guidance of their elders. They live in a culture where they can get married, borrow life-crushing sums of money to pay for college, and be forced to join the military at age eighteen . . . but they can't drink or do pot for three more years. They know these rules are stupid and so do the people who have to enforce them. But those dumb rules still have a huge impact on how safe young people feel talking to adults about what they're doing and who they're doing it with. Parties and hangouts where young people drink and get high become furtive affairs, ripe for sexual assault with few consequences. Young people are afraid to tell anyone they were at these illicit gatherings in the first place, doing illegal drugs (that aren't illegal for most adults), so they're often reluctant to tell older people if someone violated their consent at them too (Huck 2021).

ALTERNATIVE CULTURAL MODELS

If we're serious about improving sexual consent and reducing sexual assault, there are a lot of cultural changes that have to happen in the United States, especially around sex education. But countries with *much* better sex education, much more open attitudes about sex and sexuality, and much healthier attitudes toward young adults' consumption of alcohol are still (to varying degrees) struggling with all the same consent issues that the United States is. That commonality suggests there's something much deeper and more fundamental going on here, which I think is heterosexual dating norms. We tend to zero in on sexual consent as if it's an aspect of sex and dating we can simply isolate and change, and doing so can create some excellent Band-Aid solutions. But if we're looking for serious changes, the reality is that there's an entire messy web of cultural beliefs we have to untangle before such changes are possible.

In recent years, many consent advocates have turned to the BDSM subculture as a place to model what best consent practices could look like. I've spent many years studying and participating in this subculture, so I know it well.

(If you want to know more, check out my book *Please Scream Quietly: A Story of Kink* [Fennell 2022].) It's a subculture where people often enjoy hitting each other/being hit, ordering people around/being ordered around, and intentionally playing with very dark desires (from kidnapping fantasies to objectifying people as furniture to "owning" people to much more besides). Most participants in the BDSM subculture argue that the only thin line separating "abuse" from most BDSM practices is "consent," so the subculture sets ideal(istic) standards for getting and maintaining consent that are extremely high. There are rituals of "negotiation" in which people are expected to precisely name their specific desires and "limits" (meaning the things they don't want to do under any circumstances) for a given interaction. In the ideal model, people provide up-front, explicit consent for everything they want to happen to them in the course of an encounter. The strictest version of that model insists that people can withdraw consent at any time, meaning they can decide they no longer want to do what they previously agreed to. It also criticizes people who seek to expand the original agreement through "mid-scene negotiations," meaning no one should seek more leeway in the interaction than they were originally granted.

These consent rituals are fairly well established and normalized in the community, and people use them to negotiate extremely narrow forms of interaction as well as fairly broad ones (although the techniques change). People who are new to each other and/or new to the community tend to rely on "inclusive" negotiations, meaning they list things they would like for the interaction to include and expect it won't include much else. People who are more experienced and/or know each other well often use "exclusive" negotiations, meaning they list things they *don't* want the interaction to include and leave open a wide range of other possibilities. There are also fairly standard rules about who initiates these negotiations, as well as the structure and format of them. Most of the time, "tops" or "dominants" (the people who are creating the sensation and/or more in charge of the experience) solicit information and consent from "bottoms" or "submissives" (who are receiving the sensation and/or have given up control). In essence, the people who are assumed to be the least in control have an opportunity to declare in advance just how much control they're willing to give up. The format of these negotiations is so heavily ritualized in the community that it's easy to judge the experience level and competence of both tops and bottoms by the ease with which they practice them.

In practice, a very basic inclusive negotiation between Diane and Chris, a hypothetical experienced pair, might look something like this:

Diane: Hi, I heard you're a good impact top; would you like to beat me up?

Chris: That sounds fun! Have you done this before?

Diane: Many times!

Chris: Great! Let me show you some of my toys [the term for BDSM tools]. Which of these looks good to you?

Diane: Oh, the pink flogger looks fun! And the police baton. I'm not so sure about the canes, though. Could we try those a little bit and then see how much I like them?

Chris: Of course. They feel really different depending on how you hit with them, though, so just give me feedback once we start playing. Do you have any injuries I should know about?

Diane: I'm asthmatic, and my inhaler's in my purse if I need it. Otherwise, I'm good.

Chris: Where are your favorite places to be hit?

Diane: My ass and the front of my thighs. Where are your favorite places to hit someone?

Chris: I actually really love caning the bottom of people's feet, but I know that's not a really common taste. Is that something you might be into?

Diane: I'm definitely willing to try, but I don't know how much I can take. I've never done it before.

Chris: Great, thanks for being willing to try something new with me, I promise I'll go slow! Any parts of your body you definitely don't want hit?

Diane: Let's stay away from my genitals, neck, face, and arms. I'm okay with canes on the palms of my hands, though.

Chris: How will I know if you're having a good time?

Diane: I usually go through a phase where I'm really giggly, and then I kind of drift off into not making much noise. If you ask me questions and I can't answer with real words, that's a good sign.

Chris: Do you feel confident you can tell me to stop if I'm doing something you don't like at that point?

Diane: Yeah, I'll kind of flail my hands and shake my head no.

Chris: Got it. Hopefully we won't get to that point! What type of emotions or vibes would feel good for you from this?

Diane: I think we can keep it pretty casual. But I'm really into it if it feels like someone's kind of attacking me.

Chris: Oh, I love that! Is it okay if I grab your hair and shove you around some for that?

Diane: Definitely!

Chris: Do you need anything particular in the way of aftercare [taking care of after the BDSM play is complete]?

Diane: No, I'm pretty easy. I just like hugs and drinking my water. What about you?

Chris: Same! I'll try to send you a text message tomorrow to check in on you, but I always love getting pictures of your bruises!

Notice the types of information that Chris and Diane can communicate in a simple exchange. She shows enthusiastic interest in his flogger and police baton and consents to try his canes, but admits lack of experience and asks him to go slow, so he knows what he can do easily versus carefully. He knows that his interest in caning feet is unconventional in the community and checks in with her about it specifically to gauge her interest. When she explains that having a good time for her means she becomes mostly nonverbal, he asks if she's secure in her ability to get the interaction to stop if necessary, and she says yes. (When people say no, these conversations get a lot more complicated.) She describes a mood for their interaction (an attack), and he checks in to make sure his vision of that experience seems to be in line with hers, as well as seeking specific physical consent beyond what is traditionally included in "impact play" among people experienced in the community.

Exclusive negotiations are, by design, much more open-ended and tend to occur between people who know each other much better. They're more common if the bottom is seeking an experience of submission (giving up control) and/or is unfamiliar with, but very interested in, something the top is experienced at doing. A negotiation in these terms between two experienced people who know each other pretty well might look more like this:

Ethan: I'm really interested in submitting to you. I know you're good with knives [by BDSM subcultural convention "knifeplay" doesn't usually involve breaking the skin], so maybe we could start there with creating a scene [meaning an interaction of BDSM play]?

Gina: I'd love that. What kinds of things make you feel more submissive?

Ethan: I'm really into a combination of affectionate cruelty—kind of like a villain is seducing me.

Gina: That is a space I am super into. Are there any specific actions or words that encourage that for you?

Ethan: Choking me, pulling my hair, sitting me on the floor. But mostly I just really like doing the things that you enjoy.

Gina: I'm into all that. How do you feel about being stepped on? Spat on?

Ethan: Those sound hot.

Gina: What kind of limits do you have?

Ethan: Not many . . . nothing likely to put me in the hospital or get me arrested. Try not to actively break skin. No shit, blood, or vomit.

Gina: That's a lot of leeway.

Ethan: Yeah, I trust you, and I think you're hot.

Gina: I'm flattered. So you'll tell me if I do something you're not okay with?

Ethan: Yeah, I'm pretty good at communicating, I think.

Gina: Any injuries or peculiar things I should know about your body?

Ethan: My knees are pretty messed up, so I can't kneel for as long as I wish I could without support for them. I'm not particularly great at taking a lot of pain in general, so I mostly do it as an act of submission. But I like to be scared, and since I'm not great at taking pain, I'm pretty easy to scare.

Gina: That's all very good to keep in mind! So it sounds like you're okay with doing sex stuff?

Ethan: Only if you want to.

Gina: Let's see where things go.

In these types of exclusive negotiations, bottoms still usually provide some sort of starting framework but are typically actively looking for the tops to take direction of the interaction. Bottoms declare what's off-limits and leave tops to direct the rest of the encounter at will. Tops still care about how bottoms feel and what it is they're seeking, and if this conversation continued, Gina would still ask Ethan about what kind of aftercare he needed, and possibly solicit more specific information about his sexual desires and STI testing history.

I'd love to believe these standards have a lot to offer mainstream cultures in terms of consent modeling, but the subculture has many basic features that make it hard to guess how well its consent norms could generalize. For starters, you might have been frustrated that I cut that sample negotiation between Ethan and Gina off where I did, hoping I'd show them negotiating a sexual interaction, since that's presumably the thing nonkinky people would most like to learn from kinky people. But part of why I cut that conversation short is that the BDSM community offers very little in the way of models for "standard negotiation" for sex. In fact, I've taught several classes in the community on "negotiating sex for BDSM play" and people often say to me, "Oh, I never thought about doing that," because contrary to outside expectations, the BDSM community works fairly hard to separate BDSM from sex.

There's a pretty clear understanding in the community that sex should be negotiated clearly and explicitly, but the formula for that negotiation is so spectacularly absent compared to the formula for other BDSM interactions that people often end up having to kind of make it up on the fly. If even the people experienced in operating within this framework struggle to apply it to sexual interactions, I am very uncertain how well others could use it.

There are many other reasons I think the BDSM subculture can provide only a minimally useful outline for consent negotiations outside the subculture, but I think those reasons help highlight major cultural changes that might need to occur in order for mainstream culture to be able to successfully adopt idealistic explicit consent negotiation. Perhaps most importantly, the BDSM culture places such a strong emphasis on not engaging in BDSM while intoxicated that some former drug and alcohol addicts join the subculture partly to help them get sober. That alone is such a massive departure from mainstream dating sexual norms that it might almost entirely account for any observed differences in rates of sexual assault. (To the best of my knowledge, no one has ever actually measured those theoretical differences.) Second, the BDSM subculture places a strong emphasis on gender equality that is still lacking in mainstream society. Most of the evidence we have suggests that in heterosexual interactions, men are expected to ostensibly take the lead in both relationships and sexual interactions, but the BDSM subculture is a place where women are allowed to be dominant over men (although, statistically speaking, even there they rarely are [Fennell 2022]). People are much more conscientious about what gender equality means in the BDSM subculture, even in an already much more gender-equal society like Sweden (Carlström 2017). Third, and relatedly, the BDSM subculture is strongly influenced by queer subcultural norms, which, as Lamont (2020) has shown, tend to have a much more make-it-up-as-you-go approach to relationships and sexual encounters. It's also a place that tends to be skeptical about a lot of traditional social norms in general, with a strong emphasis on questioning authority and tradition for tradition's sake. Fourth, and further related to that, the social makeup of the BDSM subculture tends to be composed of extremely liberal people who value open-mindedness, with a specific focus on the free discussion of sex and sexuality.

There are many other qualities of the BDSM subculture that help it create an exceptionally supportive environment for experimenting with more ideal consent models. One of the key dimensions of mainstream society that the BDSM subculture has rejected is monogamy, which seems to bring with it a lot of cultural baggage about what it means for people (and especially women) to have extensive sexual histories and experiences. Instead of viewing people with long sexual histories negatively, my research shows that the BDSM subculture often views them as desirable partners. Women in mainstream culture are often afraid that being too open about sex will make them look "slutty" and thus undesirable as long-term partners (England and Bearak 2014). But being very open about sex is basically a requirement for having frank conversations about consent, so these two cultural norms are currently in pretty direct conflict in mainstream society. In general, the BDSM subculture cultivates a sexually open and explicit environment; it encourages people to freely have casual conversations about sex and sexual desires in general, which presumably makes it easier for them to have those kinds of conversations more intimately with specific partners. The subculture also mostly eschews the dogma and practices of most mainstream religions, which probably helps chuck some of the classically sex-negative views plaguing much of mainstream society.

The last two reasons the BDSM subculture is a very different social context for consent than mainstream society are somewhat related. The first is that it's an extremely tight-knit social world that depends on reputation as its most desirable form of social capital. As noted earlier, everyone in the BDSM subculture understands that the line between BDSM and "abuse" can be a very thin one, and one of the main ways people try to avoid the kinds of people who might be on the wrong side of that line is by talking to other people. People in the subculture ruthlessly use gossip to make sure everyone knows who's following the rules (and who isn't). And that's related to the second important difference in the BDSM subculture compared to mainstream society: there *are* clear rules for how to negotiate BDSM encounters (and, to a lesser degree, rules about how to negotiate full-blown BDSM relationships) that make it *slightly* easier to decide who's on the right and wrong side of the line. That determination gets directed very disproportionately at tops/dominants (the people directing sensations and experiences) compared to bottoms/submissives (the people receiving sensations and experiences), but the subculture tends to implicitly or sometimes even explicitly expect that tops/doms will accept greater responsibility for how interactions play out compared to bottoms/subs.

I've spent a long time telling you why I don't think the BDSM subculture presents a very easily translatable model for sexual consent for mainstream society, but I do think there are still some important things we can learn from it—more in terms of cultural modeling than the specifics of how to create a consent negotiation at the individual level. First, and probably most important, is a greater emphasis on sober sex. As we saw in previous chapters, mainstream culture really portrays drunken sex as fun, normal, and the only acceptable avenue for wild experimentation. But the BDSM subculture argues the opposite: drunk sex makes it difficult to be very experimental because it's so hard to know if you're honoring someone's boundaries and consent, and the hottest interactions you can have with someone are when you can trust them not to negatively judge you even though you're both sober. The statistics we saw previously were very much against the mainstream portrayal here; by pretty much any measure you like, the majority of people report that drunk sex is bad (Herbenick et al. 2019). It sounds like a strangely conservative slogan, but it turns out one of the most sexually radical things you can argue is, "If you wanna have a fucking good time, fuck sober." If you really want to say "fuck you" to a sex-negative culture, be a woman who stays stone-cold sober and in the light of day looks someone of any gender dead in the eyes, tells them sincerely how you want to have sex with them, asks them what they want from you . . . and then demands they respect you when you're done. That's the idealistic model the BDSM subculture offers women of what their own sexual potential can be, but even there, it's still extremely hard to actualize.

I didn't choose the gender of the person in my example there casually. The scenario I just described seems incredibly unlikely in mainstream culture, not just because of norms about tipsy sex, but because women don't expect to be sexually empowered. A huge component of what the BDSM subculture offers mainstream culture in terms of consent modeling is a real-life example of what's possible when we demand actual gender equality instead of the mere pretense of it. Gender equality is about much more than equal pay: it's also about equal respect. When straight men say they want women who are sexually experienced and know what they're doing in bed but have had fewer sexual partners than themselves, *walk the fuck away*. I've studied the US porn industry as well as the BDSM subculture, and I know how deep the cultural hypocrisy goes. Most American men seem to find the idea of dating and marrying a porn star to be laughable, but they're happy to jerk off to them. This kind of hypocrisy has to change if we want a society where women and men both understand what it means to respect what each other wants sexually.

One of the most concrete things the BDSM subculture does to help facilitate clear consent communication is to establish well-known norms about whose job it is to start a consent conversation. In the BDSM subculture, even if bottoms/submissives are the ones who asked to play with the top/dominant, tops/dominants are still the ones everyone expects to initiate and lead a consent conversation. As we saw, these conversations have a pretty strict format, too, so people don't have to constantly reinvent the wheel with them. For now, mainstream culture has mostly assumed that in heterosexual encounters, the gender role of "man" substitutes for that of "top/dominant" in basically every respect here—including being the person more responsible for initiating and having a consent conversation. Given that mainstream culture provides men with basically no models or archetypes for how these consent conversations are supposed to go, it seems especially problematic to stick them with the sole burden of initiating them. If we're trying to ditch gender norms in dating and sexual interactions (and I think we should), then we're going to have to come up with a better marker for "who should initiate this conversation" than "whoever has a penis and/or wears a tie."

I don't have an easy answer for this question, and if you're wondering, "well, how do lesbians manage it?" the answer, unfortunately, is "with great difficulty." Lesbians and bisexual women often complain that it is extremely hard to know who's supposed to make the first move (Gordon 2006). I've struggled with this so much personally dating women that I eventually started declaring in advance of dates whose job it was "to make sex happen if it's happening," and several queer women friends told me I had changed their lives for the better with this advice. Without such a declaration or some clearly predefined roles like those of top/dom and bottom/sub in the BDSM subculture, I don't know what else people are left with other than who asked someone else out or whose place they ended up at (when relevant). But I cannot emphasize enough that *having a great consent script is completely useless if no one knows their roles to play in it or cues for applying it.*

The last thing that might be relevant about the BDSM subculture for small, tight-knit social worlds like high schools and college campuses is normalizing sharing information about people's consent skills throughout social networks. As far as I can tell, this fails to happen right now partly because the networks are often too big; but in an ideal world, it should be a status element for people of both genders to have friends with good consent skills, so the "cool fraternities and sororities" would be the ones where everyone felt safe. The other reason I think this doesn't happen in the real world is most people don't feel comfortable enough talking about sex with strangers (and even many friends) to say, "I was making out with this guy last night and he tried to pressure me into blowing him" and perhaps even less to say, "I kissed this girl last night and she tried to pressure me into eating her out." Everyone has to believe they won't be judged for the mere fact of being drunk, making out with someone, and having some sex (especially relevant for women) or not wanting to have sex (especially relevant for men). Moreover, they have to believe that a friend or even a stranger will believe them when they say their partner treated them badly in order for word to get out that their partner needs to work on their consent hygiene.

CONSENT HYGIENE AND THE
CULTURE OF INTOXICATION

In their massive study on sexual consent among American college students, Hirsch and Khan (2020) argue that consent is a public health issue, and I agree. They point out that large-scale social factors, from gender norms to the physical construction of dormitories and other sexual spaces, have a massive impact on how people end up practicing sexual consent. I propose taking this concept further so we can begin to have a cultural conversation around "consent hygiene." Imagining consent as a public health issue may sound weird, given that we're mostly used to thinking of it in a criminal context. But if we've learned nothing else from the bewildering statistics in the previous chapter, surely we've learned that the criminal justice system is really only (possibly) prepared to manage issues of aggravated sexual assault, not the sexual violations that concern most of us in our daily lives. Sexual consent is a public health concern in that being bad at it can affect other people, not just yourself. Think of it like washing your hands: if you're bad about washing your hands, you could get sick more easily, but you also might *just* make other people sick or make other people sick *as well*. There are also different standards for "good enough" depending on your position—if you're a doctor or food preparer, we expect you to be more diligent about washing your hands than if you're a plumber or computer technician. You also need to wash your hands much more thoroughly in some situations than others (for instance, if you just emptied your cat's litter box compared with just eating dinner).

These situations all parallel consent. Rather than trying to pretend that we have some hard-and-fast rule for what constitutes "good consent," we need to recognize that good consent varies a lot depending on social positions and situations. Fischel (2019) argues in *Screw Consent* that there's so much variability in these situations that from a legal perspective, the concept of consent is somewhat useless. I think he's correct that there are many circumstances (particularly involving people with serious disabilities) where the concept of consent is very difficult to apply well. But for the purposes of this book, we're going to focus on the vast majority of people who are presumably able-bodied and able-minded enough to conform to conventional social standards of consent (and I'm also going to set aside the tricky issue of age). Using a concept of consent hygiene allows us to start talking about a spectrum from "possibly excessively diligent consent hygiene" to "good" to "needs improvement" to "bad" to "so bad that it probably should be illegal" to "really fucking bad and definitely illegal." We can stop painting the world purely in black-and-white terms of people who committed sexual assault and people who didn't, and people who were sexually assaulted and people who weren't. We can start acknowledging a vast grey area of people who made poor decisions, or people who suffered from a tough sexual experience—without always having to jump to "that's rape."

Developing and practicing good consent hygiene is a lifelong endeavor, and most of us will probably slip up every now and then. Ideally, we should learn good consent practices from formal education and people close to us (both romantically and otherwise). But we will almost inevitably mess up on our first few attempts, and we need to leave ourselves (and others) space to mess up and learn from our/their mistakes. We have to get in the habit of being reflexive with ourselves about an encounter, and asking ourselves if we're happy with the way we handled consent before, during, and after that encounter. We can have an ongoing conversation with our partners to make sure they also feel good. We can talk with our friends about how things went and see if they have advice or constructive criticism.

If you think I'm being cagey here by failing to create a script or a one-size-fits-all standard for what good consent should look like . . . well, maybe I am. There are no one-size-fits-all standards, especially since social circumstances can radically alter what appropriate consent looks like. People should be allowed to construct social spaces using whatever consent norms feel appropriate to them: gay men should be allowed to have sexual hookup spaces where explicit verbal sexual consent is basically nonexistent (Orne 2017); straight people should be allowed to have (consensual) drunken parties where explicit verbal sexual consent is hazy; and BDSM participants should be allowed to construct high-risk spaces where people can explicitly consent to many behaviors that would otherwise be perceived as abusive (although the standards are necessarily higher for verbal consent in those spaces, for both social and legal reasons). Adults should be allowed to make "bad decisions"—to consent to get wasted and go out partying with the full intention of having sex with strangers that they might regret later, to consent to let someone beat them until their legs are giant black-and-blue bruises, and even to consent to give up their authority over their own well-being (which some BDSM submissives consent to). These controversial consent norms only pose big problems when people don't understand them, when people don't actually agree on them, and/or when people face social pressure to participate in these activities and didn't really want to. In trying to create better consent hygiene, our social goals should emphasize making sure people understand the consent norms of the activities they're participating in and that they're actually comfortable with them. Maybe a group agrees that they like their consent norms, or maybe a group agrees they'd rather have different norms, but no one has ever been conscientious enough to detail the norms before, so real agreement or change were both impossible. Part of good consent hygiene is simply *noticing* the consent norms of your environment and making sure others are aware of them and on the same page about them.

One of the accounts in Hirsch and Khan's (2020) book is powerfully illustrative of the range of the vast grey area of consent norms in everyday life. Their book recounts the experiences of a young college man named Elliot, told from his perspective. In his version of events, one of his friends, Katie, complained that she hadn't had sex in a long time; he offered, and she declined. They went on a late-night walk together; he again asked her to have sex, and she declined. Hours later, around 5 a.m., they ended up back in their dorm common room together, and this time when he asked her to have sex, she said yes and got lube, and they did. Was his behavior ideal consent hygiene? Probably not. But having been on the receiving end of a few people repeatedly propositioning me, I can say from experience that it can be flattering to be asked repeatedly, as long as you feel empowered to say no. It can be hot to be wanted, even (or especially) at the expense of someone else's pride or dignity. Assuming Elliot's account was correct, personally, I'd say his consent hygiene could use some improvement without painting him as a rapist. Columbia University apparently disagreed. It turned out that unbeknownst to Elliot (or at least so he says), Katie had taken the sedative clonazepam and been drinking before all this transpired. The university found him guilty of sexual assault for "wearing her down and extracting a yes that she did not want to give, that she was not capable of giving" (Hirsch and Khan 2020, 161) and suspended him. Elliot was devastated and nearly suicidal at the thought he had hurt someone, and he faced social ostracism when he came back to school. His own later experiences—having sex he didn't always want with his girlfriend when they were both drunk—led him to some profound observations that I think deserve our attention. He says,

> I think there should be another term [than rape]. Not so much that I think that, like, date rape or something like that isn't rape, but I think there's culturally such a connotation with rape and physical violence, that it conjures up the wrong image of what consent is meant to be. I think in coining another term—and I'm sure a feminist will point out how this is entirely wrong of me were I to bring it up, but that's okay—in coining another term, you could kind of take the wrong connotation away from it [physical violence] and start to break down what consent actually is in the context of alcohol, drugs, and all of these altered states of mind and stuff. (163–64)

Well, I'm a feminist and I mostly agree with Elliot. I think we have too few words to discuss these experiences, which is why I'm proposing changing to the term "sexual violation." I also think that saying an adult who made their own choices "couldn't really consent" is infantilizing. (If someone else intoxicates you against your will or knowledge, that's a different story.) And yet. I also recognize there are experiences people can ostensibly consent to that they don't really have sufficient knowledge to understand what they're agreeing to (the extreme edges of BDSM come readily to mind). The lines here aren't always clear, and having a cultural, social, and legal system that recognizes that blurriness would make us all better able to productively engage with ourselves, our partners, and our friends.

This is where the difference between legal consent and social consent should matter. But regardless of which way we slice it, I'm hard pressed to think Elliot deserved much social or any legal censure based on the story he provided—although of course Katie's version of what happened might have been quite different.

IS IT ALWAYS SOMEONE ELSE'S FAULT?

When I think about gender and sexual consent, the thing I come up with again and again is that women should probably try to be a bit more like men, and men should probably try to be a bit more like women. I have been deeply discouraged in my conversations with men over the years about their experiences with sexual violation and how they've learned to downplay them. Sometimes they downplay them as being not that bad or not that bad compared to what happens to many women, and sometimes they don't even realize their experiences constituted a sexual violation at all. Many women do these things too, but at least some parts of society tell them they should be angry and indignant and stand up for their bodies and their rights. Men don't have any of these advocates, and even most of the limited sociological research I found on sexual violation still frames it almost entirely as a women's issue, falling prey to the statistical deceptions we saw in the previous chapter that lead one to mistakenly believe that sexual violations almost never happen to men. Society, most social scientists, consent advocates, and certainly the law have not really come to terms with the apparent frequency of men's experiences of sexual violation as victims, and the cultural and institutional refusal to acknowledge this lived experience is alienating for men. It tells men in these conversations that their own experiences are trivial, it removes support for them, and it also teaches them the perverse lesson that the thing that happened to them is "okay"—but they shouldn't do it to someone else. All these things are the exact opposite of what we need to happen.

Meanwhile, I think we've been teaching women to see their bodies as too vulnerable and too exposed, and to embrace a shared identity of victimhood. Sanyal (2019), writing from Germany, is one of the few feminist writers about rape to challenge us by asking, what do we gain as feminists by emphasizing women's experiences as victims (or even when we reframe this label as "survivors")—especially when we do so in a context of advocacy that largely ignores the grim reality of men as the vast majority of homicide victims? I don't by any means want to suggest that anyone of any gender who has suffered sexual violence is undeserving of sympathy. But I do want to suggest that women are encouraged to embrace an identity as victims/survivors in a way that men are not, and that this sympathy inequality harms both genders.

Men and women both need to recognize that living in a modern world with modern sexual freedoms and experimentations will almost inevitably lead to experiences that are unpleasant, unwelcome, and ambivalent—and possibly even to experiences that are bad or potentially harmful. There's an emotionally productive space in between "I was raped" and "I am so stupid and incompetent and irresponsible for failing to say no when I didn't like what was happening to me." That space is saying, "I was uncomfortable in that situation, and I would like to minimize the circumstances of that situation reoccurring in my life to the best of my ability. I will try not to let the unpleasantness of that situation define me or my sexual life, as best I am able."

There's a fine line between respecting survivors and asking people to think about the likely consequences of their actions. If you leave your car door unlocked and your wallet visible on the dashboard, someone is still guilty of a crime if they steal it. Sure, it would be great to live in a world where that wallet would just be waiting for you when you get back to your car, and let's all try to imagine the circumstances that could help promote that world. But in the meantime, most of us also understand that we need to lock our car doors and hide our valuables, because we're a long way from living in a perfect world. And the same logic applies to sex. Rather than provide false guarantees to young people about the safety of sexual experiments in a world where dating and relationship norms have become mixed up and blurry, we need to tell them, "There are choices you can make that are safer than others. If you choose to make less safe choices, you'll increase the chances that something you don't like will happen to you, or that you'll do something to someone that hurts them. Learn from that experience, reflect on it, and grow from it. Try not to let it define you." Metaphorically speaking, you can forget to lock your car or even actively decide not to lock your car, and it doesn't mean you're a bad person or irresponsible if someone steals things from your car. But it's probably worth reflecting on how much those stolen things matter to you in the first place, and whether you're willing to repeat the experience. And again, the same logic applies to taking sexual risks.

THE HARM REDUCTION APPROACH

The concept of "harm reduction" has become popular in the philosophy of drug use and law, referring to the idea that, barring very intense religious and cultural enforcement, simply banning drugs wholesale generally doesn't work well (Hawk et al. 2017). Rather than trying to ban drugs and alcohol, encouraging people to use them responsibly and providing therapies for people who become addicted—described as a harm reduction approach—have mostly worked much better. I think it's possible the same approach might be the best strategy for managing consent conversations and negotiations. There doesn't seem to be much enthusiasm among mainstream straight people (or even gay men) for a strict verbal affirmative consent approach to negotiating sexual consent. Although a few states have passed affirmative consent laws, their enforcement seems to be hazy at best (Marciniak 2015). We need to be tackling this issue with greater realism, especially since most young adults seem to strongly prefer that initial sexual encounters take place while drunk and/or high. So what *is* actually possible?

It feels a bit like a grim admission of defeat to say, "We need to lower our standards for what 'good consent' looks like as long as most initial sexual encounters occur with at least one person tipsy or drunk." But I think it's possible to reframe that sentiment more positively and say, "We need to think about what elements of consent are essential to maintaining reasonably safe and fun sexual experiments in the context of pot and alcohol." A harm reduction approach to sexual consent admits that the strict and lofty standards established by the sober and relatively gender-egalitarian BDSM subculture are probably very unrealistic (and possibly frankly unnecessary) in the much more drunken and less gender-egalitarian context of mainstream sexual inter-actions. Unfortunately, trying to answer the question, "what counts as *good enough* sexual consent?" turns out to be a lot harder than, "what clearly is *very bad* sexual consent?"

There are two basic ways to conceptualize solutions for reducing sexual violations: short-term solutions and long-term solutions. We'll start with the short-term solutions, because they seem more pressing and are probably eas-ier. However, it's important to keep in mind these short-term solutions have to function more like "defensive driving" techniques in order to teach people how to protect themselves more. For better and for worse, it's generally easier to teach people how to not get sexually violated than it is to teach people how to not violate someone else. Unfortunately, teaching people to "not rape" is a much harder and longer-term endeavor, so short-term solutions end up target-ing potential victims much more than they target potential agents of harm.

First, begin creating small-group programs that teach young people to get used to talking about sex with each other. The ideal versions of these programs would involve slightly older adults becoming peer educators to mentor slightly younger adults (e.g., graduate students with undergraduates, or undergraduates with high school students). The best sex education isn't something that happens for a few days in a classroom: it involves ongoing and reflexive conversations with peers as they're having new experiences. These kinds of conversations don't even have to teach people to talk with friends and acquaintances about what they want sexually; they just need to get them more comfortable talking about sex, period. These kinds of pro-grams would need to be conscious of gender and sexual orientation, but are still probably easier if they begin as mostly same-gender groups and then branch out to all-gender groups. One of the challenges people so often face in heterosexual interactions is that men and women just aren't used to talking about sex with someone of the opposite sex, so creating an environment that accustoms them to those kinds of conversations would be helpful. It seems unlikely that US high schools will host such programs any time soon, but colleges might, especially during freshman orientation.

Second, create sex education focused on the specific combination of drinking and sex. Even if schools and colleges continue to reject such formal education, we can post these resources online for individuals and groups to access. Cultural messaging seems to have emphasized "guard your drink" to women at the expense of also necessary advice like "try not to end up alone with someone you don't want to have sex with while you're both drunk"—advice that both men and women need to hear. Right now, our cultural messaging keeps pretending sexual consent mostly happens in a context of mutually sober interactions, but the statistics say the exact opposite. Our education programs need to acknowledge that reality and teach young people what it's realistic to expect in the context of the intoxication we pretend they're not engaging in.

Third, in sex education programs in particular and in the culture more generally, we need to create programs that focus on learning to say no—whether to food you don't want, company you don't want, or anything else you don't want. I'm seeing more parents nowadays intentionally teach their children to learn to say no to the casual touch of adults and other children that they don't want, and that kind of empowerment is beautiful. But most young adults these days didn't grow up with that, and they need to be encouraged to practice while sober and then be reminded that saying no while drunk might be much harder. This kind of training shouldn't just be about the idea of "saying no"; rather, in any voluntary interaction, we need to teach people to reframe their thinking in terms of "Are you making an active choice to participate in this interaction?"

Fourth, we need cultural reeducation programs that teach people to identify actual risky behavior and warning signs of danger. As we saw in the previous chapter, it's a matter of interpretation and debate whether women or men are more likely to be the victims of violent crime, but there's no question that men are much more often the victims of violent crimes committed by strangers—yet men often demonstrate little fear of this happening. Presumably, men need to be somewhat more afraid than they currently are and ideally demonstrate more cautious behavior to hopefully be less victimized, and women need to be less afraid than they are so they can live more freely and independently. Women are much more likely to experience extreme sexual violation at a frat party than they are walking down the street alone at night, but we've normalized their attendance at frat parties and profoundly discouraged them from walking alone at night. We also haven't taught them that one of the most reliable indicators of a habitual sexual violator is a man who is generally sexist and shows little respect for women. *Those* men—not those who happen to also be walking on the street at night—are the types of men most likely to hurt women.

Fifth, we have to educate everyone about consent in a context that makes sense to them. For example, we know straight men can better understand the idea of "non-consent" in the context of being sexually violated by other men rather than by women. As a culture, we simply don't imagine women posing much in the way of sexual threat, and so we struggle to imagine their behavior as threatening, even when we would find the same behavior threatening if it came from a man. Contrary to what we might hope and expect, lesbians still often end up in situations of domestic violence, and I strongly suspect part of the reason this happens is that our culture views violence and sexual violence from women as so unthreatening. In order for consent standards to improve for everyone, we need to adopt a more pansexual approach to education (Heer, Brown, and Cheney 2021) that challenges everyone to view themselves as a sexual threat in the same manner as whatever they personally imagine as the most threatening sexual figures. For lesbians and straight women, that's probably straight men; for straight men, it's probably gay men; and for gay men it might very well be straight women (Richardson 2022).

The long-term solutions to reduce sexual violation are much more complicated but probably require less explanation, as they hopefully logically follow from most of what I've been discussing in this book so far. None of these things are simple, and all of them probably require a lot of time and dedication from people in really different parts of society. They include:

- *Demanding institutional change from schools, churches, and other formal organizations to establish sexual values and norms in line with contemporary lives and morality.* Americans have been leaving religious institutions in droves as those institutions have failed to evolve with the rest of society, but the law requires children to attend school unless parents homeschool them. We shouldn't settle for formal institutions that teach children unrealistic sexual values, because conflicting values between formal and informal social institutions is a social problem in and of itself.
- *Convincing parents to provide more support for adolescent sexual experiences.* Although parents are often too far removed from the generational norms of the young people in front of them to be able to relate to their experiences, they still can provide meaningful emotional support and relationship training to help young people stay safer. Throwing

young people out into the world without adult guidance and supervision and hoping they'll date and have sex responsibly is a bit like putting them behind the wheel of a car without guidance and supervision and hoping they won't wreck it. Currently, we expect professionals and parents to teach their children to drive when relevant, and we should also be expecting both to work harder to teach children how to have sex and relationships.

• *Convincing the law to allow people eighteen and over to buy alcohol and marijuana.* Given that young people in countries all over the world with much more reasonable laws about purchasing drugs still struggle with consent violation, this change is certainly not a panacea. However, it would go a long way toward helping institutions guide and protect young people from sexual violation by being able to better regulate and supervise the environments where they consume substances. It would also be tremendously helpful for young people to be able to safely report instances of sexual violation without having to worry they will be officially or unofficially reprimanded for consuming alcohol or marijuana at the time.

• *Challenging society to show more respect for women's sexuality and desires.* We've certainly made a lot of progress in this fight over the last seventy years, but there's still a long way to go. Women need to be able to voice sexual desires, learn how to responsibly make sexual advances, seek sexual advice from peers, and report sexual violations without fear of judgment or repercussion.

• *Rethinking heterosexual dating norms in general.* Consent violations are the direct consequence of dating norms that expect men to make the first move in terms of asking for a date and seeking sex, pay for things, and show both personal and sexual dominance. It's hypocritical for a woman to demand equal respect in a relationship while simultaneously expecting a man to pay for dates, give her an incredibly expensive ring to symbolize an engagement, and to make all the first moves. If nothing else, expecting men to make all the first moves for sex virtually guarantees that men will be more likely to violate women's sexual consent than women are to violate men's in heterosexual interactions, just because men are the ones who are expected to do the "asking" (while also apparently expected to not explicitly verbally ask).

• *Changing a cultural conversation that talks about consent violation like it's something that happens only to women.* Adult men who get their consent violated by women are almost certainly less common than adult women who get their consent violated by men, but not by enough that they should simply be disregarded. Part of a serious social conversation about teaching men to take the sexual violation of women more seriously also involves teaching them to take their own experiences of sexual violation at the hands of others more seriously. Moreover, greater sexual empowerment for women has to be accompanied by the greater responsibility for others' safety and consent that comes with that power.

- *Shifting the cultural conversation to talk more about the sexual viola-tion of girls under age sixteen.* This book has, of course, focused on the "grey zones" of consent, which usually almost by definition occur to adults and young adults over the age of consent. There are good reasons to do that, not least that they seem to be greatly increasing as our soci-ety provides more opportunities for sexual liberation, easy dating, and concomitant higher standards for respecting boundaries and consent. But the few reliable-looking statistics we have strongly suggest that an extremely disproportionate amount of sexual abuse of women occurs when they're quite young, and girls seem to be much more vulnerable than boys to this type of abuse. Preventing the sexual abuse of children may be much more complicated than preventing the sexual violation of adults, and it may involve very few of the same underlying social causes and factors. But as we saw in the previous chapter, much of the lifetime statistical odds difference for women's and men's experience of sexual violation appears to happen before age eighteen, so if we're really con-cerned about "protecting women," a lot more of our attention needs to go toward "protecting young girls."
- *Shifting the cultural conversation for young adults and adults to talk more about consent hygiene and less about a black-and-white world of rapists and not-rapists.* Teaching young people to be reflexive with themselves and those around them so they can constantly try to improve their consent practices is probably the most effective way we can make actual large-scale social strides in improving consent practices. Most of these interactions are very private in a way that will always make intervention extremely difficult for official institutions. But in order to encourage people to admit when their consent practices could use improvement, we have to create a context where people feel like they won't be horribly judged for admitting that they (like us) are imperfect.
- *Demanding major changes to our legal system and the carceral struc-ture of our society and culture.* These changes are so vast that they will be the subject of two more chapters, so I'll conclude here simply by say-ing that social change is always most effective in society when it occurs at all levels simultaneously: the macro level of governments and major social institutions, the meso level of individual community centers and neighborhoods, and the micro level of individual family and personal interactions.

Chapter 7

Race, Sexual Identity, and the American Criminal Imagination

I want to begin this chapter by asking you to pause and guess what percentage of Americans you believe are white, Black, Hispanic, Asian, and "other"? I'll come back to these numbers shortly.

Next, I want to warn you that if you found some of the statistics in chapter 5 hard to swallow, you're probably going to find the numbers in this chapter even harder. They're even hard for me, and I cringed when I wrote some of these sentences, afraid they'll be taken wildly out of context, misunderstood, and/or misrepresented. So I want to preface everything else I'm going to say here with great emphasis: *In many respects, the American criminal justice system is terrifyingly racist.* The police harass, harm, and even sometimes kill Black men and boys in a way that is both statistically and emotionally hard to process and comprehend. Life in many poor, Black, urban areas is a literal "police state," with intense police surveillance, threats, and actual violence, constant arrests for trivial matters, and stunningly little violent crime prevention (Goffman 2015).

Most American theorists (Alexander 2010; Unnever and Gabbidon 2011) treat the criminal justice system's oppression of Black people as both a direct and indirect institutional descendant of slavery. From the *de jure* deprivation of basic human rights and dignity through slavery to the *de facto* deprivation of basic human rights and dignity through Jim Crow–era life (where Blacks and whites in the South were completely segregated, and Blacks were still treated as half citizens at best, often living as slaves in all but name through sharecropping), the United States has a long history of appalling racial oppression against Black people. After a lengthy battle, Jim Crow slowly unraveled, but in its place, the nation rapidly established a new system of Black oppression: the prison industrial complex, which became yet another way for the United States to deprive Black men of their basic rights and liberties, both with actual imprisonment, the threat of imprisonment, and treatment as barely citizens upon being branded "ex-cons."

In 2021, combining numbers from federal and state US prisons, 32 percent of prisoners were Black, 31 percent white, 24 percent Hispanic, and 3 percent Asian or other (Carson 2021). Think back to my question at the start of the chapter where I asked you to guess the racial/ethnic makeup of the United States. Whatever you guessed, you're probably not going to be surprised when I tell you the racial composition of the prison population doesn't look like the actual population of the nation. In 2021, about 13 percent of those living in the United States were Black, 59 percent white, 19 percent Hispanic, and 9 percent Asian or other (Census Bureau 2021). Sixteen percent of all male prisoners were being held for rape or sexual assault, versus 3 percent of female prisoners. By race, for males, this breaks out to 19.5 percent of white prisoners, 9.6 percent of Black prisoners, and 16 percent of Hispanic prisoners (Carson 2021). Thus, in spite of the low sexual assault conviction statistics we saw in chapter 5, many, many people (more than 160,000 people in 2021) are imprisoned for some form of sexual assault.

Many theorists have argued the long history of racial oppression in America has left a fundamental impression on our understanding of rape and sexual assault (Bourke 2007; Sanyal 2019). Before the Civil War, it wasn't a crime for white men to rape their (Black) female slaves, and it was many years before it clearly became illegal for white men to rape Black women in the South. The idea of Black men raping white women remained a looming threat within white American popular consciousness, with Black men portrayed as sexual animals who would steal the virtue of white women (Bourke 2007; Block 2009). It was often unclear in these portrayals if white women might be seduced by Black men's supposedly animalistic sexuality or if Black men would take them physically by force (with the further threat to white purity and social dominance of the resulting mixed-race children). Regardless, white men perceived and portrayed Black men's sexuality as a threat to their own sexual dominance and to the safety of white women (Sommerville 2005). Among those executed for rape from 1930 through 1972 (when the death penalty was declared unconstitutional as a punishment for rape), 89 percent—405 of the 455 who were executed—were Black men (Spohn 2017). Meanwhile, Black women were often described as sexual objects whose sexuality was never securely their own but always perceived to be the property of men.

I have read this historical narrative again and again in my research on sexual assault and race, and I have no idea how accurately it portrays a time gone by (even one of the historical citations above challenges it [Sommerville 2005]). It's hard to say how much this narrative directly affects and applies to the present. Certainly, Americans often *believe* these things are true, and their belief surely has an impact on popular consciousness. One of the famous aphorisms of sociology from W. I. Thomas goes something like "things become real because society believes they're real." The classic example of this idea is race itself, which is not a genetic or physically objective reality, but rather a socially constructed fiction held in common by members of a particular society—and most societies have very different racial categorization systems. Americans mostly believe race is real, and they mostly believe it matters *a lot*; no one seems to expect rape and sexual assault to be an exception to this pattern. Indeed, many believe race is fundamental to both our social and legal construction of rape.

Qualitatively, there's no question that race matters in how Americans imagine rape. One study of undergraduate women of color found that African American, Latina, and Asian American women all felt that both the wider culture as a whole, as well as their own ethnic subcultures, were much less supportive of them as rape victims than the larger culture was of white women; all felt like formal institutions such as the police and rape crisis services would be less helpful to them than they would be to white women (Harris 2020). For sure, the people who do the formal work of managing rape (rape crisis workers, lawyers, and to a lesser degree police officers) are predominantly white (Martin 2005). Prosecutors in Milwaukee, Wisconsin, complained that in any sexual assault trial with a Black female victim, all defense attorneys needed to do was imply the woman was a prostitute, and juries would readily return a verdict of "not guilty" (Hlavka and Mulla 2021). I could probably go on and on with many other ways that, qualitatively speaking, Americans' imagination seems to conjure up "rape" as a crime mostly committed against white women, who are imagined as the most deserving of support in their time of crisis, with a background threat of Black men as rapists (George and Martínez 2002), who are imagined as the most deserving of punishment for this heinous crime.

And yet. One of the corollary truisms in sociology to the idea that society makes things true comes from Robert Merton (the inventor of the term "self-fulfilling prophecy"), who said something along the lines of "sometimes things are true even when society doesn't believe in them." Bizarrely, when it comes to rape and sexual assault, despite a *wealth* of qualitative evidence showing that race matters *a lot*, the quantitative evidence, measure after measure, raises serious doubts about how much it affects the statistical outcomes of sexual assault and its prosecution. If you're reading that sentence with great skepticism, I can assure you I don't write it lightly; as a sociologist, the idea that race is important is practically baked into my discipline from the get-go, from the nineteenth-century writings and theorizing of W. E. B. Du Bois (Du Bois 1996). Moreover, it's extremely difficult to prove a negative, so saying that "race doesn't matter that much for sexual assault" is a dangerous claim, both scientifically and socially. The best I can accurately say is, "Given the wealth of available data, with multiple measures across time, from victimization to arrest, at the national level, race mostly doesn't seem to matter that much in analyses of sexual assault, and the ways that it does are the reverse of the direction most of us expect." I should add numerous caveats to this statement right off the bat. First, many studies of race and sexual assault are stuck measuring race as "white" or "Black," either because of small case numbers or because that's how it happened to be recorded in the data. There's some reason to believe more nuanced measures of race might find more effects from it in their outcomes (Shaw and Lee 2019). As of this writing, the FBI is in the process of overhauling its crime reporting system, and it's possible that overhaul will reveal a heretofore undiscovered role of race in sexual assault. And finally, to the best of my knowledge, there are no recent data on the role of race in prosecutorial charging practices or sentencing for sexual assault, which is why I have to specify "from victimization to arrest." Imprisonment data *strongly imply* that Black men aren't more likely to be convicted and imprisoned for sexual assault, but those data are too blunt to untangle nuance. But for now, with many caveats, available data make it appear that, contrary to what Americans imagine, race doesn't matter much (today) when it comes to sexual assault. On the other hand, as I'll discuss later in this chapter, despite the fact society doesn't seem to expect it at all, sexual orientation matters *a lot—far* more than any other demographic factor except age.

RACE, VICTIMIZATION, AND
REPORTING TO THE POLICE

There are so many points where race could affect sexual assault: victimization, offending, the relationship/interaction between victim and offender, reports to authorities and the police, likelihood of arrest/official disciplinary action, likelihood of being found guilty, and punishment if found guilty; for each of those elements, we might find effects based on the victims' race, the offenders' race, or the victims' + offenders' race. I'll walk through what available research has shown about each of those stages, again with the reminder that proving a negative is very difficult.

Most extant theorizing on racial sexual assault victimization tends to assume that Black women would be more likely to experience all forms of sexual assault (Pittman 2023). The logic here is that since the days of slavery, the United States has a long history of treating Black women as objects of sexual attention/violence, with little regard for their rights. They also are much more likely to live in communities deprived of men due to imprisonment and death (Wolfers, Leonhardt, and Quealy 2015), which might make them less likely to stand up for their sexual rights for a variety of reasons. And finally, they're less educated, on average, than white women (Anthony, Nichols, and Pilar 2021), which might make them less aware of their sexual rights. Moreover, they're generally assumed to be unlikely to report crimes to the police due to the perception that society doesn't care about their well-being, along with the general low opinion of the police in African American communities (Zaykowski, Allain, and Campagna 2019).

These theories feel intuitively logical but turn out to be almost exclusively supported by obsolete data. More modern studies, using multiple measures in different contexts, find there's either no difference in the likelihood that women will experience sexual violence based on race—or a slightly increased likelihood for white women (Shaw and Lee 2019). Baseline comparisons between race groups from the 2017–2021 National Crime Victimization Survey (which, you will remember from chapter 5, has a fairly narrow definition of sexual assault) find the only statistically significant difference by race to be that Asian Americans have a lower rate of sexual assault victimization than other groups (Thompson and Tapp 2021). Raw baseline numbers are only a vague estimate, since age distributions aren't the same across race groups, so at a bare minimum, it's important to hold age constant for racial comparisons. Sexual assaults occur very disproportionately against women ages eighteen to twenty-four, and data from the 1995–2013 NCVS show the baseline sexual assault rate against young white women not in college is actually *double* the rate against Hispanic women in or out of college (Sinozich and Langton 2014). For women in college, rates are fairly similar among race groups, and for young women not in college, the only notable difference is the higher rates among young white women (9 per 1,000, versus about 6 for white women in college and all Black women; Sinozich and Langton 2014). However, even controlling for age, we should always be careful trusting baseline statistics pertaining to race, because they often hide other factors underneath them. (In the United States, "race" often encompasses a wide range of other factors, from education and metropolitan residence to religiosity.)

Most analyses of sexual assault that include broader measures than the NCVS's narrow version of "sexual assault" have been done with college students rather than the general population. In these studies with large college samples and much more expansive measures of sexual assault, race effects are still either extremely small or nonexistent. One study found that Asian American women were less likely to experience sexual assault in college (Mellins et al. 2017); another that Hispanic women and Asian American women were less likely to experience sexual assault, with a very small increase for Black women (Coulter et al. 2017); and another, using only Black/white measures of race, that it was not significant at all (Rogers and

Rogers 2021). Rogers and Rogers (2021) point out that individual factors almost entirely overwhelm demographic measures in general for predicting who gets sexually assaulted in college: binge drinking, marijuana use, grade point average (GPA), and membership in fraternities and sororities all matter much more than most demographic factors. Another large study of college students using older data from 2006 even separated out sexual assault by force versus incapacitation and still found basically no effect of race on victimization (Krebs 2007).

I have found no recent studies that specifically analyzed the effect of race on the likelihood of reporting sexual assault to the police. However, multiple studies have looked at the effect of race on reporting violent crime victimization in general to the police and found that unquestionably, the people most likely to report violent crime victimization are . . . Black people. There may be some subtlety and nuance to this, depending on other demographic factors. One study found that impoverished and less educated Black women were the group most likely to report violent victimization to the police, while impoverished and less educated Black men were the least (Zaykowski, Allain, and Campagna 2019). Echoing those findings in a very different way, another study found that straight Black people were the most likely to report violent victimization and LGBTQ Black people were the least (Flores et al. 2023). Given well-documented qualitative and quantitative data on Black people's general distrust in the police, these statistics so utterly contradict what one might predict that scholars are largely at a loss to explain them (Zaykowski, Allain, and Campagna 2019).

RACE, OFFENDING, AND THE
"VICTIM-OFFENDER DYAD"

There are competing and contradictory theories about whether we might imagine white or Black men would be more likely to commit sexual assault. On the one hand, rape is traditionally a crime of power, and white men are more likely to be in positions of power and influence; on the other hand, some have suggested that Black men's lack of power and influence in other arenas might motivate them to commit sexual assault as a way of asserting the dominance and control they feel they lack. But yet again (at least in the modern data), we see very few effects from race. Baseline statistics from victim reports consistently find that Black men are slightly more likely than white men to commit sexual assault (Fogliato et al. 2021; Sinozich and Langton 2014). One very large study that separated out violent physical sexual assault from sexual assault by incapacitation against college women found that Black men were more likely to be accused of committing the rarer physical assaults, and white men were much more likely to be accused of committing sexual assaults by incapacitation (Krebs 2007). However, these data are quite old (from 2005), and sexual assault by incapacitation against college women had greatly increased over time, at least until 2015 (Koss et al. 2022), so it's hard to guess how much these trends still hold.

The majority of sexual assaults appear to be intraracial, meaning they're committed by someone of a race group against someone else of the same race group. However, most of the classical theorizing on rape assumes that Black men who rape white women will face the harshest penalties. While this almost certainly was true at an earlier point in American history, when lynchings of Black men were horrifically common (Sanyal 2019), there is very little evidence that this type of inequality persists in sexual assault cases today. One much older study found that intraracial rapes were generally more likely to be reported to the authorities (Fisher et al. 2003), and this may still be true. Rapes committed by Black men are slightly more likely than rapes by white men to be reported to the police (Fogliato et al. forthcoming), but this small difference might simply be the result of Black women being more likely than white women to report violent victimizations to the police (Zaykowski, Allain, and Campagna 2019).

It's important not to exaggerate the weight of small statistical differences, but it's also important to remember that the police can only act on crimes they know about. Because so few rapes are committed in broad daylight with officers nearby to witness them, the police depend almost entirely on victims to report sexual assaults. Even though victims of rapes committed by Black men are more likely to report to the police, white men are disproportionately likely to be arrested for the crime, and this trend has been true for decades (Fogliato et al. forthcoming; D'Alessio and Stolzenberg 2003). Not only are white men the most likely to be arrested for committing rape (net of other factors), the specific racial pairing most likely to result in arrest is white-against-white rape, followed by interracial dyads and lastly by Black-on-Black rapes (Stacey, Martin, and Brick 2017; Kelley et al. 2021). Once again, these differences are not large, so the main takeaway here is that white men don't just skate by if they're accused of raping Black women, as many theorists have predicted, nor do Black men face a disproportionately high likelihood of arrest for raping white women. Despite all this, controlling for other factors (including the physical violence of the crime reported), white women who report their sexual assaults to the police are the least likely to have their rapist arrested, but again, these effects are usually small and sometimes disappear when other factors are included (Fogliato et al. forthcoming; Ylang and Holtfreter 2020).

RACE FROM THE DEFENDANT'S PERSPECTIVE

Nationwide statistics can potentially cover up for all kinds of local discrimination in sexual assault statistics. For instance, one study of Los Angeles from 2007 to 2011 found that in certain parts of the city, sexual assault cases with Black victims were considerably more likely to result in arrest, net of other factors, while in other parts of the city there was no effect (Morabito, Williams, and Pattavina 2019); meanwhile, another study of Los Angeles from 2008 to 2010 found that the only statistically significant racial effect on arrest was that Black offenders with Hispanic victims were less likely to be arrested than white offenders with white victims (which were only 4 percent of cases; O'Neal et al. 2014). Sample sizes here are pretty small when analyzing local areas, so we have to approach outcomes with caution. However, it is especially important to pay attention to this kind of local variation because racial minorities are not at all evenly dispersed throughout the United States, nor even within states that have relatively high concentrations of them. For example, Asian Americans are heavily concentrated within certain regions of California, and African Americans are heavily concentrated in large cities in eastern states. If the police in just one of the largest US cities where many Black people live (New York City, Los Angeles, or Chicago) were extremely racist, that could potentially affect the entire pool of numbers on racial arrest patterns. But almost anywhere we look in the United States, arrest rates for reported violent crime are higher for white offenders than Black offenders—and in some areas the difference is quite large (Fogliato et al. 2021). For sexual assault, no state is disproportionately likely to arrest Black offenders except for New Hampshire (Fogliato et al. 2021), where only 2 percent of residents are Black (Census 2021). It's worth nothing that for all violent crimes, racial arrest patterns are the most even for rape and homicide (Fogliato et al. 2021), and they're pretty darn even for both. (That said, I would urge much greater caution in addressing the numbers there on homicide, for which we have far fewer independent data validation sources than for rape. For rape, we have independent nationwide data on arrests from victims through the NCVS, but for obvious reasons, there's no parallel way to collect data from [deceased] murder victims. The *Washington Post* [2018] collected its own vast data set on murder arrest rates by race and contends that the FBI numbers on homicide arrests are incorrect and that murder arrest rates are extremely biased toward arrests made in crimes with white victims).

Even if the police are relatively color-blind in their arresting practices for sexual assault, that still leaves three more stages in the criminal justice process for racism to rear its ugly head: whether the offense is prosecuted (and if so, for which crime), whether the accused is then found guilty, and what penalties are applied for those found guilty. Unfortunately, we have no nationwide statistics on these case outcomes. Without wide-scale numbers, calculating the effect of race on who gets charged and who is found guilty is basically impossible because large numbers of cases are required to provide stable and accurate estimates in these kinds of complex statistical analyses. No study I have seen meets the usual statistical bare minimum of five hundred cases to allow for logistic regression, which compares the likelihood of various outcomes, yet all of them employ logistic regression because it's the typical statistical tool for this type of analysis. Studies looking at Los Angeles between 2008 and 2010 (Morabito, Williams, and Pattavina 2019) have found no effect of race on criminal charging practices. Further attempts to see if there's a specific relationship between the race of the offender combined with the race of the victim and charging outcomes in Los Angeles found few effects—but again, sample sizes are *very* small for these analyses (Kelley et al. 2021; Tellis and Spohn 2008). Working with an even smaller case set from a small city in Pennsylvania between 2006 and 2010, another study found that Black suspects were significantly *much* more likely than white suspects to be charged (Colon et al. 2018). As I've said before, it's entirely possible that the justice systems in some jurisdictions are *very* racist, others are a little racist, and some are biased against white people (Franklin 2010), and when we smoosh them all together into one big nationwide statistic, we're missing a lot of information. However, we need large sample sizes to calculate complex numbers reliably, and without them, all we're really left with are educated guesses.

Yet there is one way to *roughly* gauge the racism in the latter stages of the criminal justice system nationwide: we can guesstimate inequalities by looking at the percentage of people reported to the police as suspects of rape/sexual assault for a given race, then compare that number to the percentage in prison. Unfortunately, calculating this statistic turns out to be weirdly difficult because the various government agencies that collect all this information measure "Hispanic" quite differently, and it's unclear how those differences affect reports. I'd love to have more specific numbers here focused on sexual assault, but let's work with "nonfatal violent crime" (robbery, aggravated assault, and rape and sexual assault), because that's what we have. Let's assume for a moment that Black people are mostly unaffected by the problematic "Hispanic" labeling throughout these different agencies (that's not a great assumption, since 2 percent of all Americans are Afro-Latino [Gonzalez-Barrera 2022]), but the evidence suggests they're less affected than white people (Beck 2018). In 2018, 42.8 percent of people reported to the police as offenders for nonfatal violent crime were Black (Beck 2018). By the end of 2020, 35 percent of people in prison for those crimes were

Black,[1] suggesting the criminal justice system overall actually underpenalizes violent Black offenders. Indeed, by these measures, it appears that if blatant racism in the criminal justice system overpenalizes any group for violent crime, it is Hispanics. While Hispanics are only 12 percent of offenders for nonfatal violent crime reported to police (Beck 2018), they are 29 percent of those in prison (Carson 2021). Some of this difference could be pure perception: we have the reports of victims who might not know if their assailant was Hispanic, which we must contrast against the self-reported ethnicity of offenders themselves (Beck 2018). Even with that caveat in mind, the differences here certainly warrant concern and further investigation. For example, the number of Hispanic people in prison for rape and sexual assault is higher than the number of Black people in prison for the same crime (Carson 2021), and these numbers seem wildly out of line with relative reported rates of violence, either at the population level or among crimes reported to the police (Beck 2018).

I wouldn't want anyone reading these numbers to come away with the impression the US criminal justice system isn't racist. The police just straight-up shoot and kill young Black men, often with impunity (*Guardian*, n.d.). They stop Black men at absurdly disproportionate rates compared to white men, even including children (Kramer, Remster, and Charles 2017). And the lower arrest rates for Blacks committing violent crimes could easily be interpreted as an indication that the criminal justice system doesn't take violence committed against Black people as seriously as other races (since most violent crimes are intraracial). What is reasonably clear from these data is that despite the influence of historical racism on the American cultural imagining of sexual assault, that history doesn't seem to be having a big effect on what's happening today (nor even in the recent past). If there's a significant story to tell about race in terms of recent criminal law statistics on rape and race (and we will need more and better statistics to be certain), it's a largely untold and undertheorized one about Hispanic men being excessively likely to be imprisoned for sexual assault.

THE OTHER MINORITIES: LGBTQ FOLKS

It turns out that the people who are most likely to be the victims of violent crime in general, and sexual assault in particular, are sexual minorities. It's genuinely hard to overstate the grim reality of these statistics. In raw

---

1. This statistic was calculated from table 17 in Carson (2021). According to those numbers, 436,900 people were in prison for rape/sexual assault, robbery, and aggravated assault; 153,600 of them were Black.

numbers, bisexual women are twelve times as likely to be sexually assaulted as straight women, while gay and bisexual men are about twenty times as likely to be sexually assaulted as straight men (but that number isn't necessarily as bad as it sounds because straight men are so unlikely to report being sexually assaulted; Bender and Lauritsen 2021). Bisexual women are also about thirteen times as likely to be robbed as straight women, so these differences aren't just about sex (Bender and Lauritsen 2021). Smaller sample sizes make it hard to calculate numbers for sexual assault specifically, but controlling for *many* other factors, bisexual women are still more than four times as likely as straight women to be the victims of serious (nonfatal) violent crime; indeed, with all those factors, straight women and men are about equally likely to be the victims of serious violent crime (Bender and Lauritsen 2021). (The same analysis finds at most small effects from race, with Blacks and Hispanics slightly less likely to be the victims of violent crime compared to whites [Bender and Lauritsen 2021].) No demographic factor comes close to the impact of being a bisexual woman in influencing one's likelihood of being the victim of violent crime, either in general or focusing on "serious violent crime." Lesbian and bisexual women are also eerily vulnerable to two very specific types of violent victimization: stranger violence and "multiple offender incidents" (meaning that someone was hurt by multiple people at the same time), with bisexuals fifteen times as likely as straight women to be the victims of stranger violence and twenty-four times as likely to be the victims of multiple offender crimes (with lesbians about half that; Bender and Lauritsen 2021). These numbers are not because straight women are unlikely to experience these victimizations; lesbian and especially bisexual women really are just horrifyingly likely to have these experiences.

These sexual assaults come pretty much entirely from men, at least by the measures usually employed (Murchison, Boyd, and Pachankis 2017); bisexuals aren't in some sexual assault double-jeopardy situation arising from dating and having sex with multiple genders. But their much higher overall risk of being the victims of violent crime suggests this isn't really about sex and dating at all anyway.

Multiple large-scale studies with college students further support the risk sexual orientation poses for sexual assault, with bisexual women consistently showing up as the most at-risk (Coulter et al. 2017; Mellins et al. 2017). Even after controlling for a vast array of nondemographic factors like drinking habits, number of sexual partners, GPA, and membership in fraternities and sororities, bisexual women and gay men are still at increased risk of sexual assault (Mellins et al. 2017). It might be comforting to know that these individual factors all matter much *more* than any demographics, but among college students, sexual orientation and gender are the only demographics remaining significant in predicting who gets sexually assaulted when including a wide range of individual behavioral factors (Rogers and Rogers 2021). Other analyses suggest individual factors only matter when analyzing the chances of sexual assault by intoxication, but not by physical force (Krebs 2007). When comparing those two outcomes, bisexual college women are much more likely to be the victims of physical force specifically, with no apparent differences based on incapacitation (Krebs 2007).

Not only does being LGBTQ (and particularly bisexual/trans/queer) make a person—especially a woman—much more likely to be the victim of a violent crime in general, it also has a tremendous effect on police response. Again, these numbers are not specific to sexual assault, but white LGBTQ and straight people are about equally likely to report a violent victimization to the police; Hispanic LGBTQ people are somewhat less likely than Hispanic straight people to report to the police; and Black LGBTQ people are less than half as likely as Black straight people to report to the police (Flores et al. 2023). In addition to the grim victimization figures are the arrest numbers here: among violent victimizations reported to the police, within each race group, LGBTQ folks are less than half as likely as straight people to say the person who hurt them was arrested, and for Black LGBTQ victims, the arrest rate is merely one-third of that for Black straight people (Flores et al. 2023).

In the grand scheme of criminology, these numbers are incredibly recent, and I haven't read any theorist who claims to be able to explain what makes bisexual women in particular so horrifyingly likely to be the victims of violent crime. If it was merely sexual assault they were so vulnerable to, we might be able to concoct some sort of theory based on dating behaviors, but given that they're equally disproportionately likely to be the victims of robbery, this doesn't really seem to be about sex. There's a slowly emerging body of research showing bisexuals are hugely disadvantaged in general, being vastly more likely to be bullied in school, to experience mental illness, and to be suicidal (Annor et al. 2018; Bauer et al. 2016; Taliaferro et al. 2018)—but again, no one really knows why.

It's important to add that, contrary to many people's expectations, being a racial minority doesn't seem to have a big effect on the increased violent victimization of LGBTQ folks in general. White LGBTQ folks are more likely to be the victims of violent crime in general by a fairly substantial margin and more likely to experience a criminal event where they're injured, although Hispanic LGBTQ folks are the most likely to experience serious violence (Flores et al. 2020). Straight Black people are the most likely straight racial group to experience serious violence, but especially when compared to the differences with LGBTQ people, these differences are minute (Flores et al. 2023). The actual numbers here are in events per 1,000 people: for serious violence, white straight people's rate is 6.9 compared to a straight Black rate of 9.4; for LGBTQ people, these numbers are 33.7 for white people and

35.2 for Black people (Flores et al. 2023). Even help-seeking behaviors don't easily match many theorists' expectations, with Black LGBTQ folks by far the most likely to seek professional help for dealing with their experiences as crime victims, followed by Hispanic LGBTQ, with white LGBTQ a long way down (Flores et al. 2023). Some intersectional theorists have proposed that professional organizations would be particularly unhelpful and unsympathetic toward racial minority crime victims (Martin 2005; Harris 2020), but the rates among straight people are mostly the same (Flores et al. 2023). As previously mentioned, the only place where disadvantage seems to stack up is the extremely low arrest rate of offenders reported by Black LGBTQ people, even compared to other LGBTQ race groups (Flores et al. 2023).

CONCLUDING THOUGHTS ON MINORITIES AND SEXUAL ASSAULT

Regardless of the factual or legal realities of the issue, America's cultural construction of rape as being closely tied to racial oppression is hardly unique. Throughout Europe, cultures tend to construct rapists as "other," envisioning a threat from someone the culture views as an outsider. For example, a Swedish newspaper notoriously published an article with a rather dubious claim that the majority of people in Swedish prisons for rape were immigrants (Khoshnood et al. 2021). Similarly, in Germany, cultural attention has focused very disproportionately on the supposed rape threat posed by immigrants (Sanyal 2019). Meanwhile, in England around the turn of the twentieth century, rape was largely imagined as a problem of the lower classes (Bourke 2007). Throughout Europe and the United States, rapists are imagined as People Who Aren't Us, but there has been less consistency in how we imagine rape victims—sometimes it's Our People and sometimes it's Those People. No one seems eager to accept the grim reality that everywhere, sexual violence appears to be a much greater threat from those close to us than from strangers.

It's pretty clear that the cultural and scholarly reframing of minority experiences related to sexual assault in America (and possibly violent crime in general) needs to be completely overhauled. Nearly every scholarly and scholarly-adjacent publication I have read on race and sexual assault begins with the same historical tale of the rape of Black female slaves in the United States, the lynching of Black men accused of raping white women in the post–Civil War era, and the purported continued legacy of these historical events in the modern United States. The racist underpinnings of sexual assault have influenced our cultural imagination in profound ways, and there's no doubt we should remember these past grim events and work to move away from them. The effects of this kind of racism still linger into the twenty-first century, with the early part of the century seeing many exonerations of Black men who had been wrongfully convicted of rape and murder—especially when their victims were white (Gross et al. 2022). The case evidence suggests that most of these convictions were due to wrongful identifications (stranger violence cases in which white people were bad at correctly identifying a Black offender), and DNA evidence has mostly done away with this problem; rape exonerations for crimes committed in the twenty-first century are largely unheard of (Gross et al. 2022).

Whatever the reality of historical trends may or may not have been, for the entirety of the twenty-first century thus far in the United States, there has been very little evidence that Black women were more likely to be the victims of sexual assault (and at least as much evidence that white women might be slightly more likely). There has likewise been no evidence that Black men are disproportionately likely to be arrested for sexual assault, and little to suggest they're disproportionately likely to be charged and found guilty at the national level. There really isn't enough evidence to say whether Black men are more likely to be charged and found guilty of raping white women, but they definitely aren't more likely to be arrested for doing so. And in total contradiction to what we usually imagine, the people with the highest rate of reporting violent crime to the police (and presumably that includes sexual assault) are impoverished Black women. Indeed, the best evidence for criminal justice racism is that violent offenders reported to the police by Black people are the least likely to be arrested (but it's not at all clear that applies to sexual assault [Fogliato et al. forthcoming]). The belief that Black men are disproportionately likely to be arrested for, charged with, and convicted of sexual assault has been so deeply ingrained in our cultural understanding of the issue that many feminists have expressed hesitation about making legal reforms to sexual assault laws; they, like many, assume that the brunt of such reforms would unfairly fall upon Black men. Given the historical context, these concerns are understandable, but there simply is not sufficient evidence to support those concerns in the present day.

I wouldn't want to let anyone leave this chapter feeling too cozy about the state of racial politics in American crime, so I want to pause and tally up some of the best-documented aspects of intense racism in the legal system: Black men are vastly more likely to be the victims of homicide than white men (Fogliato et al. forthcoming); Black men are vastly more likely than white men to be stopped by the police for absolutely nothing (Kramer, Remster, and Charles 2017); Black men are vastly more likely than white men to be stopped for trivial crimes like minor traffic infractions (Pierson et al. 2020); perceptions of racism itself greatly contribute to the violence of Black men (that is, feeling racially oppressed is linked to them doing more crime; Unnever and Gabbidon 2011); Black men are much more likely to commit violent crimes than any other group, controlling for other factors (Unnever and Gabbidon 2011); and even by their own report, police are much more likely to be violent toward Black men than white men, and this includes children (Kramer, Remster, and Charles 2017).

As we try to fix all these elements of criminal injustice against Black men, we also really need to be conscious of the victimization experiences of LGBTQ folks. When considering nonfatal violent crime victimization in general, and sexual assault in particular, we need to be thinking more about why LGBTQ folks (and bisexual women and trans people especially) are so much more likely to be victims. With vastly higher chances of being the victims of stranger violence and multiple offender crimes, what could possibly account for the extremely dangerous lives of queer women? We're so far from a solution to this problem because we've barely even identified that it is one. We need to spread the word, and we need to take violence against bisexuals more seriously as a society and culture.

To conclude this chapter, I want to emphasize that even if the legal system isn't terribly racist at a national level in the way it addresses nonfatal violent crime, by multiple measures, it's still very bad at dealing with violent crime in general—and sexual assault isn't exactly special for that. Even most nonfatal violent crimes reported to the police never result in arrests, and only a tiny percentage result in convictions. That said, the legal system does seem to be much *worse* at dealing with sexual assault. Buried in a study looking at the effects of race on sexual assault charging in a small Pennsylvania city is a wild statistic: during the years of observation, there were more murder cases than sexual assault cases in the city's courts (Franklin 2010). Given that eleven times as many sexual assaults as murders are reported to the police (Fogliato et al. 2021), those case numbers are extremely out of line with actual crime proportions. We shouldn't generalize too much from a single jurisdiction, but it just doesn't seem like the criminal justice system is well prepared to deal with sexual assault. It's not particularly well prepared to deal with nonfatal violent crime in general (Baughman 2020), but there are some obvious problems with the current legal construction of sexual assault, which we'll explore in the next two chapters.

Chapter 8

Why Change the Law?

In fall 2023, two scenes from very different popular media—one a movie and the other a TV show—released within weeks of each other presented good complementary examples of just how complicated trying to judge sexual assault can be. Imagine for a moment, dear reader, that you have been picked to be on a jury charged with judging sexual assault in each of the following cases.

The first case is from the Netflix film *Fair Play*. The film contains many explicit sex scenes, including one in the middle of the film in which the female main character, Emily, blatantly pressures her fiancé, Luke, into having sex with her, but the film never questions her actions. The film, which is often described in its marketing as an "erotic thriller," centers around the demise of Emily and Luke's relationship, and by the end of the movie, the characters are in such heated conflict that Emily cracks a glass bottle over Luke's head publicly at their engagement party. He aggressively follows her to the bathroom at the public venue; it's not clear how drunk either of them is. They continue arguing, and he shoves her hard enough that she's backed against a wall. She angrily taunts him, "Go on. Go on. Show me what you need to. Prove what kind of man you think you are." He kisses her, and she shoves him, yelling, "Get off me! I fucking hate you!" With her back against the wall and most of his body against hers, they stare into each others' tearful eyes. Then she leans in to passionately kiss him, and they both frantically help each other out of the relevant parts of their clothing; she bends over the sink so he can fuck her. Fairly quickly, she says, "Luke, that hurts. Luke, stop! Luke. Fuck." He does not. The camera zooms in on her unhappy face as she slowly stands up, clearly upset, with a visible bruise on her face from the sink. Neither of them touches the other as she pulls down her dress and walks slowly out of the building. It's not really clear what the movie expects the audience reaction to be. The scene plays as very passionate, and in the context of a film with so much explicit sex, it feels like the filmmakers have eroticized Emily's pain and humiliation.

Emily angrily confronts Luke the next evening, demanding an apology, pointing to her numerous bruises, and accusing Luke of raping her. Initially blasé, he begins to look panicked and says worriedly, "Okay, look, we both got a little carried away that night. Let's leave it at that, all right?" She then picks up a knife, demands an apology from him (which he makes, crying, at knife point), cuts his shoulder, and tells him to wipe his blood off the floor and get out. And the movie ends.

The second case is from a wildly different fictional context of historical fantasy, in season 2 of *Wheel of Time*, where a young man, Rand, is in a relationship with Lanfear, an older and more experienced woman. He tells her she's the first woman he's ever been with, and from the get-go, their relationship dynamic has undertones of her dominating him (with varying degrees of his consent). As the season progresses, their dynamic gains increasingly explicit kinky overtones, including a scene in which she pleasures him while he is (apparently enthusiastically and consensually) tied to a bed, and another very cinematic one where she's dressed as a dominatrix on a throne, staring at him as he's cuffed to a large wheel. Early in the season, before these kinky undertones become overtones, a scene occurs in which Rand arrives back at their bedroom looking distraught. Lanfear is seated on the bed, while Rand stands a good distance apart, saying nervously, "Listen, I don't think tonight is . . . I have to be alone." She gets off the bed, walks toward him seductively, and begins kissing his hands. She assures him that when people think they need to be alone is when they actually need other people the most. He makes no move to respond to her advances, standing awkwardly. She leans in to kiss his cheeks, saying, "We can be alone together." He says, "No, no," and pushes her violently against a wall, his hand at her throat. Instead of looking afraid, she merely looks turned on by the gesture. He ends up leaning in to kiss her. The scene cuts away, and the next thing we see is the two of them naked in bed together, with him stroking her cheek, saying, "I don't want to hurt you." She says, "You can't."

Both visually and contextually, the two scenes provide strangely similar examples of Hollywood blurring the lines between BDSM and outright violence for purposes of titillation, while also illustrating how difficult it can be to judge the real-life complexities of sexual violation. In the first case, it's clear that Luke is guilty of a commonly understood sexual violation (not stopping when Emily told him to), but it might surprise you to learn that in many US states, that wouldn't come close to meeting the standards for any sort of legal sexual assault. He has no weapon and has not obviously physically restrained or threatened her, or even coerced her. There are many states where "no means no," but "no" usually has to be protested much more vigorously from the get-go in order to qualify as a sexual assault. Meanwhile, Rand's experience perfectly matches the way our society tends to imagine the sexual violation of men: that is, "they could physically stop it if they really wanted to, but of course they don't actually want to stop it." His repeatedly and even violently saying no is insufficient to prevent a sexual encounter that he apparently decides he wants anyway. Since no one claims "rape" in that situation, presumably it would be unlikely to end up being reported to the police, which is just as well, since the court system would have no real way to deal with it. It's also worth noting that in both of these cases, the person who does engage in very explicit physical violence is the person who is the victim of the nonconsensual sex: Emily slams a bottle over Luke's head in anger, and Rand slams Lanfear against a wall and chokes her as an apparently defensive gesture. How do we, the jury, feel about sexual assault victims who have also committed (nonsexual) assault? Presumably, committing assault does not preclude being the victim of sexual assault, but the combination feels a bit awkward in the context of an adversarial criminal justice system that usually wants black-and-white criminals and victims.

These kinds of messy (admittedly fictional) examples should motivate us to think about how we'd like the legal system to frame and address sexual violation cases. Do we want a system that neatly categorizes all who go through it as "violators" and "violated"—and which ends up filtering out and simply not meaningfully dealing with most cases where that doesn't *easily* apply? Or do we want a system that can handle more nuance? In this chapter, I will begin by reviewing the current state of sexual assault law and then consider some of the general reasons why changing "rape" and "sexual assault" to "sexual violation" law would be a good idea; then, in the next chapter, I'm going to explain more of the specifics of what that should look like.

THE CURRENT STRUCTURE OF THE LEGAL SYSTEM

I should preface the next few sections with a warning that the US legal system, like that of many developed countries, is constantly changing the text of its laws, and what the textual law *means* is constantly changing as courts interpret it. The specific laws referenced in this book as it goes to press might look quite different by the time it's printed and finally reaches your hands. That said, *I want to remind you that nonconsensual sex alone is not actually illegal in many US states.*

To understand the way sexual assault laws operate, we first need to understand the basic structure of the legal system in the United States. For criminal charges related to sexual misconduct, a prosecuting government attorney (usually called a district attorney, or DA), will get information—in these cases, normally because someone (not necessarily the victim) reports it to the police. After the police investigate and decide whether or not to forward the investigation to the prosecutor, the DA decides whether to bring a case on behalf of the government against a defendant in order to seek some sort of official punishment. Civil complaints, meanwhile, are brought by an individual against another individual or entity in order to seek some form of redress, usually "damages" (that is, money), as well as occasionally injunctive relief (a court order directing that the defendant must do or must not do something) or declaratory relief (a court order officially declaring the legal status between the parties, for example, "Adam sexually assaulted Bert").

Criminal charges are resolved with a finding of either "guilty" or "not guilty," which in turn results in incarceration, fines, and other future legal interventions and consequences (for example, sex offender registration requirements). Civil claims are resolved with findings of "liable" or "not liable." To be found guilty in criminal court, the prosecution typically must establish "beyond a reasonable doubt" that the defendant committed the crime they are accused of; the standards of proof are much lower in civil court, where "a preponderance of the evidence" (meaning a better than 50 percent chance)—or, in some much rarer contexts, "clear and convincing evidence" (meaning most of the evidence)—must show that the plaintiff's complaint against the defendant is legitimate. Finally, civil suits are paid for by the people who bring them (or sometimes are eventually paid for by a defendant), while criminal charges are funded by the government itself. We typically think of sexual assaults as being handled by the criminal system, but many survivors bring lawsuits over what happened to them (and many people accused of sexual misconduct sue for defamation, for that matter). That said, because the primary goal of civil litigation is money, for many survivors, civil actions would largely be pointless because (1) they cannot afford to pay years of attorneys' fees and (2) the defendant would likely be unable to pay any amount a court awards at the end anyway.

In the vast and often byzantine US criminal legal system, there are courts belonging to different "sovereigns" (that is, federal versus state), but the vast majority of criminal complaints are handled by state courts and subject to state laws. For some criminal offenses, these state-by-state differences are trivial, but for sexual offenses, the differences are often massive. State laws pertaining to sex are so bizarrely and arbitrarily different from one another that most Americans I speak to are unaware that even something as basic as the age of sexual consent can change multiple times within a one-hour drive in some parts of the country. For example, in one cluster of US states that shares close borders with one another, ages of sexual consent vary: in Tennessee and Kentucky, it is eighteen; in Missouri and Illinois, seventeen; and in Arkansas, sixteen. That means a person can be charged with "statutory rape" (meaning the victim was assumed to be too young to give sexual consent, regardless of any other circumstances) if they have sex with a sixteen-year-old in all the listed states except Arkansas and if they have sex with a seventeen-year-old in Tennessee or Kentucky. I'm not going to try to tackle the complexities of statutory rape laws (which are very messy and hotly debated in legal circles [Fischel 2019]) specifically here; rather, my point is that having a standard national age of consent ought to be the simplest thing we could agree on in sexual violation law, but we haven't even come close—and it only gets worse from here.

Importantly for our purposes, criminal law in the United States doesn't require the victim to come forward with a complaint. Anyone can report an alleged crime and initiate an investigation; alternatively, the police or prosecutor can start an investigation all on their own (based on a news story, a hunch, or political motivations), make an arrest, and press charges—with or without the cooperation of the purported victim. Particularly in instances of domestic violence and abuse, the government often has concerns about the victim's state of mind in their emotional and/or practical attachment to the person hurting them. Thus, the government might decide to make an arrest and press charges even if the victim doesn't cooperate, based on the premise that the victim might not be in a stable position to cooperate but needs protection from the person who (is) hurt(ing) them. On one hand, this may look (and often is) paternalistic; on the other, it can theoretically protect victims assaulted by abusive partners from being threatened by their abusers for pursuing criminal charges.

While the government apparently occasionally makes sincere attempts to protect families from ongoing abusive dynamics by pressing charges without the support of the victims (Hlavka and Mulla 2021), in most cases, victims withdraw their support from cases because the criminal justice process itself is so exhausting, unfriendly, and even traumatizing (Smith and Freyd 2013). For all that rape kits and victim accounts in the immediate aftermath of a sexual assault can be conspicuously cruel to survivors, an even bigger problem seems to be simply having to repeat the same story over and over again to various officials, which can retraumatize survivors (Cossins 2020; Fohring 2020). We should ask ourselves, "Who would subject themselves to that kind of government-sponsored misery?" and the fastest answer I can come up with is, "People who have no other official channels to seek support and relief from." The statistics seem to bear this conclusion out: in general, the people who report violent victimizations to the police the most are disadvantaged minority women, in contrast to more advantaged white women who say they reported to some other official entity (such as a college security officer; Zaykowski, Allain, and Campagna 2019).

These "other official entities" now have their own complex legal(ish) system in the United States attached to schools and, to a much lesser degree, businesses. Businesses have to prevent human resources complaints, but there are relatively few businesses in the United States where people live, so opportunities for extremes of sexual violence at places of business are generally scarce. The government requires private businesses to try to maintain workplaces free of sexual harassment, or they will be open to lawsuits. For obvious reasons, when people live at the place where they spend their days (whether as an employee or as a student), the risks of sexual violence increase significantly. There are two major types of businesses where adults are very likely to live—the military and universities—and both now have their own complex systems to deal with sexual harassment and assault at "work" (which can also apply to encounters outside work that happen with a colleague or fellow student; Hattery and Smith 2019). With some caveats, the military and universities operate as their own weird little (psuedo-)legal bubbles and can thus make and try to enforce whatever rules they want about sexual conduct and harassment. Thus, for example, employees in the US Navy are strictly banned from having sex with each other (even when stuck on a ship together for months at sea), and some conservative universities like Brigham Young ban students from having sex before marriage. No one knows the exact numbers, but due to age and living conditions if nothing else, it stands to reason that a substantial percentage of all sexual violations occur among college students, military personnel, and prisoners, so having separate entities responsible for handling offenses in each of these contexts isn't necessarily unreasonable, although no one is doing much for prisoners (Hattery and Smith 2019).

In response to public outcry about sexual assault at university campuses, the federal government has instructed schools and universities since 2011 to maintain formal review policies and boards to address complaints from students and workers about issues that may have occurred between them (Sanyal 2019; Grigoriadis 2017). These boards are charged with punishing students (including expelling them) and workers (including firing them). Broadly speaking, most boards that started after that guidance (many individual institutions had their own similar systems before the guidance) tended to operate with an extremely loose standard of evidence against students and employees against whom complaints had been made (Sanyal 2019; Grigoriadis 2017); that is, they tended to operate with the generous standards of civil courts—a preponderance of the evidence. As of this writing (and the regulations around Title IX, the act used as the basis for these arrangements, are constantly changing), the US Department of Education has stated that universities are supposed to formally state whether they use a preponderance of the evidence or a more stringent clear and convincing evidence standard for all cases they oversee.

THE STATE OF THE LAW

The closest thing the United States has to a unified criminal law statute is the Model Penal Code (MPC), which isn't actually the law anywhere. Originally drafted by the American Legal Institute in 1962, the MPC was designed to be a model for state governments to use in drafting their laws in the hopes of providing more unity between states (Robinson and Dubber 2007). Its formulation of "rape" (below) was purportedly quite forward-thinking for the time, although still subject to some contemporary criticism (Denno 2003):

A male who has sexual intercourse with a female not his wife is guilty of rape if:

   a. he compels her to submit by force or by threat of imminent death, serious bodily injury, extreme pain or kidnapping, to be inflicted on anyone; or

   b. he has substantially impaired her power to appraise or control her conduct by administering or employing without her knowledge drugs, intoxicants or other means for the purpose of preventing resistance; or

   c. the female is unconscious; or

   d. the female is less than 10 years old. (American Law Institute 1985)

Most US states eventually adopted some version of this language in their own laws. Over the subsequent decades, the two aspects that received the most pushback were whether a man could in fact be guilty of raping his wife, and whether sexual acts other than vaginal intercourse should be counted as rape. The answers to these questions have mostly been, respectively, "Yes, but the offense has to be absolutely egregious to have any chance of being taken seriously" and, "It varies wildly by state." As we've discussed before, an important dimension of the limits of sexual acts countable as "rape" here was gender, since only women could be raped in this classical formulation.

Although the United States was far ahead of most other countries in its timeline for making marital rape illegal (it was technically illegal in all fifty states by 1993), many states have been or remain very slow to make the same things illegal for married (or sometimes cohabiting) and unmarried/nonco-habiting partners (Anderson 2002). For example, until 2023, in Maryland, marital rape was illegal only if someone "use[d] force or threat of force and the act [was] without the consent of the spouse." Many other states continue to require similar acts of physical violence from married or cohabiting part-ners in order to charge someone with rape (or sexual assault), even though such acts of violence are not required for other nonconsensual encounters in those states.

As we saw in chapter 2, several states did away with the term "rape" entirely in their rape reform laws and replaced it with various degrees of "sexual assault" as a way to avoid the problematic connotations of the term "rape." Some states updated their statutes to include an increasingly large number of sexual acts, while others did not. The states that failed to make such changes have occasionally ended up with court rulings that seem bizarre to people outside of the legal profession. For example, former president Donald Trump was found liable by a civil jury for "deliberately and forcibly [penetrating] [E. Jean] Carroll's vagina with his fingers" in the mid-1990s. Carroll had publicly claimed that Trump "raped" her, and he sued her for defamation on the grounds that in the state of New York, where the crime took place, only penis-in-vagina sex legally constitutes rape. In 2023, a New York judge ruled that Trump's suit was baseless on the grounds that both forcible penetration with fingers *or* penis constitutes rape in "common modern parlance," in "some dictionaries," and in many other criminal statutes (*Carroll v. Trump* 2023), New York's actual law notwithstanding. If we translate the judge's ruling out of legalese, it seems to me to read, "We all know the state of New York is frustratingly behind the times in its labeling of 'rape,' and we're not going to accuse its citizens of making libelous claims just because the state hasn't updated its laws to the twenty-first century."

In 2012, the American Law Institute began a much-needed project to update its Model Penal Code to the twenty-first century (American Law Institute 2023). Focusing on the changes to its rape law section, we can find major alterations emphasizing consent more than violence. Like many contemporary state laws, it removes the term "rape" entirely in favor of graded "sexual assault" down to "sexual misconduct" offenses. It uses much more gender-neutral language, stating that an offense can occur in the absence of consent, when "the actor engages with another person in, or causes another person to engage in, submit to, or perform, an act of sexual penetration or oral sex" where "sexual penetration" refers to "an act involving penetration, however slight, of the anus or genitalia by an object or a body part." These graded offenses largely refer to the contextual nature of the acts, such as physical violence or the threat of violence, an incapacitated victim, an otherwise "vulnerable" victim (for example, due to intellectual disability), or coercion or deception. The draft is even sufficiently modern in its sensibilities that it functionally includes extensive language allowing for BDSM activities by creating an "affirmative defense" for a defendant to state they had "explicit prior permission" to engage in acts of violence in the context of a sexual encounter.

Everything in this proposed revision is a huge improvement over the 1962 MPC, to be sure, and even a huge improvement over most existing US state statutes. I'll suggest a major critique/shift in the next chapter, but I want to be clear that even though I think this proposed statute could be a lot better than it is, it's a huge improvement over what we currently have. That said, as of this writing, it has not been approved, and the entire process of approving the new MPC has been held up for years specifically because of arguments about the changes to the sexual statutes, so who knows what effect the proposed suggestions will have on actual US law (Murphy 2020).

Thus, for now (and the foreseeable future), in most states, the current state of the law means that for the government to convict someone of rape (or in states without "rape," "first-degree sexual assault"), it must prove (1) that the person committed a sexual act, often assuming the worst (or only) kind of violation is penis-in-vagina sex by a man with a woman he isn't married to; (2) that the sexual act was accompanied by the use of force, lack of consent, young age of the victim, or another factor; and (3) some very basic level of intention (for example, that the person knew they were engaging in the sexual act, as opposed to doing so accidentally, and knew the other person did not consent).

WHAT DOES THE LAW REALLY DO, ANYWAY?

Decades ago, anti-rape activism in the United States (Bevacqua 2000) and more recently abroad (Sanyal 2019) was heavily focused on changing the law. Moving away from the rape-as-theft legal model that assumed women were property to a more modern rape-as-nonconsent legal model has required a lot of work on the part of activists, lawyers, scholars, and politicians. Unfortunately, a kind of legal cynicism seems to have set in among many young activists, and the idea of changing the law as a means of activism when not focused on specific legal rights has started to feel a bit quaint and old-fashioned. But in very much the same way that liberals have begun engaging in intense activism in the last decade or so by taking over district attorneys' offices in an effort to curb "tough on crime" rhetoric and instead get tough on police corruption (Otterbein 2021), we need to seriously consider the idea that *legal change matters for its own sake*. Anti-rape activists who actively sought to increase conviction rates for rape were labeled "carceral feminists" by others in the movement (Whalley and Hackett 2017), and the label stung. However, we should be more expansive in our reformist attitudes: legal reforms and even increasing conviction rates don't have to result in more people in prison/on parole/on probation if those reforms are accompanied by concomitant reforms in sentencing. Moreover, surely there is general agreement that two of the worst crimes individuals can commit are homicide and rape, so it seems a bit backward to start prison reform with rape.

The best way to gauge the success or failure of a law is to see what it does versus what it is ostensibly supposed to accomplish. The traditional theory is that criminal laws and their accompanying systems of punishment accomplish five things: retribution, individual deterrence, general deterrence, incapacitation, and rehabilitation (Karstedt 2007). Retribution is supposed to contain the principle that the government is responsible for punishing criminals for you; this concept is specifically partly intended to prevent cycles of revenge justice, such as fathers and brothers assaulting or killing men who raped their daughters and sisters. It's supposed to serve a general sense of justice in an idea of punishment (you did wrong, so you should suffer, but your suffering should be based on a set of equally applied laws and principles that individuals would never be able to apply on their own). Individual deterrence refers to the idea that we as a society are trying to keep *this specific person* from doing crime (so, for example, courts might issue restraining orders to prevent someone from going near a specific person they've threatened or hurt). General deterrence refers to the idea that we want to stop people in general from doing something we deem problematic, especially when prevailing moral codes might not prevent them from doing so; thus, even if people don't necessarily feel that stealing candy is wrong, they might choose not to do it based on the fear of being arrested. Incapacitation refers to the idea that we want to make it basically impossible for a person to physically commit a crime by limiting mobility and access. This principle is foundational for prisons, since people ostensibly can't commit more crimes while in prison. Rehabilitation is the idea that the criminal legal system should help encourage criminals to stop committing future crimes by changing their values and opportunities. This logic is another major reason why prisons were established and is indeed the source of the word "penitentiary" (e.g., a place used for penitence; Foucault 1979).

But in addition to the obvious practical effects of punishment, laws can provide an important set of ethical guidelines for our social worlds. As a matter of philosophical principle, ethics are supposed to provide the foundation for laws. In practice, most citizens aren't philosophers, and they learn a lot of their general outline of what's right and what's wrong based on their (and their friends') understanding of the law. For example, to return to the age of sexual consent, most Americans I speak with believe it to be eighteen, and most people seem to support this idea; when I ask them why, they say, "Because it's when you're an adult"—which is, of course, entirely a product of other sets of laws. In short, people learn to define the morality of an act (consent to sex) based on an arbitrary distinction (legal adulthood) carved out by law.

When laws are inconsistent or illogical, people take them less seriously and often straight-up ignore them. Thus the United States tells its young people that they're legal adults at age eighteen; but then it illogically tells them they're not allowed to drink alcohol or buy marijuana until they're twenty-one, and pretty much everyone goes, "This is a really dumb law, and I'm not going to pay much attention to it." However this lack of sense is really important because *another important function of the law is to provide legitimacy* (Hahn 2022), and when the law lacks internal consistency, it looks less legitimate. When the law is obviously wrong, we start to question the whole structure and system of it, because the law legitimizes the authority of the government itself. It also legitimizes the nature of people's complaints against one another. If I say, "Ted stole $10,000 from me," the law provides a legitimate process for me to try to prove that Ted stole that money from me and to seek redress for its loss.

In the case of sexual violation law, the current legal structure has failed us in every conceivable way. With so few violators being convicted, most survivors never see their experiences validated by the justice system. And despite its myriad problems, society views the criminal justice system as our primary means of showing something "really happened" (Johnson 2017; Lorenz, Kirkner, and Ullman 2019). Reporting a sexual assault to the police is a crucial step for many victims in trying to prove to others (and perhaps even to themselves) that a violation actually took place, and they weren't just lying or exaggerating. But without that societal recognition, what do survivors tell themselves and others happened to them? These low conviction rates also, of course, mean that the law is failing to provide useful enforcement, especially deterrence. Moreover, even on the rare occasions when convictions occur, many survivors report that seeing their violator hauled off to prison was far less satisfying than they expected it to be, so the retributive element here seems pretty weak (Koss 2006). It's true that prison punishment can achieve the goal of incapacitation in that violators often can't commit another offense against the person they originally hurt, but given the mind-boggling statistics about how many sexual violations occur in prisons (both between prisoners and from guards against prisoners; Stemple, Flores, and Meyer 2017), it's clear the government has functionally created its own hotbeds of sexual violation. While that might qualify as retributive in some sense, it definitely doesn't qualify as rehabilitative, nor does it qualify as meaningful incapacitation if imprisoned people are committing those acts of violation.

The law has also failed to provide us with a set of contemporary ethical guidelines in keeping with modern sexual morals. It still overemphasizes physical violence, even as general moral understandings have come to emphasize consent. Young people have mostly been left to muddle along for themselves, trying to conform to a set of moral behaviors (now sometimes officially enforced at universities and places of work) that are pretty far out-side the scope of most formal legal statutes. Even setting aside the disastrous inconsistency of sexual assault laws between US states, they also fail to be consistent with other criminal laws in their basic underlying structure. We'll tackle this issue thoroughly in the next chapter, but for now I just want to ask, conceptually, why does the legal structure treat sexual violation so differently from homicide? Several famous philosophers (most notably Michel Foucault [Taylor 2009]) have even argued that "sexual assault" shouldn't be a separate crime from "assault," although this view is certainly not very popular.

WHAT BEHAVIOR DO WE WANT TO BE LEGALLY ACTIONABLE?

As we contemplate legal reforms, it's essential that we ask ourselves how much we want the law to be involved in criminal issues in general, and with regard to sexual violation in particular. Presumably, there's a certain level of violence and/or coercive behavior we're generally on board with being criminally liable for nonconsensual sex (which the law in pretty much all states currently addresses, although we probably would ideally like it to be more expansive in what it counts as "sex"). If someone drugs your drink so you'll be unconscious and unable to object to them having sex with you, I think most people would agree that warrants involvement from the criminal justice system, because the behavior is especially egregious and warrants punishment (retribution), and because we want to try to prevent that person from doing it again (incapacitation and individual deterrence), as well as discouraging others from doing it (general deterrence). And the same gener-ally goes for nonconsensual sex involving weapons as well as blatant threats and coercion.

But what about everything else? What about the kinds of "grey zone" cases I opened this chapter with where we, the hypothetical jury, rarely have a video account to try to assess the accuracies of one person's account against the oth-ers'? What about those grey zones where someone initially said yes and then later said no? What about encounters where someone initially said no and then later said yes? What about drunken encounters where someone said no, but the other person never even heard it? What about sober encounters where someone thought they were engaging in a seduction, but the other person felt like they were being psychologically manipulated and attacked? Do we think sexual violations should be treated differently if they occur between partners who are currently in a romantic and sexual relationship? What about exes? What about people in on-again/off-again relationships?

We need to work out these questions together as a society to decide collectively how we feel about them. Of course, this isn't a book about how to overhaul the criminal justice system in general (although it's certainly a book that presents plenty of evidence on why we should!). But we can't provide really good answers to these questions without thinking outside the box of police/jail/courtroom/prison with the goal of trying to achieve more inclusive versions of community healing and safety. A decent metric for conceptualizing this problem is asking ourselves, "Is this a situation where a person with a gun is likely to be helpful?" At the end of the day, that's what the police in the United States mostly are: people with guns who are ostensibly tasked with helping us in difficult situations but who have no enforceable legal obligation to actually do so (*Castle Rock v. Gonzales* 2005). A person with a gun might be helpful in interrupting a sexual violation in progress, but the odds of that happening aren't very high. Are the police the appropriate people to be dealing with the grim aftermath of survivors? I genuinely don't have an easy answer to that question. I have no doubt that we need to alter the way the criminal justice system handles survivors overall, and activists in British Commonwealth countries have been spending a lot more time than Americans have thinking about these types of reforms (e.g., Cossins 2020; Daly 2022). But I don't think a responsible society can get away without doing something to formally chastise, incapacitate, and attempt to rehabilitate people who intentionally and even dangerously recklessly violate the sexual consent of others.

It's important to remember that the criminal justice system is a blunt instrument for dealing with offenses against and by members of our society. Consider drunk driving: currently, the legal blood alcohol limit for driving in most of America is .08. This measure is hardly perfect, and many agree it's far more intoxicated than we actually want anyone behind the wheel of a car (Fell and Voas 2006). Instead of ticketing and arresting people driving drunker than we really want them to, we employ social shaming and stigma to negatively and positively encourage people not to drive when they're even somewhat intoxicated. We only legally punish people who go far beyond our general social tolerance for driving drunk. And the scope of our punishment for drunk driving is designed to address not only how drunk the person was, but also how much damage they caused. In my opinion, we should employ similar standards with regard to sexual violations (which, not coincidentally, also often occur while people are intoxicated). As I noted in chapter 6, we should set standards for sexual consent hygiene ranging from "excessively cautious" to "excellent" to "good" to "good enough" to "dubious" to "unacceptable" to "technically criminally bad" to "punishably criminally bad"—and "technically criminally bad" should be well past "unacceptable." By "technically criminally bad," I'm referring to sexual consent hygiene that might technically be illegal based on the way we construct the law, but in much the same way as stealing $20 is from a store: it's illegal because we need the law to be logically consistent and theoretically enforceable, but it probably just warrants a scolding from a manager, not a phone call to the police and a public punishment. (Obviously, this attitude toward legal punishment assumes less police surveillance and less dramatic punishment for crimes like stealing $20 than we currently have in most places).

As a society, we ideally want to intervene to improve people's consent hygiene at the point where it hits "dubious," not at the point where it's gone all the way to "criminally bad." That's why it's so important to think beyond the criminal justice system as we conceptualize the management of consent. We want a social system where all parts of it serve to reinforce the idea that practicing good sexual consent hygiene is important to all of us. I would argue that in a well-organized system, any adversarial criminal justice system (meaning one in which one person has been harmed and the other person has unambiguously harmed them and deserves to be punished) would ideally always be the place of last resort for dealing with any sexual violations outside of the "punishably criminally bad" category. By its nature, an adversarial criminal justice process will always be slow and invasive for everyone involved, because fundamental civil rights have to (at least attempt to) be honored when civil liberties are at stake. And the necessary honoring of the rights of violators is probably always going to result in making survivors incredibly uncomfortable because the criminal justice process is supposed to be organized to protect the rights of the defendant, not to help victims feel protected or vindicated.

Institutions outside the criminal law system are probably better suited to dealing with many "technically criminally bad" offenses. As I mentioned above, two major institutions—the military and universities—already have official means of dealing with sexual violation offenses. Given that *many* sexual violations occur in these institutional contexts, merely fortifying these existing systems (many of which are so overtaxed as to be largely useless) might be helpful. Much closer to the context of the violations and the specific circumstances surrounding them than a traditional court, these institutional boards seem theoretically better equipped to handle incidents that would probably falter in an adversarial criminal justice system. While the consequences of being expelled from the military or a university can seriously negatively impact a person's life, the consequences are small compared to being found guilty of a crime and sent to prison. That said, we will always need to have alternatives in place, because these institutional boards will probably have the institution's best interests at heart, not those of the people in their proceedings. And in very small institutions, concerns about familiarity and nepotism become even more pressing.

The next level down from major institutional authorities are the heads of clubs and organizations (such as fraternities) and religious institutions, who may be in a good position to monitor poor consent hygiene and even to intervene at the "unacceptable" level, not just the "technically criminally bad" level. These organizations might choose to expel or discipline members for engaging in unacceptable consent behaviors, or they might recommend problematic members for therapies and counseling. And the next level down from that is any tight-knit friend group, where gossip and social scolding can serve to punish dubious consent hygiene and beyond. Most of us listen to our friends and care what they think of us; we can aspire to hold each other accountable without being pointlessly cruel. Our goal should always be to encourage the people we care about to be reflexive and thoughtful in their consent hygiene, not to demand perfection.

WHAT KINDS OF LEGAL REFORMS ARE POSSIBLE?

When considering the idea of legal reforms, it's probably always worthwhile to take a moment and ask, "What do we want in an ideal world . . . and what will we settle for?" In an ideal world, I think more and more people would like to see a legal system that is focused more on active rehabilitation and less on retribution and incapacitation. This philosophy is a major part of the argument for restorative justice, which has become an increasingly important component of many advocates' perspectives on managing crime in general, including sexual violations (Burns and Sinko 2023). I like to imagine a system where a survivor can call a hotline after a sexual violation and make choices, in conjunction with legal authorities and social workers, to decide: whether to pursue voluntary counseling or receive other resources for themselves, mandatory counseling (with or without the survivor) for the person being accused of the violation, and/or punitive adversarial measures. Throughout the process, the central guiding principles would be helping the survivor feel safe and protected, and trying to protect others from further offenses by the violator—while also trying to respect the basic humanity of both people.

These are very big ideas, and they are the subject of entire books themselves (Daly 2022; Cossins 2020)—far beyond the scope of this particular book. For now, I simply want to say that revising the law ideally means more than just changing some words in a book: in the best possible world, it means a systemic overhaul that is less about people with guns and briefcases, and more about mental health, social work, and the general philosophy of helping people feel better about themselves and safely participate in our society.

Thankfully, there are a lot of things we can do to reform sexual assault laws other than totally overhauling the justice system. Relatively simple and straightforward solutions include recording victims' initial detailed testimonial statements, and then never subjecting them to further questioning and cross-examination (Cossins 2020). Most authorities on the subject agree that we appear to gain little through the process of repeatedly grilling victims other than discouraging them from continuing their cases. We could also try to channel more complaints into civil, rather than criminal, courts, since civil courts have a much lower burden of proof and potentially provide tangible benefits for the victim. Handling more cases in civil court also could address concerns about more people ending up in prison, since civil rulings do not result in prison terms.

If the prospect of changing the law seems daunting, it's important to remember that rape and sexual assault laws have been changed many times in the distant and recent past. Indeed, the fact that I wrote "rape and sexual assault laws" instead of just "rape laws" in the last sentence is the result of major activist legal reforms. Indeed, these laws change so often that it's difficult to talk about them in a book because books don't update quickly. Major legal reforms have been instituted in the past, from bans on discussing a victim's sexual history in court to bans on the death penalty being applied to rape cases. We can and should do more.

In my vision, the law is both the starting point and the end point. It should be a starting point inasmuch as it should serve as a reliable guidepost for measuring our own and others' behavior; it should also ideally help other organizations and groups formulate their own codes of conduct. For example, following the suggested legal changes in the next chapter would not necessarily force institutions like colleges and the military to revise their own codes of conduct accordingly, but it would certainly give them guidance for how to do so if they chose. (And because of the way they face certain kinds of liability, they would have major incentives to at least ensure their systems covered all the criminalized conduct.) When I say the law should be the end point, I mean that it should ideally be summoned only when things have gotten very bad indeed. In a perfect world, we should have a lot of unofficial and official mechanisms for resolving problems with others that don't involve a person with a gun (aka a police officer). And we should have a much more sophisticated way to think and talk about sexual violations than the law presently gives us.

Chapter 9

Actual Legal Changes

As the attempts by the American Law Institute to overhaul sexual assault laws in the Model Penal Code suggest, many people in legal circles, at least, are increasingly aware of the need to make some big changes. This chapter isn't going to be a step-by-step guide for how to make those changes, and it's not going to provide word-for-word suggestions for what model statutes might look like. Instead, I'm going to provide general principles the heavily revised versions of these statutes could be based on, and discuss why these specific changes could be so helpful.

WORDS MATTER!

Twentieth-century anti-rape activists were cognizant that words matter. Their activism led to changing legal wording in some states to avoid the word "rape" entirely in favor of "sexual assault," and also introduced the terms "date rape" and "acquaintance rape" into the popular vocabulary (Bevacqua 2000). I think trying to change popular vocabulary from "rape" to "sexual assault" was a savvy political move, but the problem with the term "sexual assault" is that it still implies an act of physical violence (and in fact, many statutes define physical violence as an essential part of the crime). But as our social ideas about "rape" and "sexual assault" have moved further and further away from acts of physical violence, the time has come to introduce new legal (and ideally social) terminology that holds fewer connotations of overt violence.

I suggest the term "sexual violation" as an umbrella category, intended to refer to the thing that violent "stranger rape" has in common with pushed boundaries within a relationship: *a violation of the autonomy of another human, as experienced by that person.* In other words, calling these things "violation" offenses focuses on the effect on the person who experienced them, much in the same way the umbrella term "homicide offenses" focuses on the fact that negligent homicide, manslaughter, and murder all involve someone dying.

As it stands, US states have a dizzying patchwork of terminology for many crimes of sexual violation, and this inconsistency confuses juries and even creates absurd legal drama—for example, the defamation case filed by Donald Trump against E. Jean Carroll mentioned in the previous chapter. For now, as far as the state of New York is concerned, being nonconsensually anally penetrated at gunpoint doesn't legally qualify as "rape" but the same act with vaginal penetration does. These wild legal and terminological inconsistencies are the legacies of older ideas that still linger in our culture but have also become very old-fashioned. Culturally speaking, it will undoubtedly take a very long time to get rid of these associations, but we could go a long way toward doing so simply by passing new legal statutes—changing our legal and cultural vocabulary to emphasize "sexual violation" instead of "rape" and "sexual assault."

MENS REA AND DEFINING THE "CRIME" OF SEXUAL VIOLATION

Criminal laws in the United States are traditionally broken down into three basic components:

1. *Actus reus* (literally "guilty act," which we'll call the "act"): This is what act someone must do to commit the crime.
2. *Mens rea* (literally "guilty mind," which we'll call the "state of mind"): This is what state of mind someone must have toward the act. In order for the act to be deemed criminal, the state of mind is traditionally something like "knowingly," "intentionally," and so on—suggesting the person knew what they were doing and intentionally committed a crime.
3. Punishment: This is the defined range of what the government is permitted to do to a defendant if the state can show the required act and state of mind, sometimes with maximums (e.g., "no more than five years in prison") and sometimes with minimums (e.g., "no less than five years").

We can think of states of mind along a continuum from most culpable (and therefore tied to more severe punishments) to least culpable (and therefore tied to the least severe, if any, punishments). The traditional set of states of mind runs from most culpable to least:

- Purposely—the goal was to do the act.
- Knowingly—the person knew the act was going to happen.

- Recklessly—the person knew there was a real risk the act was going to happen.
- Negligently—the person was not actually aware of the risk the act was going to happen, but should have been.
- None or so-called strict liability—just doing the act is enough for criminal liability (often used for drug possession and other regulatory offenses, as well as being frequently used for statutory rape).

Most criminal statutes care about temporality and spontaneity in their assignment of state of mind designations: did someone put a lot of time and effort into planning the crime or did they do it basically on a whim? Was that whim to do a criminal thing or was it a dumb idea that happened to have criminal consequences?

We can see these gradations reflected well in the way our criminal law system treats homicide. As I've observed several times, our criminal law system seems best set up in every way to manage homicide: the adversarial justice system seems to prefer not having to actually deal with a victim or trying to make a victim feel better, and the law itself is quite nuanced and sophisticated in delineating many different ways and means that someone might cause the death of someone else. Thus, almost all jurisdictions have legally different charges for "murder," which is often defined as "purposely or knowingly causing the death of another human being." Even this condition can be further exacerbated with separate charges that show more evidence of criminal intent, such as conspiring with others, possession and use of an illegal weapon, and committing another crime. These conditions of premeditation often result in charges of murder or a high-degree form of homicide in many jurisdictions, whereas merely causing the death of another intentionally but without obvious premeditation usually results in charges of lower degree like second-degree homicide. Meanwhile, "manslaughter" is usually defined by the same act (causing a death), but with reckless intent, or for some other reason the actor was not necessarily in their right mind. In most states, merely being voluntarily intoxicated is specifically not sufficient grounds to disqualify someone from being charged with behaving criminally recklessly. And finally, we have "negligent homicide," which is often defined as causing the death of another with negligence. In layman's terms, negligent homicide basically means someone caused the death of another by being criminally stupid. State of mind is so fundamental to our understanding of homicide and its severity that in many jurisdictions, it's simply not a crime to cause the death of another person if the government can't prove any particular criminal state of mind.

Structurally, there are also important exceptions, even when the government proves an act and state of mind, called "affirmative defenses." When someone pleads an affirmative defense, they admit to both the act and state of mind of the crime (that's the "affirmative" part—they're affirming the crime) while arguing that there's some reason those together are still not criminal. Common criminal affirmative defenses include things like "justification," "entrapment," "duress," and so on, usually claiming that some set of circumstances required the individual to commit the crime. The most popularly understood of these is "self-defense." When you say you killed another person in self-defense, you're specifically affirming (1) that you did the act (caused the death of another human being) and (2) that you did it purposely (you meant to kill them). But you're arguing that you only killed someone because protecting yourself required you to do so, and therefore the law cannot penalize you.

That was a lot of structural information, but let's try to apply it. Getting back to the topic we're here to discuss, it might surprise you to realize that we don't currently treat rape and sexual assault at all the way we treat homicide. That difference partly starts with the assumption that no one ever wants to be killed (and indeed, that assumption gets us in a lot of trouble when it comes to trying to construct laws around assisted suicide), while simultaneously reasonably assuming that many people want to have sex. There are more or less only two violent crimes where the *victim's* state of mind could be treated as paramount: theft/robbery and sexual assault. In the case of theft, a defendant can (theoretically) try to argue, "I thought they were giving that to me!" just as in the case of sexual assault, the defendant can try to argue, "I thought she wanted it!" But note that there are still crucial differences in the way this plays out: little, if any, theft jurisprudence (e.g., case law, decisions, and so on) actually focuses much on victims' states of mind. But despite the fact that rape laws technically tell courts to focus on a defendant's state of mind (e.g., the whole *mens rea* thing we talked about), much US sexual assault jurisprudence has flipped things on their head, ignoring the defendant's state of mind in favor of focusing on what the alleged victim thought or believed.

An (in)famous 1979 case from Maryland, *State v. Rusk*, provides a grim illustration of the extremes this legal mentality can reach (Gersen 2010). The facts of the case were a bit peculiar. A man (Rusk) got a ride to his home from a woman at a bar, then invited her up to his apartment; she said no, and he grabbed her car keys and repeated the "invitation." So she followed him up to his place but immediately asked to leave. He said no, apparently without making any violent moves to prevent her from doing so. She said, "If I do what you want, will you let me go without killing me?" By her account, "he said nothing," and, crying, she then proceeded to have oral and vaginal sex with him. At some point in all this, he "lightly choked" her. A jury convicted Rusk of rape, but the intermediate appellate court reversed and found that Rusk could not be guilty as a matter of law, because Maryland's rape statute at the time (which was only updated to remove this requirement in 2017!) required "force or threat of force" to be present for there to be a crime. Given that there were neither weapons, serious acts of physical aggression, nor even explicit threats involved, the intermediate court argued there was not, in fact, a plausible threat of force. The discussion focused, therefore, not on what *the defendant believed or intended*, but instead on whether the victims' fear of force in this context was "reasonable" (and on whether "lightly chok[ing]" counted as any force—the intermediate appellate court said it didn't). Ultimately, the state's high court reversed the intermediate court and affirmed the initial guilty verdict, albeit over a vigorous dissent. And as appalling as this debate looks to modern readers, the legal reasoning in the intermediate court decision and the dissent remains plausible today, given how the law was drafted.

But imagine if the law were constructed differently: instead of centering around the victim's state of mind (was it reasonable for her to think that Rusk would hurt her if she tried to leave without having sex with him?), centering it around what Rusk must have been thinking in this situation. Surely outside of some *very carefully negotiated and well-documented* BDSM situations, it's pretty hard to make a persuasive case that a sobbing sexual partner who just asked if you will let her live if she lets you fuck her is a meaningfully consenting one. What kind of person thinks, "Well, she'd rather have sex with me than die, so I guess that's enthusiastic consent"? I hope we can all agree—as the jury and at least a decent number of judges in the state of Maryland in 1979 ultimately did (though quite a few judges didn't)—that such a person is someone who is willing to commit a crime. But for that idea to be manifest, we need laws that elucidate the nature of that criminal intent, not merely imply it.

TAKING *MENS REA* SERIOUSLY ISN'T A NEW IDEA

For American legal scholars, the idea of taking *mens rea* more seriously in the sexual assault context seems to be relatively novel. A major exception is an article by Hong (2018), who wrote an in-depth critique of the American Law Institute for failing to significantly alter the MPC's rape provisions, and argued that the same logic of intentionality we apply to homicide should also apply to rape. Hong argues that we need to stop focusing so much on victims' attitudes, beliefs, and behaviors, and focus more on those of defendants. In particular, she notes that we should interpret defendants' state of mind from their overall behavior before, during, and even *after* their encounters. She offers an example of a case where a college football quarterback was acquitted on charges for rape, largely for a lack of evidence that he knew he was having sex with a woman without her consent. In his version of events, he showed up drunk to the room of a woman he had never had sex with before, didn't use a condom during sex, did not believe the woman orgasmed, and immediately left her room after orgasming himself. Despite many texts before this encounter, he never contacted her by phone afterward. Hong describes this man as demonstrating a "callous indifference" (307) toward his partner's enthusiasm and consent to their encounter, arguing that this kind of callous indifference should be criminalized. (Although Hong's article has generated considerable academic interest, most of the attention has focused on its *other* excellent point that US rape laws are excessively punitive compared both to rape laws in other countries and to the nation's own homicide laws.)

It's extremely strange that US legal discourse on rape laws has had so little to say about *mens rea* while most other Anglophone countries have long and argumentative histories about it (Biebel 1995). As previously discussed in chapter 2, UK law has emphasized the importance of intentionality for rape for most of modern history, and most former Commonwealth countries have followed suit. The arguments in these cases have often boiled down to: How do we know what goes on in the mind of the defendant? What constitutes a "reasonable belief" that someone has consented (or not) to sex (Alexander 1995)? If anything, many critics seem to feel that British courts have *over-*emphasized the *mens rea* of rape defendants, and the earlier era of British law that failed to demand a "reasonable" belief that someone had consented to sex clearly created some serious legal problems (Bourke 2007; Alexander 1995). The legal arguments around these cases in the UK should not discourage Americans from changing our own laws; rather, they should serve as cautionary tales about the specific changes we need to make, and a reminder that law and cultural changes must come together. The most important lesson the United States can learn from the UK here is the importance of situating *mens rea* within the larger context of a case and the defendant's behavior, not making it the sole focus.

WHAT ACTS AND STATES OF MIND DO WE ACTUALLY WANT CRIMINALIZED?

These lessons from the UK are an excellent starting point for imagining what sexual violation offenses we want to criminalize. Remember that criminal statutes are usually composed of both an act and a state of mind. Well, it turns out there's not a lot of consistency about either element when it comes to sexual violation laws. For years, as per Blackstone, "rape" was simply "carnal knowledge of a woman forcibly and against her will." I would suggest, gener-ally speaking, that we as a culture have now decided that "sexual violation" is "sustained or attempted genital contact with another person against their will." I think that's an accurate characterization of our cultural approach to understanding sexual violation, and there are problems with it—namely, just like the US construction of the law, it overemphasizes the experiences of the victim with little reference to the intentionality or perspective of the actor/defendant. But the law has generally lagged behind that understanding.

Many states continue to have language in their laws claiming that in order for an act to count as rape, it must include "force or the threat of force" on the part of the defendant. In other words, in many states, if someone screams, "No!" the sex that follows isn't rape unless it's accompanied by force or threats. As if that wasn't limiting enough, the threats can't just be any threat; they must be threats where (predominantly older, white, male) judges find the (almost always female) victim's fear of the threat is reasonably grounded (as previously discussed). Prosecutors also filter out cases based on how believable they find the force or threat of force, meaning that many cases never even get to court. This situation is hardly hypothetical: Indiana changed its rape statutes in 2022 thanks in part to the activism of Stephanie Stewart, who recounted a harrowing tale of being drugged and violated by a salesman who came to her house in 2019. Despite screaming "No!" at this stranger and subsequently subjecting herself to a full rape kit and police investigation, she says the prosecution apologized, admitting in frustration that Indiana's rape laws were so restrictive that without force or the threat of force, they couldn't successfully charge rape in the state. Fed up with the situation, she repeatedly emailed state legislators until they changed the law to make all nonconsensual sex illegal (Kenney 2021).

At present, most laws around the "act" portion of rape and sexual assault include: (1) a sexual act, often (but not always) restricted by the body parts involved (e.g., things like "vaginal intercourse" or "vaginal or anal penetration with a body part or foreign object") and (2) lack of consent, sometimes with explanation of how it might be shown. Additionally, many statutes continue by listing (3) an additional factor, usually something like force or threat of force, the age of the victim, drugging the victim, and/or the victim being unconscious. As discussed previously, there have also been exceptions (that is, it can never be rape or sexual assault) based on marital status. And of course, limitations based on biological sex (namely, having a penis for some things and having a vagina for others), and to a lesser degree gender, persist in many of these statutes.

We should of course consider how the "lack of consent" dimension necessarily brings some element of analyzing the state of mind of the victim into the offense. To be sure, violation is certainly not alone in criminal law doing that: wire fraud, minus fraudulently obtained consent, is simply a wire transfer. Yet—to make the point perhaps somewhat flippantly—those defending people accused of wire fraud (whether in court or in the public sphere) do not get up with a straight face and say, "Well, did you see how that bank account was dressed?" It's true that there are plenty of cases of sexual violation where the victim's demonstration of non/consent might be complicated or question-able—for example, in instances where they consented to sex but not *that sex*, or where they were both drunk and no one said no but no one said yes either. Moreover, we need to come to terms with the idea that someone can legiti-mately and sincerely feel violated—but that doesn't *always* mean someone else is "guilty" of violating them. "I regret having sex with you" is not the same as "you accidentally violated my consent," which is in turn not the same as "you violated my consent and should have known better," which is not the same as "you violated my consent because you get high on power"—and I'm sure we've all encountered people who seem a bit confused on these points. But—*but*—there are plenty of cases where the victims' lack of consent is not really a serious question, and we need to remain cognizant of that fact.

Continuing to hyperfocus on the victim's consent while ignoring the behavior of the defendant in cases where lack of consent is pretty clear is socially problematic, intellectually disingenuous, and legally chaotic. In that sense, cases of clear nonconsent ought to be relatively simple. But the more complicated question is: as a culture, do we want the legal system to take on the responsibility for adjudicating cases of complex consent, or do we want the criminal justice system to stick to the cases where the victim obvi-ously didn't consent? It's clear that not all instances of sexual violation a are good fit for an adversarial criminal legal system and that many need to be addressed in other ways, but we have to decide where we as a society want to draw that line. We also have to think about who we want drawing those lines, given that victims "opt in" to a civil suit but can get opted in by the govern-ment to a criminal case. And we need to think about the impact of having law that says certain clearly bad conduct is not criminal at all, when a lot of people think about sex as if "legal" is the same thing as "okay." (Just think of how some people talk about age of consent.)

There are plenty of cases where we could argue that theft isn't entirely clear either (to continue to be glib, imagine someone claiming, "She handed me the keys to her car! I didn't realize she wanted it back!"). And examples like this for theft illustrate why it's so important to put less emphasis on the victim's precise behaviors (in the instances of either theft or sexual violation) and more emphasis on *what a reasonable person would have understood in the defendant's position.* Yes, handing someone the keys to your car is clearly consent to drive it, but without further negotiation and clarification, it's not consent to drive it indefinitely. Nor is it consent to drive it recklessly, get speeding tickets, or otherwise damage it. And while most of us seem to be in general agreement on these points about cars, we seem to be a lot more hesitant to accept the idea that sexual violations can occur under similar circumstances: "I agreed to go watch a movie at his place, not have sex with him," and "I agreed to have sex with him, not to let him fuck my ass, choke me, and spit on my face." Are there people who probably sincerely confuse these consent dynamics? Yes, just as there are probably people who sincerely believe that permission to drive a car is permission to own it. But do we think their beliefs are *reasonable*? I hope not.

GRADING STATES OF MIND

In sum, someone commits a sexual violation at the point where they've committed a commonly understood sexual act upon another person who does not consent to that act. I think we can all agree that this act itself is a social problem, regardless of any other mitigating circumstances or contextual factors. And we should address it as a social problem, regardless of any of those other factors, devoting more resources than we currently do to training counselors to help *both* survivors and the people who hurt them (especially with the goal of helping those violators not hurt anyone else), as well as providing more institutional support in situations where sexual violations are extremely common (particularly prisons, the military, and universities). However, it's not merely the act, but the state of mind of the violator that should move a situation from "let's address this with counselors and mediators" to "let's take this to court and prosecute it as a crime."

Historically, the idea of intentionality in rape and sexual assault crimes was just kind of assumed. Going back to the MPC's original draft from the 1960s, the broader code had a default state of mind requirement that essentially said if a state of mind was not otherwise specified in a statute, then it should be assumed that in order for a crime to be committed, it must be done purposely, knowingly, or recklessly (basically, "recklessly or above"). Since the MPC never bothered to specify states of mind with regards to rape, that default applied. Thus, whereas homicide statutes are largely graded based on the defendant's state of mind, rape and sexual assault statutes in the United States have been almost entirely graded on the nature of sexual act, age of the victim, and whether violence or coercion were used.

Having a single state of mind for all of rape does not meaningfully divide the crime into degrees of moral culpability. In other words, it does not distinguish at all in terms of punishment or gradation between rape offenses committed *purposefully* ("I set out to do this because I wanted to rape someone"), *knowingly* ("I really wanted to fuck someone, and it doesn't matter to me that I know this person said they do not consent"), or *recklessly* ("all the signs she didn't consent were there, but somehow I missed them"). The space between each of those three seems to me to be an ocean: the law should certainly differentiate between a person who sets out to rape someone and a person whose consent radar is criminally bad. While it's true that the current system allows for taking state of mind into account in assigning punishment, that really seems insufficient for formally clarifying our social position on what the actual underlying crime is. At the end of the day, doesn't it seem like the person who purposefully violates another person's sexual consent (that is, sets out to violate another person's consent because they want to violate that consent) is fundamentally committing a different crime than someone who does the same act because they are criminally reckless about consent?

We can even imagine a case for "sexual violation by negligence," in which, say, a person gives every indication they subjectively thought they were on a date with another person and believed their sexual advances were welcome and enjoyed in spite of plenty of evidence to the contrary. To go back to Hong's (2018) point that a defendant's behavior before, during, and after an encounter are all relevant in determining their state of mind, negligent sexual violation presumably occurs when someone seems to have been trying to be good to the other person but just really missed the message. For example, thanks to the problematic gender norms we've discussed throughout this book, it's depressingly easy to imagine a woman who thinks a guy saying no "doesn't really mean it" and to unintentionally violate his consent (especially if one or both of them is drunk). If she behaves in every other way like she thinks he's having a good time (cuddling him, trying to give him sexual plea-sure, texting him afterward to ask about another date, etc.), we might label such behavior "negligent."

We haven't gotten to a more modern understanding about any of these nuanced issues yet. Even looking to the proposed MPC reform draft we discussed in the previous chapter, sexual assault is still distinguished solely by acts, not states of mind. The current draft differentiates between "sexual assault by physical force" (for which it recommends a prison sentence of ten years) and "sexual assault in the absence of consent" (for which it recom-mends three years), and it uses a "reckless" state of mind for both. But the MPC does the exact opposite for murder: state of mind makes all the differ-ence in gradation. Grading crimes by states of mind makes a lot of sense: we intuitively understand a profound difference in the moral dimension of a person who is texting and accidentally (but recklessly) kills someone with their car and a person who sets out and makes a plan over many months to kill someone. Indeed, we understand that they are quite literally committing a dif-ferent crime. But for rape, even after a long revision process, that understand-ing remains absent. Instead, read most charitably, the "physical force" portion seems to be serving the role that "state of mind" would for most other crimes.

In principle, the traditional gradations for "rape" based on physical violence should basically be irrelevant to the fundamental crime if we rewrote the statutes more logically. Focusing only on legal adults, "sexual violation" could easily stand as its own charge, and depending on the circumstances, other charges—assault, assault with a deadly weapon, drugging another person with criminal intentions, and so on—could be added to it. If someone rapes someone else at gunpoint, the most offensive elements of the crime are that (1) they threatened someone else's life and (2) their actions demonstrate malicious intent to violate consent. Those are actually two separate crimes: "threat with a deadly weapon" and what should be called "sexual violation in the first degree." Likewise, drugging someone to unconsciousness and then forcing sex upon them would get charges for "criminal intoxication with an illegal substance" and "sexual violation in the first degree" (as acquiring and using "date-rape drugs" clearly constitutes premeditation).

To highlight how problematic the current legal construction is, let's consider two hypothetical examples:

> *Situation 1:* Al knows Bob does not want any kind of sexual relationship. Bob says so. Bob has rejected Al's numerous advances and made abundantly clear that Al should back off. Nonetheless, Al engineers a situation in which Bob is not looking in his direction, and he masturbates and ejaculates on Bob, then rushes forward and grabs Bob's genitals while trying to kiss him.

> *Situation 2:* Al and Bob are sharing a hotel room at a convention. Al is asleep and sober, but Bob comes back to the room, wakes Al up, and very obviously drunkenly demands Al fuck him in the ass. Bob has previously rejected Al's advances emphatically and has made abundantly clear that Al should back off. Happy with this apparent change of heart and not asking any questions, Al fucks Bob in the ass, and Bob passes out in the course of the encounter.

Using the current MPC draft, in situation 1 here, Al would be guilty of "offensive sexual contact," with a maximum of a misdemeanor conviction and six months in jail. By contrast, situation 2, given the intoxication and Bob's repeated past refusals, could be charged as "sexual assault of an incapacitated person," which would be a felony with up to ten years in prison. These penalties seem very strangely applied, since most of us would agree that the blatantly nonconsensual sexual behavior in situation 1 seems like a worse offense than having sex with a drunk person who is demanding it in situation 2. Indeed, given that Al was sleeping in situation 2, it seems like he is at least partly a victim himself. But a legal construction that focuses on acts at the expense of intentionality loses all sense of the relative moral repugnance of these situations.

AFFIRMATIVE DEFENSES

Recall from the previous chapter that affirmative defenses are ones that involve the defendant admitting to committing the accused act and having the required state of mind, but offering some argument the law recognizes as removing culpability for it. Traditionally, most rape and sexual assault statutes have functionally included a formal or informal "affirmative defense" of being married to the victim (that is, a husband could not be found guilty of raping his wife). In general, affirmative defenses in these situations are a solid way to make sure new statutes don't end up criminalizing behavior we don't want to be criminal. For example, the MPC proposal's draft is an impressively rare example of an attempt to functionally formalize BDSM norms and practices in a legal statute through affirmative defense. The current draft says that consent is a complete affirmative defense, so long as it "identif[ies] the specific forms and extent of force, restraint, or threats that are permitted." Translated into laymen's terms, it functionally says, "It's fine to choke your partner or stick a knife to their throat while you have sex with them, as long as they obviously agreed to that, even though those things would result in much more serious charges if the activity weren't consensual."

Affirmative defenses could also be helpful in cases of extreme intoxication. We could imagine an affirmative defense like "mutual intoxication and incapacity" to address potential sexual violations that occurred when both people were not in a position to ensure good consent hygiene (or at least to encourage those cases be addressed outside the criminal law system). Obviously, such a defense would need limits, such as requiring that both people had similar levels of intoxication, and one person didn't plan to get both people drunk for the purpose of nonconsensual sex. Moreover, we can continue to draw on the idea that behavior before, during, and after an encounter could be evidence of intentionality under these circumstances (Hong 2018), since presumably a person who intended to get someone illicitly intoxicated would behave differently than a person who ended up getting drunk with someone else and practicing less-than-ideal consent hygiene. It would be extremely counterproductive to criminalize what is functionally normal behavior (i.e., getting drunk and having sex), because the whole point of crime is supposed to be calling out and penalizing nonnormative behavior that is harmful to society. Even though we might ideally want to discourage drunken sex in order to facilitate better overall consent hygiene, the law (or, at the least, criminal law) is not the best means to do that.

OTHER CONSIDERATIONS

The traditional construction of most rape statutes has prioritized puritanical ideas of chastity over actual physical risk, and thus tended to make penis-in-vagina sex the most egregious offense when grading rape laws. If we're going to grade sexual violation laws by physical acts (and I can see good arguments on both sides for doing so or not doing so), we should do so based on physical risks, not standards of sexual purity. For years, the laws in many states have taken the perspective that a nonconsensual penis in a vagina is rape, but a nonconsensual broken bottle shoved up someone's ass isn't. Both potentially pose pretty serious risks to someone (pregnancy and STIs versus serious injury), and trying to weigh the relative risks there is probably not helpful. But surely most of us in this day and age recognize that there are far greater physical risks associated with penis-in-vagina and penis-in-anus sex without a condom than from either act with a condom, or from forcing someone to receive cunnilingus. Indeed, in some countries like Germany and the United Kingdom, removing a condom without consent during an otherwise consensual sexual encounter (popularly known as "stealthing") is a crime; in the state of California, it's a civil offense. Note that the intentionality in stealthing is part of what makes it so repellent: it demonstrates a gross disregard for a partner's consent and potentially their health and well-being. (In the real world, stealthing can make for some messy cases because it can sometimes be very hard to prove the difference between an accidentally broken condom and an intentional stealth maneuver, but the hypothetical remains important.) These added elements of risk might simply constitute "assault" or aggravating factors in determining someone's level of guilty mind. Regardless, if sexual violation statutes are graded by act, it should be based on a combination of intentionality and risk rather than puritanical ideas of offensiveness.

In addition to guiding principles about intention and risk, it is essential that we make modern sexual violation statutes more gender neutral. While I generally prefer language such as "sustained or attempted genital contact," I do understand the desire to include more traditional language about "penetration" (with additional mentions of oral sex) as a way to clearly distinguish between sex acts and casual grabbing. If statutes include language about penetration, they *also* need to include language about "forced to penetrate" so we can show that the law takes *everyone's* consent seriously.

Since we're a long way from a world where we've gotten rid of our old cultural ideas about rape, any jurisdiction that tries to implement these legal changes in their statutes would need to include what are called "model jury instructions." These are instructions a judge gives a jury before they deliberate to make sure they correctly understand the law they're trying to decide some-one's guilt about. These instructions might look something like: "I also want to advise you on how to think about the charges you have been asked to decide on. In [State], there is no crime specifically called 'rape.' Instead, the set of acts that you might call 'rape' in an everyday sense are made illegal under the heading of [whatever the state uses for violation offenses], along with a set of things you might not call 'rape.' You should draw no particular inference from the name given to the charges." (Instructions like these might also be helpful in states that have "sexual assault" without "rape").

WIDER SOCIAL EFFECTS

On the one hand, what I have proposed here is mostly a codification of more modern ideas about sexual morality. Our laws seem to be wildly out of sync with contemporary beliefs about sexual consent and respect for people's bod-ies. When laws don't reflect morals, people tend to lose faith in the laws in general and also to experience greater anxiety and less social trust overall. Changing laws to reflect changing values is normal and necessary in any progressive society. We're a long way from a time when most sex occurred in the context of marriage or prostitution, and our social conceptualization of rape has evolved away from that—but our legal conceptualization remains bounded by this much older historical context. I think it's relatively easy to agree that we need major new changes, but, as the American Legal Institute's years-long struggle to change the MPC for sexual assault suggests, it can be very difficult to decide what exactly those changes should be.

On the other hand, I am proposing legal shifts with the explicit inten-tion of trying to modify general social understanding and perception. By philosophical principle and design, the law is never intended to be anyone's moral compass to guide right and wrong actions; rather, the law is supposed to reflect and codify some subset of generally held, preexisting moral ideas. However, in practice, the law and morality in a highly literate society tend to be in a rather circular relationship, with morality shaping law, and law in turn shaping morality. Especially as society becomes less and less religious, legal authority's ideas about right and wrong have more and more sway. We might not love the idea that the law affects how people understand moral action, but the simple fact is that it often does. So having laws that explicitly say, "It's more of a crime to intentionally go out and violate someone's sexual consent than it is to do so accidentally; it's actually a crime to force someone to penetrate you; and the crime of sexual violation is independent from the amount of physical harm caused to a person" might usefully inform and shape people's moral understandings of these dynamics.

If we look back at the social history of crimes like sexual harassment and stalking, these weren't even really terms in common use until the 1980s. It took a lot of activism to convince people that these things were actually problems, but activists persuading legislators that these things were criminal acts still made a huge difference in how we came to understand and perceive them (Spohn and Horney 2013). As it stands, I think most people have a confusing mish-mashed idea of "violent rape," "acquaintance rape," "date rape," and "sexual assault" being wrong. Our laws lack cohesion, with some state statutes having been repeatedly modified and going on for pages, and our common vocabulary is similarly confused. Rather than constantly trying to shove more acts and experiences under the heading of "rape," why don't we just do away with that altogether and look for the thing that all those offenses have in common: sexual violation?

The law is a system by which governments and people resolve legal claims, but it is also a symbolic marker for the way we as a society understand certain acts. When we punish criminals together, we engage in social acts of condemnation against both an individual and their actions: we announce publicly, "This behavior is wrong." As a society we've said, "Rape is bad" for a very long time (although "rape" meant only physically violent sex procured by force with a woman who wasn't a man's wife). But our system has been very weak in enforcing that claim—so weak that many people seem to have just given up on the idea that the system is likely to do anything about their experiences as survivors of sexual violation. Part of why that enforcement has been so weak is that practically and conceptually, we've done a *terrible* job at defining what "rape" is. I hope the information in this book as a whole, and this chapter in particular, has provided guidance for better conceptualizing "the problem formerly known as 'rape,'" which perhaps we will start calling "sexual violation." Obviously, laws change only with activism, and I hope I have inspired some activists to demand legal change, and possibly to change the way they themselves talk about and understand this issue.

Conclusion

Don't Settle for Simple Solutions

CHANGING THE LAW IS NECESSARY,
BUT NOT SUFFICIENT

Sexual violation is an incredibly complex problem, and as with so many social problems, most of us instinctively want to believe there's one magic solution that will somehow take care of the whole issue. This desire for simplicity helps breed misguided campaigns telling men, "Don't rape!"—as if most men were intentionally violating consent and just needed a public service announcement to remind them they weren't supposed to do that. Of course, the naivete of that kind of campaign is also shaped by our cultural and legal failure to distinguish between intentional, knowing, reckless, and negligent acts of sexual violation.

I've spent a lot of time talking about the law here, and I wouldn't want anyone to walk away from this book with the impression that I think changing the law is all we need to do to fix the problem of sexual violation. I definitely hope the law changes, but my larger goal in encouraging that change is to reinforce different social perspectives and shift the broader cultural discourse, not to treat changing the law as the sole end in itself. I have very conflicted opinions about the idea of securing more convictions in an adversarial criminal justice system, with prison penalties for sexual violations. The adversarial criminal justice system seems to mostly be a grim place for victims; meanwhile, prisons themselves are one of the grimmest hotbeds of sexual violation, so it's hard to justify the idea of reducing sexual violation overall by locking more people in them. I think the overall shape and scope of our legal system needs to change, with more focus on ideals of restorative justice, victim advocacy, legitimate concern for the humanity of criminals themselves, stopping cycles of violence, and the well-being of communities. As important as these goals are, I want to emphasize my strong belief that all those goals are more achievable if we rewrite our laws on rape and sexual assault than if we leave them as they are.

I think it's extremely problematic, both practically and symbolically, for society to leave so many sexual violators unaddressed (which may or may not involve "punishment"). Most of our evidence suggests that a substantial percentage of all sexual violations of women are caused by a much smaller percentage of men repeatedly offending. One way or another, practically speaking, we need some sort of intervention to stop these repeat offenders—perhaps those are therapeutic interventions, and perhaps they are incapacitating and/or punitive interventions. Without solid institutional management, we're currently depending on untrained and unmanaged social networks to take on a lot of the burden of managing problems that are better suited to professionals. But it's also important symbolically for society to demonstrate collectively that we take this issue seriously, both to generally prevent the crime from happening in the first place and to show we value sexual rights and well-being.

WE NEED TO MAKE A COLLECTIVE DECISION ABOUT GENDER AND THE FOUNDATIONS OF CONSENT

As mentioned briefly in chapter 3, I think many of our social and legal struggles around consent and sexual violation come down to arguments about whether we think all sex is rape unless someone provides consent, or whether we think all sex is consensual unless someone objects. To a large degree, there simply is no criminal parallel to sexual violation. We do not, for example, assume all slapping and choking is BDSM unless someone objects—we assume it's assault without explicit and direct consent. Nor do we assume that, say, inviting someone into your house for a glass of water constitutes permission for them to take your television with them—we generally assume it's theft without explicit and direct consent. But the complication here is that we generally start with a base assumption that most people don't want to be hit or choked, and most people want to keep their belongings—and that most men want to have sex all the time, most women want to have sex some of the time, and neither particularly wants to admit it. We have no other violent crimes that are "fun except when they're crimes." (Indeed, BDSM and sports like boxing are exactly the opposite, being "crimes except when they're fun.") So we don't have an easy reference point for saying, "Sexual violation is like this thing over here."

I don't have an easy solution to this puzzle. To some degree, it just feels like a philosophical quandary, but since it's the foundation of law and policy, it's really much more than that. This quandary is the logical basis for determining whether the best foundation for legal and institutional approaches to determining who is guilty of committing sexual violations is "affirmative consent" (meaning it's a problem unless someone demonstrates clear consent) or "negative consent" (meaning it's only a problem if someone demonstrates nonconsent or can't consent). I generally tend to think that sexual violation *mostly* only belongs in the criminal legal system when someone has explicitly said no, has been rendered incapable of doing so, has been taken by surprise, or is in a situation with fundamental power imbalances—but it's still a problem when someone doesn't give active and voluntary consent to what's happening to them. That is, the legal standard should probably be negative consent, but the social standard should be affirmative consent. (This logic returns us to the same basis as the legal limits for drunk driving, which are far beyond where we actually want people to get behind the wheel of the car, but we encourage people to socially pressure one another not to drive well before that point.)

We need to make a collective social choice about which of those standards we want to employ and under what conditions, and then we need to apply it regardless of gender. It just doesn't work (and isn't fair) to operate with separate consent standards for men and women—socially or legally. Actual gender equality in the context of sexual consent would mean that women have to take real responsibility in sexual situations for ensuring the other person's consent and not take men's desire for sex for granted. It would mean that men are allowed to be really upset when their bodies and consent are violated. It would mean that everyone has to be conscious of their consent hygiene—both in terms of protecting their own bodies and interests to the degree they feel they need to *and* in terms of protecting others.' It would mean that if a man and a woman are both consensually drunk, and they have sex she didn't want but never overtly objected to, it's not automatically his "fault."

Our assumptions about equal responsibility and vulnerability have to extend beyond ideas about gender in heterosexual interactions. Even gay men seem to (incorrectly) assume that being penetrated makes someone more vulnerable and often imagine that men who top don't become victims of rape (Meyer 2022). Sexual roles don't really provide much protection in the end because power is much more complicated than who penetrates whom. But the cultural belief in the power and protective benefits of penetration remains strong. We need to establish consistent cultural and legal standards of responsibility for sexual violation that apply to everyone—and stay cognizant that anyone's consent can be violated—regardless of genitalia, sexual role, or gender.

MOST OF US WILL NEVER SIT ON A
JURY FOR A SEXUAL CRIME

No matter what criminal justice reforms we make, most of us will never sit on a jury for a sexual crime—and that's okay, because that wouldn't be a good distribution of our social resources in terms of people, time, or money. But due to the present state of social confusion around sexual norms in general, I think we're going to be left with a world where sexual violations remain common for the indefinite future. Developing very good consent hygiene is a learning process, and it's a learning process we've mostly left young people to muddle through on their own with little guidance from their elders. And even if we improved our guidance, we'd still have to change norms that expect so much sexual activity to occur while intoxicated. So what do we do about all these violations in the land of sexual confusion?

Instead of sitting in a courtroom, advised by a judge, we're far more likely to find ourselves in situations where we're judging the actions of friends, lovers, strangers, and ourselves in informal conversations. Our responses in these everyday situations can make a world of difference in how our society comes to treat sexual violation. For example, I used to have conversations with friends that went something like this all too often:

Friend: I was raped last week.

Me: I'm so sorry that happened to you! Do you want to tell me more about what happened?

Friend: [Relays a story in the context of broader physical intimacy in which a sexual experience occurred that they didn't want, which someone hadn't explicitly asked them permission for, and which they didn't try to stop]

When those types of encounters occur, most survivors seem to respond with a mixture of depression, guilt (because they never tried to stop it), and anger (at the other person for not asking and/or for not reading their signals correctly). I was young and inexperienced myself when I had most of those conversations, and what I *wish* I had said in response was, "Unfortunately, it's normal to freeze up in those kinds of situations and not say the things you wished you'd said. That's just the way many people respond in unexpected situations like that. Let's get you in touch with a therapist, and see if they can help you work through your own feelings and how you want to manage things with the other person." Alas, being young and inexperienced, I'm pretty sure what I actually said was exactly the wrong thing: "Is it really helpful to call that 'rape'?"

Those conversations from my youth have haunted me well into my middle age for so many reasons. For starters, I wish I'd been a more helpful friend.

Lacking support after a sexual violation makes someone much more likely to be traumatized by the experience (DeKeseredy et al. 2019), and I hate feeling like I may have contributed to those traumatic cycles. But I also recognize that my failure to be supportive was due to other massive institutional failures: as discussed earlier, I went to a high school where my sex education classes began with our teacher announcing she was still a virgin and encouraging us to remain abstinent until marriage. I researched contraception on the internet myself, but I never got around to researching empathy until I was much older.

Another reason those conversations haunt me is because, like Sanyal (2018) and Hirsch and Khan (2020), I'm appalled and frustrated that Western cultures spend so little time teaching young people how to say no to sex they don't want, in spite of considerable evidence that doing so *massively* reduces their chances of being sexually violated. If we think about sexual violation as a public health problem, that's like society refusing to vaccinate teenagers against a very serious illness that could easily plague them for the rest of their lives—it is, in short, a grim waste of young lives and opportunities. And this resistance to better education is buffeted in part by our misguided belief that *all* "rapes" are intentionally committed by bad people instead of understanding that *many* "rapes" are actually committed by ignorant, intoxicated, and/or naive people who really didn't understand what they were doing or what was happening. Using a single word and a single concept to describe both of those things obfuscates the fact that those are almost certainly two fundamentally different problems with fundamentally different solutions. Presumably the kind of violator who is a genuinely bad person is either actively excited by or really doesn't care about violating someone's else's consent, while the other type of person never wanted to hurt anyone and would be horrified to know they had done so.

And that is the third reason those conversations haunt me: because I think I was technically correct in saying that framing those experiences as "rape" was unhelpful in the broader context of personal narratives and social experiences (but that was hardly the moment to be mentioning it). These were sexual violations, to be sure, but these particular stories were exactly the same kinds of collegiate violations that Grigoriardis (2017) profiled in her book *Blurred Lines*, lacking the intentional malice or even reckless disregard for consent that the concept of "rape" usually implies in our culture. Grigoriardis admits that she was surprised to find in her interviews with college men who had been officially reprimanded by their universities for sexual assault that the majority were lacking malice or reckless disregard (but of course, college sexual violations may or may not be representative of the problem as a larger whole). We need more words and better concepts for framing these types of experiences. As a culture, we seem to really struggle with the idea that bad things can happen to people without it being anyone's "fault." This concept applies as much to sexual encounters as it does to more mundane interactions like tripping over someone and breaking your leg. In either case, it's possible for someone to be really hurt without someone else being totally responsible for that hurt. In the case of sexual violations, survivors often blame themselves for what happened to them, which is terrible. But *sometimes* it's no one's fault they got hurt—theirs or the other person's.

Even more confusing, we may have to acknowledge that people who feel the worst about being assaulted sometimes really do have the least "criminal" experiences, because not saying no when you felt like you should have can make you feel *especially* traumatized. Again, if we try to get past a judge-and-jury perspective, where everything about consent is viewed through a cultural lens of criminal justice, we can simply provide sympathy for someone who experienced a terrible but incredibly common experience without having to blame anyone or cast aspersions. It's normal to freeze in certain sexual situations. It's normal to occasionally make bad choices. It's normal to fail to speak up for yourself just because you're afraid of the social consequences or hurting someone's feelings or looking foolish. We can validate someone's distress in those experiences without having to turn it into a criminal case and without "blaming the victim." We may not sit as a jury in a box, but we often sit as a jury in a living room, and we have not been given good model instructions from a judge. We need a social vocabulary to support one another without necessarily being immediately asked to blame someone, but we also need to be able to gauge the types of offenses that probably warrant a phone call to authorities. We haven't prepared most eighteen-year-olds well to handle these types of situations (and they're one of the most at-risk age groups), and we also don't give them much in the way of direct assistance from their elders. We do a lot of work to teach them to drive responsibly before they get behind the wheel of a car alone, but we do next to nothing to teach them how to fuck responsibly. We should do both.

BAND-AID SOLUTIONS

The term "Band-Aid solution" carries a very pejorative connotation of being something done to inadequately and very temporarily handle a serious problem that needs much greater attention. But what many people often forget is that Band-Aids can still help *a little*, even if they don't help a lot. In the case of sexual violation, there's no single solution—large or small—that's going to fix everything, at once or even over time. Throughout this book, we've mostly focused on big, longer-term solutions like rethinking heterosexual dating norms, demanding that major institutions adopt more realistic attitudes and advice about sex, adopting a more relativistic approach to understanding consent, creating a culture where it's normal and accepted to talk about sex, changing our thinking about men's experiences of consent, and changing the law. There's no world where we snap our fingers and just magically manifest those kinds of massive social changes. But while we work toward those long-term goals, there are some short-term things we as a society can do to lessen the problems.

The first is to make sure that young people have easy access to good sex education online. If institutions and families and peers all fail, most young people can still find their way to the internet eventually. I'd love to see a "how to say no" campaign online that teaches young people how to say no to sex—without being abstinence-based and without blaming the victim. It can be hard to say no to lots of things people want from us, and we need education in how to do it.

The second, relatedly, is to encourage young people on the internet to start coming up with sexier and more creative ways to say yes. Currently, the most popular strict verbal affirmative consent model doesn't integrate well into conventional dating scripts for straight people or gay men. So in addition to a "how to say no" campaign, we also need a campaign that helps young people learn how to say yes—especially when intoxicated.

The third, very different solution is potentially to demand more creativity from prosecutors. While sexual assault laws remain horribly outdated in many states, there's no good reason why motivated prosecutors can't charge violators with other, related crimes, such as assault, aggravated assault, unlawful intoxication, and a host of other offenses to ensure perpetrators don't just get away entirely. Prosecutors have historically been hesitant to pursue sexually assault cases vigorously because they're so afraid they'll lose. But very tentative analyses from the UK suggest that juries are much more eager to convict sexual violators in the post-#MeToo world than they were in the past (Thomas 2023).

The fourth, possibly counterintuitively, is to stop putting so much emphasis on statistics about the low conviction rates for sexual assault, which are basically made-up numbers. Especially if we narrow our focus to sexual assaults reported to the police, there just isn't much evidence to support the idea that conviction rates for sexual assault are much worse than they are for most violent crimes—and that should be our cultural headline. Moreover, the belief in these low conviction rates is one of many factors that discourages victims from reporting to the police, which just ends up reinforcing the idea that the criminal justice system doesn't do much about sexual violation.

I'm sure this isn't a comprehensive list of quick solutions, and I hope you have gotten your own inspiration from reading this book. This book was intended as a self-help book for society, but since we all live in society, there are things we can all do to help, and I want people who feel very motivated to have a list of things they could do *right now*.

IN AN IDEAL WORLD . . .

I think perhaps the greatest challenge we face in trying to address the problem of sexual violation is that we lack a common vision for what "solving" this problem would look like. Of course, in an ideal world, no one would ever experience any type of sexual violation, just like no one would ever experience a car wreck. But neither one is likely to happen in a world where people have sex for pleasure and drive often. However, in both cases, there are things that both society can do (e.g., encourage more helpful dating norms to prevent sexual assault; build safer and better roads and intersections to prevent wrecks) and things individuals can do (e.g., take classes on improving consent practices; take classes on defensive driving).

Culturally speaking, before we can ever hope to "solve" the problem of sexual violation, we first have to define it. I hope this book has given you some ideas about how to do that more precisely. It's impossible to solve a social problem when everyone has a different personal definition of the problem. By focusing on issues of intentionality and consent violation, we can come much closer to the heart of what we're trying to get at with so many other terms like "date rape" and "sexual assault."

Our ideal-real-world solutions for sexual violation also have to take into account all the complexities of gender, youth, and alcohol we discussed throughout this book. Drunk people aren't great at managing consent on either side, and people who are drunk and high seem to be especially bad at it. We can yell at young people until we're blue in the face to try to limit their sexual exploration to sober experiences, but there's little cross-cultural evidence they'll listen. I think many people drink to have sex because it's fun for them, many people do it because it's the only way they know to get laid, and many people do it because that's just what's expected of them. Right now, the consequences of drunk sex just don't feel the same for women and men. I hear lots of people complain that men can get drunk without being sexually assaulted, and women deserve the same basic right. But it's more accurate to say that men get drunk without *the fear of being sexually assaulted* than it is to say they get drunk without being sexually assaulted, because men experience sexual violations from both women and men pretty regularly. Human communication in general is an extremely imperfect thing and worse when the people attempting to communicate are intoxicated; the fact that so much of our already fraught sexual communication occurs while intoxicated just makes it that much harder. And trying to make open sexual communication happen without real gender equality just adds a whole other layer of complexity.

So given the challenges of gender, intoxication, nebulous sexual and dating norms, and all the rest, what are we left with? I suggest that rather than specifically working toward an unattainable goal of eliminating sexual violation, let's instead work toward a sexual social climate where people don't feel pressured to say yes *or* no to sex and where the social and personal consequences of having mediocre sex are very low for everyone (as they presently appear to be for men). If we could achieve that enormous goal, I think we would have eliminated a sizable chunk of our sexual violations against adults, and then we can figure out what to do about what's left.

In the meantime, let's all go talk to our friends and children about improving consent hygiene . . . and go change some very outdated laws.

Bibliography

Alexander, Dolly F. 1995. "Twenty Years of Morgan: A Criticism of the Subjectivist View of Mens Rea and Rape in Great Britain." *Pace International Law Review* 7, no. 1: 207. https://doi.org/10.58948/2331-3536.1301.

Alexander, Michelle. 2010. *The New Jim Crow: Mass Incarceration in the Age of Colorblindness*. New York: New Press.

Allison, Rachel, and Barbara J. Risman. 2013. "A Double Standard for 'Hooking up': How Far Have We Come toward Gender Equality?" *Social Science Research* 42, no. 5: 1191–1206. https://doi.org/10.1016/j.ssresearch.2013.04.006.

American Law Institute. 1985. *Model Penal Code: Official Draft and Explanatory Notes: Complete Text of Model Penal Code as Adopted at the 1962 Annual Meeting of the American Law Institute at Washington, D.C., May 24, 1962*. Philadelphia: American Law Institute.

———. 2023. "Model Penal Code: Sexual Assault and Related Offenses." https://www.ali.org/projects/show/sexual-assault-and-related-offenses/.

Amnesty International. 2019. "Nordic Countries Do Not Define Rape on the Basis of Lack of Consent." April 3. https://www.amnesty.org/en/latest/press-release/2019/04/rape-and-sexual-violence-in-nordic-countries-consent-laws/.

———. 2020. "Sex without Consent Is Rape. It's That Straightforward." December 17. https://www.amnesty.org/en/latest/campaigns/2020/12/consent-based-rape-laws-in-europe/.

Anderson, Michelle J. 2002. "Marital Immunity, Intimate Relationships, and Improper Inferences: A New Law on Sexual Offenses by Intimates." *Hastings Law Journal* 54: 1465.

Anderson, RaeAnn E., Erica L. Goodman, and Sidney S. Thimm. 2020. "The Assessment of Forced Penetration: A Necessary and Further Step toward Understanding Men's Sexual Victimization and Women's Perpetration." *Journal of Contemporary Criminal Justice* 36, no. 4: 480–98. https://doi.org/10.1177/1043986220936108.

Annor, Francis B., Heather B. Clayton, Leah K. Gilbert, Asha Z. Ivey-Stephenson, Shalon M. Irving, Corinne David-Ferdon, and Laura K. Kann. 2018. "Sexual Orientation Discordance and Nonfatal Suicidal Behaviors in US High School

Students." *American Journal of Preventive Medicine* 54, no. 4: 530–38. https://doi
.org/10.1016/j.amepre.2018.01.013.

Anthony Jr., Marshall, Andrew Howard Nichols, and Wil Del Pilar. 2021. "Raising
Undergraduate Degree Attainment among Black Women and Men Takes on New
Urgency Amid the Pandemic." Education Trust, May 13. https://edtrust.org/
resource/national-and-state-degree-attainment-for-black-women-and-men/.

Armstrong, Elizabeth A., Paula England, and Alison C. K. Fogarty. 2012.
"Accounting for Women's Orgasm and Sexual Enjoyment in College Hookups and
Relationships." *American Sociological Review* 77, no. 3: 435–62. https://doi.org/10
.1177/0003122412445802.

Barber, Jill. 1993. "'Stolen Goods': The Sexual Harassment of Female Servants in
West Wales during the Nineteenth Century." *Rural History* 4, no. 2: 123–36. https:
//doi.org/10.1017/S095679330000025X.

Bauer, Greta R., Corey Flanders, Melissa A. MacLeod, and Lori E. Ross. 2016.
"Occurrence of Multiple Mental Health or Substance Use Outcomes among
Bisexuals: A Respondent-Driven Sampling Study." *BMC Public Health* 16, no.
1: 497. https://doi.org/10.1186/s12889-016-3173-z.

Baughman, Shima. 2020. "How Effective Are Police? The Problem of Clearance
Rates and Criminal Accountability." *Alabama Law Review* 72: 47–113. http://doi
.org/10.2139/ssrn.3566383.

Beck, Allen. 2018. "Race and Ethnicity of Violent Crime Offenders and Arrestees,
2018." US Department of Justice Statistical Brief. https://bjs.ojp.gov/content/pub/
pdf/revcoa18.pdf.

Beck, Allen, David Cantor, John Hartge, and Tim Smith. 2013. "Sexual Victimization
in Juvenile Facilities Reported by Youth, 2012." Bureau of Justice Systems Report.
https://bjs.ojp.gov/library/publications/sexual-victimization-juvenile-facilities
-reported-youth-2008-09.

Bender, Annah K., and Janet L. Lauritsen. 2021. "Violent Victimization among
Lesbian, Gay, and Bisexual Populations in the United States: Findings from the
National Crime Victimization Survey, 2017–2018." *American Journal of Public
Health* 111, no. 2: 318–26. https://doi.org/10.2105/AJPH.2020.306017.

Beres, Melanie A. 2022. "From Ignorance to Knowledge: Sexual Consent and Queer
Stories." *Feminism and Psychology* 32, no. 2: 137–55. https://doi.org/10.1177
/09593535211059003.

Bevacqua, Maria. 2000. *Rape on the Public Agenda: Feminism and the Politics of
Sexual Assault*. Boston: Northeastern University Press.

Biebel, John H. 1995. "I Thought She Said Yes: Sexual Assault in England and
America." *Suffolk Transnational Law Review* 19, no. 1: 153–84.

Bjarnason, Thoroddur. 2009. "Anomie among European Adolescents: Conceptual
and Empirical Clarification of a Multilevel Sociological Concept 1." *Sociological
Forum* 24: 135–61. https://doi.org/10.1111/j.1573-7861.2008.01089.x.

Bleakley, Amy, Atika Khurana, Michael Hennessy, and Morgan Ellithorpe. 2018.
"How Patterns of Learning about Sexual Information among Adolescents Are
Related to Sexual Behaviors." *Perspectives on Sexual and Reproductive Health* 50,
no. 1: 15–23. https://doi.org/10.1363/psrh.12053.

Block, Mary R. 2009. "Rape Law in 19th-Century America: Some Thoughts and Reflections on the State of the Field." *History Compass* 7, no. 5: 1391–99. https://doi.org/10.1111/j.1478-0542.2009.00623.x.

Bourke, Joanna. 2007. "Rape: Sex, Violence, History." In *Rape: Sex, Violence, History*. Berkeley, CA: Counterpoint.

Brooks-Hay, Oona. 2020. "Doing the 'Right Thing'? Understanding Why Rape Victim-Survivors Report to the Police." *Feminist Criminology* 15, no. 2: 174–95. https://doi.org/10.1177/1557085119859079.

Burgin, Rachael. 2019. "Persistent Narratives of Force and Resistance: Affirmative Consent as Law Reform." *British Journal of Criminology* 59, no. 2: 296–314. https://doi.org/10.1093/bjc/azy043.

Burns, Courtney Julia, and Laura Sinko. 2023. "Restorative Justice for Survivors of Sexual Violence Experienced in Adulthood: A Scoping Review." *Trauma, Violence, and Abuse* 24, no. 2: 340–54. https://doi.org/10.1177/15248380211029408.

Burton, Olivia, Patrick Rawstorne, Lucy Watchirs-Smith, Sally Nathan, and Allison Carter. 2023. "Teaching Sexual Consent to Young People in Education Settings: A Narrative Systematic Review." *Sex Education* 23, no. 1: 18–34. https://doi.org/10.1080/14681811.2021.2018676.

Campbell, Bradley A., Tasha A. Menaker, and William R. King. 2015. "The Determination of Victim Credibility by Adult and Juvenile Sexual Assault Investigators." *Journal of Criminal Justice* 43, no. 1: 29–39. https://doi.org/10.1016/j.jcrimjus.2014.12.001.

Campbell, Rebecca, Debra Patterson, and Deborah Bybee. 2012. "Prosecution of Adult Sexual Assault Cases: A Longitudinal Analysis of the Impact of a Sexual Assault Nurse Examiner Program." *Violence against Women* 18, no. 2: 223–44. https://doi.org/10.1177/1077801212440158.

Carlström, Charlotta. 2017. "Gender Equal BDSM Practice—A Swedish Paradox?" *Psychology and Sexuality* 8, no. 4: 268–79. https://doi.org/10.1080/19419899.2017.1383302.

Carroll v. Trump. 20-cv-7311 (SDNY 2020).

Carson, E Ann. 2021. "Prisoners in 2021, Statistical Tables." Report NCJ 305125 for US Department of Justice. https://bjs.ojp.gov/sites/g/files/xyckuh236/files/media/document/p21st.pdf.

Castle Rock v. Gonzales. 545 US 748 (2005).

Census Bureau. 2021. "Quickfacts." Accessed July 3, 2023. https://www.census.gov/quickfacts/.

Centers for Disease Control and Prevention. 2022a. "Fast Facts: Preventing Child Sexual Abuse." April 6. https://www.cdc.gov/violenceprevention/childsexualabuse/fastfact.html.

———. 2022b. "Fast Facts: Preventing Sexual Violence." June 22. https://www.cdc.gov/violenceprevention/sexualviolence/fastfact.html.

Colon, Katy M., Philip R. Kavanaugh, Don Hummer, and Eileen M. Ahlin. 2018. "The Impact of Race and Extra-Legal Factors in Charging Defendants with Serious Sexual Assault: Findings from a Five-Year Study of One Pennsylvania Court

Jurisdiction." *Journal of Ethnicity in Criminal Justice* 16, no. 2: 99–116. https://doi.org/10.1080/15377938.2018.1439791.

Conley, Terri D., Amy C. Moors, Jes L. Matsick, Ali Ziegler, and Brandon A. Valentine. 2011. "Women, Men, and the Bedroom: Methodological and Conceptual Insights That Narrow, Reframe, and Eliminate Gender Differences in Sexuality." *Current Directions in Psychological Science* 20, no. 5: 296–300. https://doi.org/10.1177/096372141141846.

Corrigan, Rose. 2013. "The New Trial by Ordeal: Rape Kits, Police Practices, and the Unintended Effects of Policy Innovation." *Law and Social Inquiry* 38, no. 4: 920–49. https://doi.org/10.1111/lsi.12002.

Cossins, Anne. 2020. *Closing the Justice Gap for Adult and Child Sexual Assault: Rethinking the Adversarial Trial*. London: Palgrave Macmillan UK.

Coulter, Robert W. S., Christina Mair, Elizabeth Miller, John R. Blosnich, Derrick D. Matthews, and Heather L. McCauley. 2017. "Prevalence of Past-Year Sexual Assault Victimization Among Undergraduate Students: Exploring Differences by and Intersections of Gender Identity, Sexual Identity, and Race/Ethnicity." *Prevention Science* 18, no. 6: 726–36. https://doi.org/10.1007/s11121-017-0762-8.

Cowley, Amanda D. 2014. "'Let's Get Drunk and Have Sex': The Complex Relationship of Alcohol, Gender, and Sexual Victimization." *Journal of Interpersonal Violence* 29, no. 7: 1258–78. https://doi.org/10.1177/0886260513506289.

Crenshaw, Kimberlé. 1989. "Demarginalizing the Intersection of Race and Sex: A Black Feminist Critique of Antidiscrimination Doctrine, Feminist Theory and Antiracist Politics." *University of Chicago Legal Forum* 1: 139–67.

D'Alessio, Stewart J., and Lisa Stolzenberg. 2003. "Race and the Probability of Arrest." *Social Forces* 81, no. 4: 1381–97. https://doi.org/10.1353/sof.2003.0051.

Daly, Kathleen. 2022. *Remaking Justice after Sexual Violence*. The Hague: Boom Eleven.

Daly, Kathleen, and Brigitte Bouhours. 2010. "Rape and Attrition in the Legal Process: A Comparative Analysis of Five Countries." *Crime and Justice* 39 (January): 565–650. https://doi.org/10.1086/653101.

Davies, Michelle, and Paul Rogers. 2006. "Perceptions of Male Victims in Depicted Sexual Assaults: A Review of the Literature." *Aggression and Violent Behavior* 11, no. 4: 367–77. https://doi.org/10.1016/j.avb.2006.01.002.

Davies, Michelle, Paul Rogers, and Lisa Whitelegg. 2009. "Effects of Victim Gender, Victim Sexual Orientation, Victim Response and Respondent Gender on Judgements of Blame in a Hypothetical Adolescent Rape." *Legal and Criminological Psychology* 14, no. 2: 331–38. https://doi.org/10.1348/978185408X386030.

DeKeseredy, Walter S., Martin D. Schwartz, James Nolan, Nicholas Mastron, and Amanda Hall-Sanchez. 2019. "Polyvictimization and the Continuum of Sexual Abuse at a College Campus: Does Negative Peer Support Increase the Likelihood of Multiple Victimizations?" *British Journal of Criminology* 59, no. 2: 276–95. https://doi.org/10.1093/bjc/azy036.

Denno, Deborah W. 2003. "Why the Model Penal Code's Sexual Offense Provisions Should Be Pulled and Replaced." *Ohio State Journal of Criminal Law* 1: 207. http://doi.org/10.2139/ssrn.467965.

Department of Justice Canada. 2022. "Government of Canada Acts Quickly to Address Extreme Intoxication with Proposed Changes to the Criminal Code." News release, June 17. https://www.canada.ca/en/department-justice/news/2022 /06/government-of-canada-acts-quickly-to-address-extreme-intoxication-with -proposed-changes-to-the-criminal-code.html.

De Zutter, Andre W. E. A., Robert Horselenberg, and Peter J. Van Koppen. 2017. "The Prevalence of False Allegations of Rape in the United States from 2006–2010." *Journal of Forensic Psychology* 2, no. 2. https://doi.org/10.4172/2475-319X .1000119.

Doezema, Marie. 2018. "France, Where Age of Consent Is up for Debate." *Atlantic*, March 10. https://www.theatlantic.com/international/archive/2018/03/frances -existential-crisis-over-sexual-harassment-laws/550700/.

Du Bois, W. E. B. 1996. *The Souls of Black Folk*. New York: Oxford University Press.

Edin, Kathryn, and Maria Kefalas. 2005. *Promises I Can Keep: Why Poor Women Put Motherhood before Marriage*. Berkeley: University of California Press.

England, Paula, and Jonathan Bearak. 2014. "The Sexual Double Standard and Gender Differences in Attitudes toward Casual Sex among US University Students." *Demographic Research* 30: 1327. http://www.jstor.org/stable/26348237.

Faiola, Anthony, and Michelle Boorstein. 2014. "U.N. Panel Blasts Vatican Handling of Clergy Sex Abuse, Church Teachings on Gays, Abortion." *Washington Post*, February 5. https://www.washingtonpost.com/world/europe/un-panel-blasts -vatican-handling-of-clergy-sex-abuse-church-teachings-on-gays-abortion/2014 /02/05/2a6f1b26-8e75-11e3-84e1-27626c5ef5fb_story.html.

Farvid, Panteá, Virginia Braun, and Casey Rowney. 2017. "'No Girl Wants to Be Called a Slut!': Women, Heterosexual Casual Sex and the Sexual Double Standard." *Journal of Gender Studies* 26, no. 5: 544–60. https://doi.org/10.1080 /09589236.2016.1150818.

Federal Bureau of Investigation. 2019. "Uniform Crime Reports, Table 25: Percent of Offenses Cleared by Arrest or Exceptional Means." US Department of Justice. https://ucr.fbi.gov/crime-in-the-u.s/2019/crime-in-the-u.s.-2019/topic-pages/tables /table-25.

Fell, James C., and Robert B. Voas. 2006. "The Effectiveness of Reducing Illegal Blood Alcohol Concentration (BAC) Limits for Driving: Evidence for Lowering the Limit to .05 BAC." *Journal of Safety Research* 37, no. 3: 233–43. https://doi .org/10.1016/j.jsr.2005.07.006.

Fennell, Julie L. 2022. *Please Scream Quietly: A Story of Kink*. Lanham, MD: Rowman & Littlefield.

Ferguson, Claire E., and John M. Malouff. 2016. "Assessing Police Classifications of Sexual Assault Reports: A Meta-Analysis of False Reporting Rates." *Archives of Sexual Behavior* 45, no. 5: 1185–93. https://doi.org/10.1007/s10508-015-0666-2.

Finkel, Eli J., and Paul W. Eastwick. 2009. "Arbitrary Social Norms Influence Sex Differences in Romantic Selectivity." *Psychological Science* 20, no. 10: 1290– 95. https://doi.org/10.1111/j.1467-9280.2009.02439.x.

Fischel, Joseph J. 2019. *Screw Consent: A Better Politics of Sexual Justice*. Oakland: University of California Press.

Fisher, Bonnie S., Leah E. Daigle, Francis T. Cullen, and Michael G. Turner. 2003. "Reporting Sexual Victimization to the Police and Others: Results from a National-Level Study of College Women." *Criminal Justice and Behavior* 30, no. 1: 6–38. https://doi.org/10.1177/0093854802239161.

Fisher, Terri D., Zachary T. Moore, and Mary-Jo Pittenger. 2012. "Sex on the Brain? An Examination of Frequency of Sexual Cognitions as a Function of Gender, Erotophilia, and Social Desirability." *Journal of Sex Research* 49, no. 1: 69–77. https://doi.org/10.1080/00224499.2011.565429.

Flores, Andrew R., Lynn Langton, Ilan H. Meyer, and Adam P. Romero. 2020. "Victimization Rates and Traits of Sexual and Gender Minorities in the United States: Results from the National Crime Victimization Survey, 2017." *Science Advances* 6, no. 40: eaba6910. https://doi.org/10.1126/sciadv.aba6910.

Flores, Andrew R., Bianca D. M. Wilson, Lynn L. Langton, and Ilan H. Meyer. 2023. "Violent Victimization at the Intersections of Sexual Orientation, Gender Identity, and Race: National Crime Victimization Survey, 2017–2019." *PLOS ONE* 18, no. 2: e0281641. https://doi.org/10.1371/journal.pone.0281641.

Fogliato, Riccardo, Arun Kuchibhotla, Zachary Lipton, Daniel Nagin, Alice Xiang, and Alexandra Chouldechova. Forthcoming. "Estimating the Likelihood of Arrest on Police Records in Presence of Unreported Crimes." *Annals of Applied Statistics*.

Fogliato, Riccardo, Alice Xiang, Zachary Lipton, Daniel Nagin, and Alexandra Chouldechova. 2021. "On the Validity of Arrest as a Proxy for Offense: Race and the Likelihood of Arrest for Violent Crimes." *Proceedings of the 2021 AAAI/ACM Conference on AI, Ethics, and Society*, 100–11. https://doi.org/10.48550/arXiv .2105.04953.

Fohring, Stephanie. 2020. "Reporting as Risk: The Dangers of Criminal Justice for Survivors of Sexual Violence." In *Preventing Sexual Violence: Problems and Possibilities*, edited by Charlotte Barlow and Stephanie Kewley, 79–94. Bristol, UK: Bristol University Press.

Foubert, John, and Johnathan T. Newberry. 2006. "Effects of Two Versions of an Empathy-Based Rape Prevention Program on Fraternity Men's Survivor Empathy, Attitudes, and Behavioral Intent to Commit Rape or Sexual Assault." *Journal of College Student Development* 47, no. 2: 133–48. https://doi.org/10.1353/csd.2006 .0016.

Foucault, Michel. 1979. *Discipline and Punish: The Birth of a Prison*. New York: Vintage.

Fox, Ashley M., Georgia Himmelstein, Hina Khalid, and Elizabeth A. Howell. 2019. "Funding for Abstinence-Only Education and Adolescent Pregnancy Prevention: Does State Ideology Affect Outcomes?" *American Journal of Public Health* 109, no. 3: 497–504. https://doi.org/10.2105/AJPH.2018.304896.

Fox, Keely, Alexandria M. Ashley, Lacey J. Ritter, Tara Martin, and David Knox. 2022. "Gender Differences in Sex Secret Disclosure to a Romantic Partner." *Sexuality and Culture* 26, no. 1: 96–115. https://doi.org/10.1007/s12119-021 -09880-3.

Frank, David John, Tara Hardinge, and Kassia Wosick-Correa. 2009. "The Global Dimensions of Rape-Law Reform: A Cross-National Study of Policy Outcomes."

American Sociological Review 74, no. 2: 272–90. https://doi.org/10.1177/000312240907400206.

Franklin, Travis W. 2010. "The Intersection of Defendants' Race, Gender, and Age in Prosecutorial Decision Making." *Journal of Criminal Justice* 38, no. 2: 185–92. https://doi.org/10.1016/j.jcrimjus.2009.12.001.

Fridel, Emma E., and James Alan Fox. 2019. "Gender Differences in Patterns and Trends in U.S. Homicide, 1976–2017." *Violence and Gender* 6, no. 1: 27–36. https://doi.org/10.1089/vio.2019.0005.

Fried, Joshua Mark. 1995. "Forcing the Issue: An Analysis of the Various Standards of Forcible Compulsion in Rape." *Pepperdine Law Review* 23: 1277.

George, William H., and Lorraine J. Martínez. 2002. "Victim Blaming in Rape: Effects of Victim and Perpetrator Race, Type of Rape, and Participant Racism." *Psychology of Women Quarterly* 26, no. 2: 110–19. https://doi.org/10.1111/1471-6402.00049.

Gersen, Jeannie Suk. 2010. "'The Look in His Eyes': The Story of *State v. Rusk* and Rape Reform." In *Criminal Law Stories*, edited by Robert Weisberg and Donna Coker. Harvard Public Law Working Paper No. 10-23. https://papers.ssrn.com/abstract=1546602.

Giddens, Anthony. 1992. *The Transformation of Intimacy: Sexuality, Love, and Eroticism in Modern Societies*. Stanford, CA: Stanford University Press.

Giordano, Peggy C., Monica A. Longmore, and Wendy D. Manning. 2006. "Gender and the Meanings of Adolescent Romantic Relationships: A Focus on Boys." *American Sociological Review* 71, no. 2: 260–87. https://doi.org/10.1177/000312240607100205.

Goffman, Alice. 2015. *On the Run: Fugitive Life in an American City*. London: Picador.

Goldfarb, Eva S., and Lisa D. Lieberman. 2021. "Three Decades of Research: The Case for Comprehensive Sex Education." *Journal of Adolescent Health* 68, no. 1: 13–27. https://doi.org/10.1016/j.jadohealth.2020.07.036.

Gonzalez-Barrera, Ana. 2022. "About 6 Million U.S. Adults Identify as Afro-Latino." Pew Research Center, May 2. https://www.pewresearch.org/short-reads/2022/05/02/about-6-million-u-s-adults-identify-as-afro-latino/.

Gordon, Liahna E. 2006. "Bringing the U-Haul: Embracing and Resisting Sexual Stereotypes in a Lesbian Community." *Sexualities* 9, no. 2: 171–92. https://doi.org/10.1177/1363460706063118.

Grigoriadis, Vanessa. 2017. *Blurred Lines: Rethinking Sex, Power, and Consent on Campus*. Boston: Houghton Mifflin Harcourt.

Griswold, Stephanie R., Cynthia Neal Kimball, and Alexandra J. Alayan. 2020. "Males' Stories of Unwanted Sexual Experiences: A Qualitative Analysis." *Psychology of Men and Masculinities* 21: 298–308. https://doi.org/10.1037/men0000247.

Gross, Samuel R., Maurice Possley, Ken Otterbourg, Klara Stephens, Jessica Paredes, and Barbara O'Brien. 2022. "Race and Wrongful Convictions in the United States 2022." University of Michigan Public Law Research Paper No. 22-051. https://doi.org/10.2139/ssrn.4245863.

Guardian. n.d. "The Counted." Accessed October 3, 2023. https://www.theguardian.com/us-news/series/counted-us-police-killings.

Hahn, Judith. 2022. "Functions of the Law." In *Foundations of a Sociology of Canon Law*, edited by Judith Hahn, 77–116. Cham: Springer International.

Harding, Kate. 2015. *Asking for It: The Alarming Rise of Rape Culture—and What We Can Do about It*. New York: Da Capo Lifelong Books.

Harris, Jessica C. 2020. "Women of Color Undergraduate Students' Experiences with Campus Sexual Assault: An Intersectional Analysis." *Review of Higher Education* 44, no. 1: 1–30. https://doi.org/10.1353/rhe.2020.0033.

Hattery, Angela J., and Earl Smith. 2019. *Gender, Power, and Violence: Responding to Sexual and Intimate Partner Violence in Society Today*. Lanham, MD: Rowman & Littlefield.

Hawk, Mary, Robert W. S. Coulter, James E. Egan, Stuart Fisk, M. Reuel Friedman, Monique Tula, and Suzanne Kinsky. 2017. "Harm Reduction Principles for Healthcare Settings." *Harm Reduction Journal* 14, no. 1: 70. https://doi.org/10.1186/s12954-017-0196-4.

Heer, Brooke de, Meredith Brown, and Julianna Cheney. 2021. "Sexual Consent and Communication Among the Sexual Minoritized: The Role of Heteronormative Sex Education, Trauma, and Dual Identities." *Feminist Criminology* 16, no. 5: 701–21. https://doi.org/10.1177/15570851211034560.

Henao, Steven, Beth Montemurro, and Meghan M. Gillen. 2022. "Exploring the Impact of Age and Relationship Status on Heterosexual Men's Discussion of Sexuality." *Sexuality and Culture* 26, no. 2: 449–64. https://doi.org/10.1007/s12119-021-09900-2.

Hequembourg, Amy L., and Ronda L. Dearing. 2013. "Exploring Shame, Guilt, and Risky Substance Use among Sexual Minority Men and Women." *Journal of Homosexuality* 60, no. 4: 615–38. https://doi.org/10.1080/00918369.2013.760365.

Herbenick, Debby, Tsung-Chieh Fu, Brian Dodge, and J. Dennis Fortenberry. 2019. "The Alcohol Contexts of Consent, Wanted Sex, Sexual Pleasure, and Sexual Assault: Results from a Probability Survey of Undergraduate Students." *Journal of American College Health* 67, no. 2: 144–52. https://doi.org/10.1080/07448481.2018.1462827.

Herbenick, Debby, Lucia Guerra-Reyes, Callie Patterson, Yael R. Rosenstock Gonzalez, Caroline Wagner, and Nelson Zounlome. 2022. "'It Was Scary, But Then It Was Kind of Exciting': Young Women's Experiences with Choking during Sex." *Archives of Sexual Behavior* 51, no. 2: 1103–23. https://doi.org/10.1007/s10508-021-02049-x.

Hine, Benjamin A., Anthony D. Murphy, Julia A. Yesberg, Daniela Wunsch, Barry Charleton, and Bimsara K. S. Widanaralalage Don. 2021. "Mapping the Landscape of Male-on-Male Rape in London: An Analysis of Cases Involving Male Victims Reported between 2005 and 2012." *Police Practice and Research* 22, no. 1: 109–26. https://doi.org/10.1080/15614263.2020.1843458.

Hirsch, Jennifer S., and Shamus Khan. 2020. *Sexual Citizens: A Landmark Study of Sex, Power, and Assault on Campus*. New York: Norton.

Hirst, Julia. 2013. "'It's Got to Be about Enjoying Yourself': Young People, Sexual Pleasure, and Sex and Relationships Education." *Sex Education* 13, no. 4: 423–36. https://doi.org/10.1080/14681811.2012.747433.

Hlavka, Heather R., and Sameena Mulla. 2021. *Bodies in Evidence: Race, Gender, and Science in Sexual Assault Adjudication.* New York: New York University Press.

Hong, Kari. 2018. "A New Mens Rea for Rape: More Convictions and Less Punishment." *American Criminal Law Review* 55: 259. https://ssrn.com/abstract =3060709.

Huck, Jennifer L. 2021. *Campus Rape Culture: Identity and Myths.* Abingdon, UK: Routledge.

Hunt, Geoffrey, Emile Sanders, Margit Anne Petersen, and Alexandra Bogren. 2022. "'Blurring the Line': Intoxication, Gender, Consent, and Sexual Encounters Among Young Adults." *Contemporary Drug Problems* 49, no. 1: 84–105. https:// doi.org/10.1177/00914509211058900.

Johnson, Holly. 2017. "Why Doesn't She Just Report It? Apprehensions and Contradictions for Women Who Report Sexual Violence to the Police." *Canadian Journal of Women and the Law* 29, no. 1: 36–59. https://doi.org/10.3138/cjwl.29 .1.36.

Jones, Jeffrey S., Barbara N. Wynn, Boyd Kroeze, Chris Dunnuck, and Linda Rossman. 2004. "Comparison of Sexual Assaults by Strangers versus Known Assailants in a Community-Based Population." *American Journal of Emergency Medicine* 22, no. 6: 454–59. https://doi.org/10.1016/j.ajem.2004.07.020.

Jozkowski, Kristen N., Tiffany Marcantonio, Malachi Willis, and Michelle Drouin. 2023. "Does Alcohol Consumption Influence People's Perceptions of Their Own and a Drinking Partner's Ability to Consent to Sexual Behavior in a Non-Sexualized Drinking Context?" *Journal of Interpersonal Violence* 38, no. 1–2: 128–55. https: //doi.org/10.1177/08862605221080149.

Julian, Kate. 2018. "Why Are Young People Having So Little Sex?" *Atlantic*, November 13. https://www.theatlantic.com/magazine/archive/2018/12/the-sex -recession/573949/.

Kapungu, Chisina Tsvakai, Donna Baptiste, Grayson Holmbeck, Cami McBride, Melissa Robinson-Brown, Allyse Sturdivant, Laurel Crown, and Roberta Paikoff. 2010. "Beyond the 'Birds and the Bees': Gender Differences in Sex-Related Communication among Urban African-American Adolescents." *Family Process* 49, no. 2: 251–64. https://doi.org/10.1111/j.1545-5300.2010.01321.x.

Karney, Benjamin R. 2021. "Socioeconomic Status and Intimate Relationships." *Annual Review of Psychology* 72, no. 1: 391–414. https://doi.org/10.1146/annurev -psych-051920-013658.

Karstedt, Susanne. 2007. "Explorations into the Sociology of Criminal Justice and Punishment: Leaving the Modernist Project Behind." *History of the Human Sciences* 20, no. 2: 51–70. https://doi.org/10.1177/0952695107076199.

Kelley, Shamika M., Jessica C. Fleming, Brittany L. Acquaviva, Katherine A. Meeker, and Eryn Nicole O'Neal. 2021. "The Sexual Stratification Hypothesis and Prosecuting Sexual Assault: Is the Decision to File Charges Influenced by the Victim-Suspect Racial-Ethnic Dyad?" *Crime and Delinquency* 67, no. 8: 1165– 94. https://doi.org/10.1177/0011128721991821.

Kenney, Kara. 2021. "Carmel Woman on a Mission to Change Indiana's Rape Law after She Says Man Sexually Assaulted Her." WRTV Indianapolis, October

22. https://www.wrtv.com/news/wrtv-investigates/carmel-woman-on-a-mission-to-change-indianas-rape-law-after-she-says-man-sexually-assaulted-her.

Ketting, Evert, Laura Brockschmidt, Ilona Renner, Lena Luyckfasseel, and Olena Ivanova. 2018. "Sexuality Education in Europe and Central Asia: Recent Developments and Current Status." In *Sex Education*, edited by Raquel Alicia Benavides-Torres, Dora Julia Onofre-Rodríguez, and María Aracely Márquez-Vega, 75–120. Happauge, NY: Nova Science Publishers.

Khoshnood, Ardavan, Henrik Ohlsson, Jan Sundquist, and Kristina Sundquist. 2021. "Swedish Rape Offenders—A Latent Class Analysis." *Forensic Sciences Research* 6, no. 2: 124–32. https://doi.org/10.1080/20961790.2020.1868681.

Kinsler, Janni J., Deborah Glik, Sandra de Castro Buffington, Hannah Malan, Carsten Nadjat-Haiem, Nicole Wainwright, and Melissa Papp-Green. 2019. "A Content Analysis of How Sexual Behavior and Reproductive Health Are Being Portrayed on Primetime Television Shows Being Watched by Teens and Young Adults." *Health Communication* 34, no. 6: 644–51. https://doi.org/10.1080/10410236.2018.1431020.

Klein, Richard. 2008. "An Analysis of Thirty-Five Years of Rape Reform: A Frustrating Search for Fundamental Fairness." *Akron Law Review* 41. https://ssrn.com/abstract=2341690.

Koh, Steven Arrigg. 2022. "'Cancel Culture' and Criminal Justice." *Hastings Law Journal* 74, no. 1: 79–122. https://ssrn.com/abstract=4294887.

Kosciw, Joseph G., Emily A. Greytak, Adrian D. Zongrone, Caitlin M. Clark, and Nhan L. Truong. 2018. *The 2017 National School Climate Survey: The Experiences of Lesbian, Gay, Bisexual, Transgender, and Queer Youth in Our Nation's Schools.* New York: GLSEN. https://eric.ed.gov/?id=ED590243.

Koss, Mary P., Kevin M. Swartout, Elise C. Lopez, Raina V. Lamade, Elizabeth J. Anderson, Carolyn L. Brennan, and Robert A. Prentky. 2022. "The Scope of Rape Victimization and Perpetration among National Samples of College Students across 30 Years." *Journal of Interpersonal Violence* 37, no. 1–2: NP25–47. https://doi.org/10.1177/08862605211050103.

Kramer, Rory, Brianna Remster, and Camille Z. Charles. 2017. "Black Lives and Police Tactics Matter." *Contexts* 16, no. 3: 20–25. https://doi.org/10.1177/1536504217732048.

Krebs, Christopher P. 2007. *The Campus Sexual Assault (CSA) Study*. Washington, DC: National Institute of Justice.

Lamont, Ellen. 2020. *The Mating Game: How Gender Still Shapes How We Date*. Berkeley: University of California Press.

Lange, Kaitlin. 2022. "'No Means No': Senate Passes Bill to Close Rape Law Loophole about Definition of 'Consent.'" *Indianapolis Star*, March 1. https://www.indystar.com/story/news/politics/2022/03/01/indiana-lawmakers-pass-hb-1079-attempting-close-rape-law-loophole/6944615001/.

Larcombe, Wendy. 2011. "Falling Rape Conviction Rates: (Some) Feminist Aims and Measures for Rape Law." *Feminist Legal Studies* 19, no. 1: 27–45. https://doi.org/10.1007/s10691-011-9169-2.

Laverty, Erin K., Shireen M. Noble, Antonella Pucci, and Rachel E. D. MacLean. 2021. "Let's Talk about Sexual Health Education: Youth Perspectives on Their Learning Experiences in Canada." *Canadian Journal of Human Sexuality* 30, no. 1: 26–38. https://doi.org/10.3138/cjhs.2020-0051.

Lee, Harper. 2014. *To Kill a Mockingbird.* New York: Harper Perennial.

Lehmiller, Justin. 2018. *Tell Me What You Want.* Boston: Da Capo.

Lindberg, Laura D., and Leslie M. Kantor. 2022. "Adolescents' Receipt of Sex Education in a Nationally Representative Sample, 2011–2019." *Journal of Adolescent Health* 70, no. 2: 290–97. https://doi.org/10.1016/j.jadohealth.2021.08 .027.

Lipson, Sarah Ketchen, Sasha Zhou, Sara Abelson, Justin Heinze, Matthew Jirsa, Jasmine Morigney, Akilah Patterson, Meghna Singh, and Daniel Eisenberg. 2022. "Trends in College Student Mental Health and Help-Seeking by Race/Ethnicity: Findings from the National Healthy Minds Study, 2013–2021." *Journal of Affective Disorders* 306 (June): 138–47. https://doi.org/10.1016/j.jad.2022.03.038.

Lisak, David, Lori Gardinier, Sarah C. Nicksa, and Ashley M. Cote. 2010. "False Allegations of Sexual Assault: An Analysis of Ten Years of Reported Cases." *Violence against Women* 16, no. 12: 1318–34. https://doi.org/10.1177 /1077801210387747.

Livingston, Tyler N., Peter O. Rerick, and Deborah Davis. 2022. "Relationships between Sexual Arousal, Relationship Status, and Men's Ratings of Women's Sexual Willingness: Implications for Research and Practice." *Violence and Gender* 9, no. 3: 127–34. https://doi.org/10.1089/vio.2020.0042.

Lonsway, Kimberly A. 2010. "Trying to Move the Elephant in the Living Room: Responding to the Challenge of False Rape Reports." *Violence against Women* 16, no. 12: 1356–71. https://doi.org/10.1177/1077801210387750.

Lorenz, Katherine, Anne Kirkner, and Sarah E. Ullman. 2019. "Qualitative Study of Sexual Assault Survivors' Post-Assault Legal System Experiences." *Journal of Trauma and Dissociation: The Official Journal of the International Society for the Study of Dissociation (ISSD)* 20, 3: 263–87. https://doi.org/10.1080/15299732 .2019.1592643.

Luker, Kristin. 2007. *When Sex Goes to School: Warring Views on Sex—and Sex Education—since the Sixties.* New York: Norton.

Lundrigan, Samantha, Mandeep K. Dhami, and Kelly Agudelo. 2019. "Factors Predicting Conviction in Stranger Rape Cases." *Frontiers in Psychology* 10. https: //doi.org/10.3389/fpsyg.2019.00526.

MacAulay, Margaret, Michele L. Ybarra, Elizabeth M. Saewyc, T. Richard Sullivan, Lauren A. Jackson, and Shannon Millar. 2022. "'They Talked Completely about Straight Couples Only': Schooling, Sexual Violence and Sexual and Gender Minority Youth." *Sex Education* 22, no. 3: 275–88. https://doi.org/10.1080 /14681811.2021.1924142.

Marcantonio, Tiffany L., and Malachi Willis. 2023. "Examining Substance-Involved Sexual Experiences and Consent Communication by Sexual Identity." *Psychology and Sexuality* 14, no. 1: 279–93. https://doi.org/10.1080/19419899.2022.2106884.

Marcantonio, Tiffany L., Malachi Willis, Kelley E. Rhoads, Mary E. Hunt, Sasha Canan, and Kristen N. Jozkowski. 2022. "Assessing Models of Concurrent Substance Use and Sexual Consent Cues in Mainstream Films." *Journal of American College Health* 70, no. 3: 645–48. https://doi.org/10.1080/07448481.2020.1764962.

Marciniak, Allison L. 2015. "The Case against Affirmative Consent: Why the Well-Intentioned Legislation Dangerously Misses the Mark." *University of Pittsburgh Law Review* 77: 51.

Marks, Michael J., and R. Chris Fraley. 2005. "The Sexual Double Standard: Fact or Fiction?" *Sex Roles* 52, no. 3–4: 175–86. https://doi.org/10.1007/s11199-005-1293-5.

Martin, Kate, and Frank Taylor. 2019. "How Carolina Public Press Analyzed NC Court Data on Sexual Assaults." Carolina Public Press, March 18. http://carolinapublicpress.org/28698/how-carolina-public-press-analyzed-nc-court-data-on-sexual-assault/.

Martin, Patricia Yancey. 2005. *Rape Work: Victims, Gender and Emotions in Organization and Community Context*. New York: Routledge.

McKeever, Natasha. 2019. "Can a Woman Rape a Man and Why Does It Matter?" *Criminal Law and Philosophy* 13, no. 4: 599–619. https://doi.org/10.1007/s11572-018-9485-6.

McKie, Raymond M., Shayna Skakoon-Sparling, Drake Levere, Sage Sezlik, and Terry P. Humphreys. 2020. "Is There Space for Our Stories? An Examination of North American and Western European Gay, Bi, and Other Men Who Have Sex with Men's Non-Consensual Sexual Experiences." *Journal of Sex Research* 57, no. 8: 1014–25. https://doi.org/10.1080/00224499.2020.1767023.

McMillan, Lesley. 2018. "Police Officers' Perceptions of False Allegations of Rape." *Journal of Gender Studies* 27, no. 1: 9–21. https://doi.org/10.1080/09589236.2016.1194260.

Mellins, Claude A., Kate Walsh, Aaron L. Sarvet, Melanie Wall, Louisa Gilbert, John S. Santelli, Martie Thompson, et al. 2017. "Sexual Assault Incidents among College Undergraduates: Prevalence and Factors Associated with Risk." *PLOS ONE* 12, no. 11: e0186471. https://doi.org/10.1371/journal.pone.0186471.

Meslow, Scott. 2018. "Does *Wedding Crashers* Hold Up?" *GQ*, January 17. https://www.gq.com/story/does-wedding-crashers-hold-up.

Meyer, Doug. 2022. *Violent Differences*. Berkeley: University of California Press.

Miller, Amanda Jayne, and Sharon Sassler. 2019. "'Don't Force My Hand': Gender and Social Class Variation in Relationship Negotiation." *Arizona State Law Journal* 51: 1369.

Miller, Brandon, and Elizabeth Behm-Morawitz. 2016. "'Masculine Guys Only': The Effects of Femmephobic Mobile Dating Application Profiles on Partner Selection for Men Who Have Sex with Men." *Computers in Human Behavior* 62: 176–85. https://doi.org/10.1016/j.chb.2016.03.088.

Montemurro, Beth, Jennifer Bartasavich, and Leann Wintermute. 2015. "Let's (Not) Talk about Sex: The Gender of Sexual Discourse." *Sexuality and Culture* 19, no. 1: 139–56. https://doi.org/10.1007/s12119-014-9250-5.

Morabito, Melissa S., Linda Meyer Williams, and April Pattavina. 2019. *Decision Making in Sexual Assault Cases: Replication Research on Sexual Violence Case Attrition in the US*. NCJ 252689. Washington, DC: US Department of Justice. https://www.ojp.gov/pdffiles1/nij/grants/252689.pdf.

Morgan, Rachel E. and Jennifer L. Truman. 2020. "Criminal Victimization, 2019." Bureau of Justice Statistics Bulletin, September. NCJ 255113. https://bjs.ojp.gov/content/pub/pdf/cv19.pdf.

Moussawi, Ghassan. 2011. "Negotiating Non-Heterosexual Masculinities in Beirut." In *Introducing the New Sexuality Studies*, edited by Steven Seidman, Nancy L. Fischer, and Chet Meeks, 152–59. New York: Routledge.

Murchison, Gabriel R., Melanie A. Boyd, and John E. Pachankis. 2017. "Minority Stress and the Risk of Unwanted Sexual Experiences in LGBQ Undergraduates." *Sex Roles* 77, no. 3: 221–38. https://doi.org/10.1007/s11199-016-0710-2.

Murphy, Erin. 2020. "Writing on an Unclean Slate: Challenges in Substantive Reform of a Penal Code." *New York University Annual Survey of American Law* 76: 473.

O'Neal, Eryn Nicole, Cassia Spohn, Katharine Tellis, and Clair White. 2014. "The Truth behind the Lies: The Complex Motivations for False Allegations of Sexual Assault." *Women and Criminal Justice* 24, no. 4: 324–40. https://doi.org/10.1080/08974454.2014.890161.

Orne, Jason. 2017. *Boystown: Sex and Community in Chicago*. Chicago: University of Chicago Press.

Otterbein, Holly. 2021. "Left-Wing Prosecutors Hit Fierce Resistance." POLITICO. April 8. https://www.politico.com/news/2021/04/08/homicide-surge-progressives-district-attorneys-479966.

Palamar, Joseph J., Marybec Griffin-Tomas, Patricia Acosta, Danielle C. Ompad, and Charles M. Cleland. 2018. "A Comparison of Self-Reported Sexual Effects of Alcohol, Marijuana, and Ecstasy in a Sample of Young Adult Nightlife Attendees." *Psychology and Sexuality* 9, no. 1: 54–68. https://doi.org/10.1080/19419899.2018.1425220.

Papp, Leanna J., Charlotte Hagerman, Michelle A. Gnoleba, Mindy J. Erchull, Miriam Liss, Haley Miles-McLean, and Caitlin M. Robertson. 2015. "Exploring Perceptions of Slut-Shaming on Facebook: Evidence for a Reverse Sexual Double Standard." *Gender Issues* 32, no. 1: 57–76. https://doi.org/10.1007/s12147-014-9133-y.

Paquette, Danielle, and Weiyi Cai. 2021. "Why American Teenagers Are Having Much Less Sex." *Washington Post*, November 25. https://www.washingtonpost.com/news/wonk/wp/2015/07/22/why-american-teenagers-are-having-much-less-sex/.

Pariera, Katrina L., and Brianna Abraham. 2020. "'We Talked about Our Hookups': A Diary Study of Sexual Communication among U.S. College Women." *Journal of Social and Personal Relationships* 37, no. 8–9: 2620–33. https://doi.org/10.1177/0265407520933002.

Pascoe, Cheri J. 2011. *Dude, You're a Fag: Masculinity and Sexuality in High School*. Berkeley: University of California Press.

Pattavina, April, Melissa S. Morabito, and Linda M. Williams. 2021. "Pathways to Sexual Assault Case Attrition: Culture, Context, and Case Clearance." *Victims and Offenders* 16, no. 8: 1061–76. https://doi.org/10.1080/15564886.2021.1970661.

Pedersen, Willy, Sébastien Tutenges, and Sveinung Sandberg. 2017. "The Pleasures of Drunken One-Night Stands: Assemblage Theory and Narrative Environments." *International Journal of Drug Policy* 49 (November): 160–67. https://doi.org/10.1016/j.drugpo.2017.08.005.

Perelli-Harris, Brienna, Ann Berrington, Nora Sánchez Gassen, Paulina Galezewska, and Jennifer A. Holland. 2017. "The Rise in Divorce and Cohabitation: Is There a Link?" *Population and Development Review* 43, no. 2: 303. https://doi.org/10.1111/padr.12063.

Pierson, Emma, Camelia Simoiu, Jan Overgoor, Sam Corbett-Davies, Daniel Jenson, Amy Shoemaker, Vignesh Ramachandran, Phoebe Barghouty, Cheryl Phillips, and Ravi Shroff. 2020. "A Large-Scale Analysis of Racial Disparities in Police Stops across the United States." *Nature Human Behaviour* 4, no. 7: 736–45. https://doi.org/10.1038/s41562-020-0858-1.

Pittman, Jacqueline. 2023. "Constructing Race and Gender in Modern Rape Law: The Abandoned Category of Black Female Victims." *Michigan Journal of Gender and Law* 30: 151. https://doi.org/10.36641/mjgl.30.1.constructing.

Pound, Pandora, Rebecca Langford, and Rona Campbell. 2016. "What Do Young People Think about Their School-Based Sex and Relationship Education? A Qualitative Synthesis of Young People's Views and Experiences." *BMJ Open* 6, no. 9: e011329. https://doi.org/10.1136/bmjopen-2016-011329.

RAINN. n.d. "The Criminal Justice System: Statistics." Accessed December 28, 2023. https://www.rainn.org/statistics/criminal-justice-system.

Reiling, Denise M. 2002. "The 'Simmie' Side of Life: Old Order Amish Youths' Affective Response to Culturally Prescribed Deviance." *Youth and Society* 34, no. 2: 146–71. https://doi.org/10.1177/004411802237861.

Richards, Tara N., Marie Skubak Tillyer, and Emily M. Wright. 2019. "When Victims Refuse and Prosecutors Decline: Examining Exceptional Clearance in Sexual Assault Cases." *Crime and Delinquency* 65, no. 4: 474–98. https://doi.org/10.1177/0011128719828351.

Richardson, Jacob W. 2022. "'It Doesn't Include Us': Heterosexual Bias and Gay Men's Struggle to See Themselves in Affirmative Consent Policies." *Sexuality, Gender and Policy* 5, no. 1: 69–86. https://doi.org/10.1002/sgp2.12040.

Robinson, Paul H., and Markus D. Dubber. 2007. "The American Model Penal Code: A Brief Overview." *New Criminal Law Review* 10, no. 3: 319–41. http://doi.org/10.1525/nclr.2007.10.3.319.

Rogers, Sarah A., and Baker A. Rogers. 2021. "Expanding Our View: Demographic, Behavioral, and Contextual Factors in College Sexual Victimization." *Journal of Interpersonal Violence* 36, no. 23–24: NP13094–120. https://doi.org/10.1177/0886260520905076.

Rotenberg, Christine. 2017. "From Arrest to Conviction: Court Case Outcomes of Police-Reported Sexual Assaults in Canada, 2009 to 2014." Statistics Canada,

October 26. https://www.statcan.gc.ca/n1/pub/85-002-x/2017001/article/54870 -eng.htm.

Rothman, Emily F., Jonathon J. Beckmeyer, Debby Herbenick, Tsung-Chieh Fu, Brian Dodge, and J. Dennis Fortenberry. 2021. "The Prevalence of Using Pornography for Information About How to Have Sex: Findings from a Nationally Representative Survey of U.S. Adolescents and Young Adults." *Archives of Sexual Behavior* 50, no. 2: 629–46. https://doi.org/10.1007/s10508-020-01877-7.

Rubin, Lillian B. 1990. *Erotic Wars: What Happened to the Sexual Revolution?* New York: Farrar, Straus and Giroux.

Rupp, Leila J., Verta Taylor, Shiri Regev-Messalem, Alison C. K. Fogarty, and Paula England. 2014. "Queer Women in the Hookup Scene: Beyond the Closet?" *Gender and Society* 28, no. 2: 212–35. https://doi.org/10.1177/0891243213510782.

Santore, Daniel. 2008. "Romantic Relationships, Individualism and the Possibility of Togetherness Seeing Durkheim in Theories of Contemporary Intimacy." *Sociology* 42, no. 6: 1200–1217. https://doi.org/10.1177/0038038508096941.

Sanyal, Mithu. 2019. *Rape: From Lucretia to #MeToo*. New York: Verso.

Saunders, Candida L. 2012. "The Truth, the Half-Truth, and Nothing Like the Truth: Reconceptualizing False Allegations of Rape." *British Journal of Criminology* 52, no. 6: 1152–71. https://doi.org/10.1093/bjc/azs036.

Schalet, Amy T. 2011. *Not under My Roof*. Chicago: University of Chicago Press.

Schilt, Kristen, and Laurel Westbrook. 2015. "Bathroom Battlegrounds and Penis Panics." *Contexts* 14, no. 3: 26–31. https://doi.org/10.1177/1536504215596943.

Scott, Rachel H., Kaye Wellings, and Laura Lindberg. 2020. "Adolescent Sexual Activity, Contraceptive Use, and Pregnancy in Britain and the US: A Multidecade Comparison." *Journal of Adolescent Health* 66, no. 5: 582–88. https://doi.org/10.1016/j.jadohealth.2019.11.310.

Scully, Diana, and Joseph Marolla. 1985. "'Riding the Bull at Gilley's': Convicted Rapists Describe the Rewards of Rape." *Social Problems* 32, no. 3: 251–63. https://doi.org/10.2307/800685.

Sharkey, Betsy. 2010. "Movie Review: 'Get Him to the Greek.'" *Los Angeles Times*, June 4. https://www.latimes.com/archives/la-xpm-2010-jun-04-la-et-greek -20100604-story.html.

Shaw, Jessica, Rebecca Campbell, Debi Cain, and Hannah Feeney. 2017. "Beyond Surveys and Scales: How Rape Myths Manifest in Sexual Assault Police Records." *Psychology of Violence* 7, no. 4: 602–14. https://doi.org/10.1037/vio0000072.

Shaw, Jessica, and HaeNim Lee. 2019. "Race and the Criminal Justice System Response to Sexual Assault: A Systematic Review." *American Journal of Community Psychology* 64, no. 1–2: 256–78. https://doi.org/10.1002/ajcp.12334.

Shumlich, Erin J., and William A. Fisher. 2020. "An Exploration of Factors That Influence Enactment of Affirmative Consent Behaviors." *Journal of Sex Research* 57, no. 9: 1108–21. https://doi.org/10.1080/00224499.2020.1761937.

Sinozich, Sofi, and Lynn Langton. 2014. "Rape and Sexual Assault Victimization among College-Age Females, 1995–2013." Bureau of Justice Statistics, December. NCJ 248471. https://bjs.ojp.gov/content/pub/pdf/rsavcaf9513.pdf.

Slominski, Kristy L. 2021. *Teaching Moral Sex: A History of Religion and Sex Education in the United States*. Oxford: Oxford University Press.

Smith, Carly Parnitzke, and Jennifer J. Freyd. 2013. "Dangerous Safe Havens: Institutional Betrayal Exacerbates Sexual Trauma." *Journal of Traumatic Stress* 26, no. 1: 119–24. https://doi.org/10.1002/jts.21778.

Sommerville, Diane Miller. 2005. *Rape and Race in the Nineteenth-Century South*. Chapel Hill: University of North Carolina Press.

Sowisdral, Alicia. 2010. "Get Him to the Greek." Elevate Difference, June 15. http://elevatedifference.com/review/get-him-greek.html.

Spohn, Cassia. 2017. "Race and Sentencing Disparity." *Reforming Criminal Justice: A Report of the Academy for Justice on Bridging the Gap between Scholarship and Reform* 4: 169–86

Spohn, Cassia C., and Julie Horney. 1996. "The Impact of Rape Law Reform on the Processing of Simple and Aggravated Rape Cases." *Journal of Criminal Law and Criminology (1973–)* 86, no. 3: 861. https://doi.org/10.2307/1143939.

———. 2013. *Rape Law Reform: A Grassroots Revolution and Its Impact*. New York: Springer Science and Business Media.

Spohn, Cassia, and Jeffrey Spears. 2006. "The Effect of Offender and Victim Characteristics on Sexual Assault Case Processing Decisions." *Justice Quarterly* 3, no. 4: 649–79. https://doi.org/10.1080/07418829600093141.

Spohn, Cassia, and Katharine Tellis. 2019. "Sexual Assault Case Outcomes: Disentangling the Overlapping Decisions of Police and Prosecutors." *Justice Quarterly* 36, no. 3: 383–411. https://doi.org/10.1080/07418825.2018.1429645.

Spohn, Cassia, Clair White, and Katharine Tellis. 2014. "Unfounding Sexual Assault: Examining the Decision to Unfound and Identifying False Reports." *Law and Society Review* 48, no. 1: 161–92. https://doi.org/10.1111/lasr.12060.

Stacey, Michele, Kimberly H. Martin, and Bradley T. Brick. 2017. "Victim and Suspect Race and the Police Clearance of Sexual Assault." *Race and Justice* 7, no. 3: 226–55. https://doi.org/10.1177/2153368716643137.

Statista. n.d. "U.S. Forcible Rape/Sexual Assault Victims, by Weapon Presence 2020." Accessed January 11, 2023. https://www.statista.com/statistics/251931/usa—reported-forcible-rape-cases-by-weapon-presence/.

Stemple, Lara. 2008. "Male Rape and Human Rights." *Hastings Legal Journal* 60: 605.

Stemple, Lara, Andrew Flores, and Ilan H. Meyer. 2017. "Sexual Victimization Perpetrated by Women: Federal Data Reveal Surprising Prevalence." *Aggression and Violent Behavior* 34: 302–11. https://doi.org/10.1016/j.avb.2016.09.007.

Stemple, Lara, and Ilan H. Meyer. 2014. "The Sexual Victimization of Men in America: New Data Challenge Old Assumptions." *American Journal of Public Health* 104, no. 6: e19–26. https://doi.org/10.2105%2FAJPH.2014.301946.

Stevick, Richard A. 2014. *Growing up Amish: The Rumspringa Years*. Baltimore: Johns Hopkins University Press.

Taliaferro, Lindsay A., Kari M. Gloppen, Jennifer J. Muehlenkamp, and Marla E. Eisenberg. 2018. "Depression and Suicidality among Bisexual Youth: A

Nationally Representative Sample." *Journal of LGBT Youth* 15, no. 1: 16–31. https://doi.org/10.1080/19361653.2017.1395306.

Taylor, Chloë. 2009. "Foucault, Feminism, and Sex Crimes." *Hypatia* 24, no. 4: 1–25. https://doi.org/10.1111/j.1527-2001.2009.01055.x.

Tellis, Katharine M., and Cassia C. Spohn. 2008. "The Sexual Stratification Hypothesis Revisited: Testing Assumptions about Simple versus Aggravated Rape." *Journal of Criminal Justice* 36, no. 3: 252–61. http://dx.doi.org/10.1016/j.jcrimjus.2008.04.006.

Thomas, Cheryl. 2023. "Juries, Rape and Sexual Offences in the Crown Court 2007–21." *Criminal Law Review* 3: 197–222.

Thomas, John C., and Jonathan Kopel. 2023. "Male Victims of Sexual Assault: A Review of the Literature." *Behavioral Sciences* 13, no. 4: 304. https://doi.org/10.3390/bs13040304.

Thompson, Alexandra, and Susannah Tapp. 2022. "Criminal Victimization, 2021." Bureau of Justice Statistics Bulletin, September. NCJ 305101. https://bjs.ojp.gov/content/pub/pdf/cv21.pdf.

Tutenges, Sébastien, Sveinung Sandberg, and Willy Pedersen. 2020. "Sexually Violent Effervescence: Understanding Sexual Assault among Youth." *Sexualities* 23, no. 3: 406–21. https://doi.org/10.1177/1363460719830342.

US Department of Justice. 2012. "An Updated Definition of Rape." January 6. https://www.justice.gov/archives/opa/blog/updated-definition-rape

Unnever, James D., and Shaun L. Gabbidon. 2011. *A Theory of African American Offending: Race, Racism, and Crime.* New York: Taylor and Francis.

Venema, Rachel M., Katherine Lorenz, and Nicole Sweda. 2021. "Unfounded, Cleared, or Cleared by Exceptional Means: Sexual Assault Case Outcomes From 1999 to 2014." *Journal of Interpersonal Violence* 36, no. 19–20: NP10688–719. https://doi.org/10.1177/0886260519876718.

Wade, Lisa. 2017. *American Hookup: The New Culture of Sex on Campus.* New York: Norton.

Washington Post. 2018. "Murder with Impunity." Accessed July 31, 2023. https://www.washingtonpost.com/graphics/2018/investigations/where-murders-go-unsolved/.

Weare, Siobhan. 2018. "'Oh You're a Guy, How Could You Be Raped by a Woman, That Makes No Sense': Towards a Case for Legally Recognising and Labelling 'Forced-to-Penetrate'Cases as Rape." *International Journal of Law in Context* 14, no. 1: 110–31. https://doi.org/10.1017/S1744552317000179.

Weiss, Karen G. 2010. "Male Sexual Victimization: Examining Men's Experiences of Rape and Sexual Assault." *Men and Masculinities* 12, no. 3: 275–98. https://doi.org/10.1177/1097184X08322632.

Wentz, Ericka, and Kelsey Keimig. 2019. "Arrest and Referral Decisions in Sexual Assault Cases: The Influence of Police Discretion on Case Attrition." *Social Sciences* 8, no. 6: 180. https://doi.org/10.3390/socsci8060180.

Whalley, Elizabeth, and Colleen Hackett. 2017. "Carceral Feminisms: The Abolitionist Project and Undoing Dominant Feminisms." *Contemporary Justice Review* 20, no. 4: 456–73. https://doi.org/10.1080/10282580.2017.1383762.

Willig, Lauren. 2005. *The Secret History of the Pink Carnation.* New York: Penguin.

Willis, Malachi, Tsung-Chieh (Jane) Fu, Kristen N. Jozkowski, Brian Dodge, and Debby Herbenick. 2022. "Associations between Sexual Precedent and Sexual Compliance: An Event-Level Examination." *Journal of American College Health* 70, no. 1: 107–13. https://doi.org/10.1080/07448481.2020.1726928.

Willis, Malachi, Kristen N. Jozkowski, and Julia Read. 2019. "Sexual Consent in K–12 Sex Education: An Analysis of Current Health Education Standards in the United States." *Sex Education* 19, no. 2: 226–36. https://doi.org/10.1080/14681811.2018.1510769.

Willis, Malachi, Tiffany L. Marcantonio, Kristen N. Jozkowski, Malachi Willis, Tiffany L. Marcantonio, and Kristen N. Jozkowski. 2021. "Internal and External Sexual Consent during Events That Involved Alcohol, Cannabis, or Both." *Sexual Health* 18, no. 3: 260–68. https://doi.org/10.1071/SH21015.

Wolfers, Justin, David Leonhardt, and Kevin Quealy. 2015. "1.5 Million Missing Black Men." *New York Times*, April 20. https://www.nytimes.com/interactive/2015/04/20/upshot/missing-black-men.html.

Ylang, Norah, and Kristy Holtfreter. 2020. "The Decision to Arrest in Sexual Assault Case Processing: A Test of Black's Theory of the Behavior of Law." *Violence against Women* 26, no. 10: 1141–63. https://doi.org/10.1177/1077801219862632.

Yoshida, Akiko. 2023. "Anomie, Gender, and Inequality: Developing Sociological Theory of Singlehood from Japanese Experiences." *Journal of Family Theory and Review* 15, no. 3: 542–61. https://doi.org/10.1111/jftr.12493.

Zaykowski, Heather, Erin Cournoyer Allain, and Lena M. Campagna. 2019. "Examining the Paradox of Crime Reporting: Are Disadvantaged Victims More Likely to Report to the Police?" *Law and Society Review* 53, no. 4: 1305–40. https://doi.org/10.1111/lasr.12440.

Index

191

www.ingramcontent.com/pod-product-compliance
Lightning Source LLC
Chambersburg PA
CBHW031547260326
41914CB00002B/305